1001
advertising
tips

Transcontinental Books
1100 René-Lévesque Blvd West
24th floor
Montréal (Québec) H3B 4X9
Tel.: 514 340-3587
Toll-free: 1 866 800-2500
www.livres.transcontinental.ca

For information on special rates for corporate libraries and wholesale purchases,
please call 1 866 800-2500.

Distribution in Canada
Random House of Canada
2775 Matheson Blvd East
Mississauga (Ontario)
L4W 4P7

Library and Archives Canada Cataloging in Publication
Dupont, Luc, 1964-
1001 Advertising Tips
Translation of the 3rd ed.: 1001 trucs publicitaires.
ISBN 0-9738355-1-6

1. Publicity - Handbooks, manuals, etc. 2. Advertising - Handbooks, manuals, etc. I. Title.
II. Title: One thousand and one advertising tips.

HF5823.D8613 2006   659.1'1   C2005-942394-3

This book was originally published in French as *1001 trucs publicitaires* (Les Éditions
Transcontinental Inc.), and has been translated into Spanish (Robinbook) and into Korean
(Yekyong Publishing).

Editing: K. David Brody, Matt Sendbuehler
Proofreading: Immanuel Legorburu
Cover design and layout: Studio Andrée Robillard

Printed in Canada
© Transcontinental Books, 2006
Legal deposit — 1st Quarter 2006
National Library of Québec
National Library of Canada
ISBN 0-9738355-1-6

We acknowledge the financial support of our publishing activity by the Government of
Canada through the BPDIP program of the Department of Canadian Heritage, as well as by
the Government of Québec through the SODEC program Aide à la promotion.

LUC DUPONT

1001 advertising tips

Translated by Josh Walllace, C.Tr. (Canada)

Transcontinental Books

BY THE SAME AUTHOR

Images That Sell, White Rock Publishing, 2000.

To Sabrina,
Bianca
and Anais

"Advertising is not an art form.
It's about selling more stuff more often
to more people for more money.
Success is the result of a scientific, disciplined process,
and absolutely *every single* expenditure must generate a return."

Sergio Zyman, former director of marketing at Coca-Cola

An excellent memory tool for advertisers in a hurry

By Claude Cossette*

A dvertising has become a tool for merchants and activists alike in a world of ever more complex urban centers and increasingly competitive marketplaces. *1001 Advertising Tips* by Luc Dupont is a ready reference for anyone who has to create an ad and is not a professional— or who is simply "under the gun" of time or other pressures.

I wrote a preface to the first edition of Luc's book because I was so impressed by the quality of work by this young graduate who had asked for my feedback. At the time, I wrote that the text "...includes dozens of scientific articles and studies in which the great masters of advertising reveal to us the secrets of their success." This student has

---

* Instructor, advertiser and businessman, Claude Cossette is the founder of Cossette Communication Marketing and has presided over the company as it became Canada's largest ad agency. Mr. Cossette is a full professor of social marketing at Laval University.

subsequently gone on to become an eminent colleague of mine and holds a Ph.D., has published numerous books, has himself become a professor of advertising, and is also recognized in the field as an able media player.

The world of advertising has changed between these three editions. Messages of every kind that are disseminated by influential persons, different levels of government, humanitarian organizations and common citizens, increasingly find their ways into our lives. Getting people to believe in your message, or just attracting their attention, is becoming more difficult all the time.

These are some of the reasons why Dupont has updated this book on the latest advertising techniques. He places much more emphasis on the online world, stresses the critical role of image, provides new caveats on the use of such topics as humor and sex, has expanded his lists of "proven tips", and gives more examples for his ideas.

Dupont is not only a university graduate who is fascinated by the world of advertising, but a seasoned researcher who knows how to write well. These factors have combined to produce *1001 Advertising Tips*, an excellent reference for advertisers who don't have a moment to waste.

I believe this third edition can look forward to even greater success than its two predecessors.

Acknowledgements

When I wrote the first edition of *1001 Advertising Tips* some 15 years ago, I had no idea that my book would end up being translated into Spanish and Korean! I would thus like to thank Jean Paré, publisher of Transcontinental Books, for his outstanding work, his unflagging energy and his constant encouragement. Jean has made it possible for businesspeople from around the globe to read *1001 Advertising Tips*.

I would also like to thank Sylvain Bédard, associate publisher and editor-in-chief of *Finance and investment*, for his enthusiasm, courage and determination. In 1990, when Sylvain took the reins of Transcontinental Books, he was delighted to publish the first edition of this book.

I would also like to thank the following individuals:

- Two professors of advertising whom I have had the good fortune to meet: one at university, the other in business. The first is Claude Cossette, founding president of Cossette Communication Marketing and Professor at Université Laval, for his encouragement, his suggested improvements to the text and his very kind preface. The other is Pierre Delagrave, vice-president of Media and Research at Cossette Communication Group, who introduced me to marketing research and to media strategies.

- I would also like to thank Raymond Boisvert, publisher of *Québec Scope* magazine; Jocelyn Bernier, photographer and director of Focus 1; my parents Jeanne Pomerleau and Jean-Claude Dupont; my wife, Julie Tanguay; and my three children, Anais, Bianca and Sabrina.

I would like to conclude by thanking the staffs of the libraries of the University of Ottawa, the Université de Montréal, Concordia University, McGill University and SUNY, Albany.

Luc Dupont

Contents

INTRODUCTION 17

Chapter 1

PLANNING YOUR AD CAMPAIGN 21

    The 5 keys to your strategy 22

    Review 32

Chapter 2

55 WAYS OF POSITIONING YOUR PRODUCT 33

    Positioning your message 37

    How to determine product positioning? 84

    Review 95

Chapter 3

WHAT KINDS OF IMAGES ATTRACT THE MOST ATTENTION?

WHAT KINDS OF IMAGES ATTRACT
THE MOST ATTENTION? 97

Catching the eye 101

What topics get the most attention? 125

Do pretty models help? 126

Testimonials from stars 131

Interpreting images 142

Chapter 4

WRITING CATCHY HEADLINES

WRITING CATCHY HEADLINES 145

Better than average headlines 148

The magic words 159

Long or short headlines? 164

Review 166

Chapter 5

WRITING AD COPY THAT SELLS

WRITING AD COPY THAT SELLS 167

Writing copy that works 169

Long or short texts? 181

How to boost the credibility of your advertising 183

Does humor sell? 191

Pluses and minuses of promotional campaigns 193

Sponsorship 207

Product placement 213

Chapter 6

WHAT TYPEFACES TO USE FOR YOUR AD 217

Selecting a typeface 220

Chapter 7

THE MOST EFFECTIVE LAYOUTS 227

Seven layout styles that work 234

Size and format 239

The best positions for being noticed 241

Color or black-and-white ads? 246

Conclusion 249

Chapter 8

THE HIDDEN MEANINGS OF DIFFERENT COLORS 251

The hidden meanings of colors 255

Love is red and sex is pink 264

Color combinations 266

What colors are most liked—and hated? 273

The symbolism of lines and shapes 274

Review 278

Chapter 9

**WHEN TO USE AND WHEN TO AVOID
COMPARATIVE ADVERTISING** 279

Better than average performance 281

Worse than average performance 284

Should you clearly identify your competitor? 285

Warning 286

Chapter 10

THE 5 EFFECTS OF REPETITION 287

What repetition can do for you 289

22 good leads 296

Do ads work better in some seasons than in others? 301

One or more types of media? 302

How often should you repeat your message? 303

Distributing your repeat ads 304

Conclusion

ADVERTISING: ART OR SCIENCE? 311

NOTES 315

BIBLIOGRAPHY 339

Introduction

Welcome to this new edition of *1001 Advertising Tips*! The following pages will describe what does and does not work in the world of advertising. It will explain:

- How to plan your ad campaign
- How consumers respond to different kinds of ad stimuli
- How to position your products
- What advertising images are most likely to grab consumer attention
- What kinds of headlines produce the best results
- How to write ad copy that really sells
- How to write lengthy texts
- How to boost the credibility of your message

- What words sell best

- Using color to boost your sales

- Why the right typeface matters so much in advertising

- The best layouts for drawing attention

- When to use comparisons, humor and sex in advertising

- The right times to consider product placement, sponsorship and promotion

- How often you should repeat your ad to sell your product... and more

The principles outlined in this book are based on the research and the experiences of hundreds of US and Canadian experts.

Some specialists will, however, say that the best ads fail to observe these rules. This may be true—*one time in a thousand*. But consumers virtually always respond to the same techniques in the same manner.

- Women spend more time looking at photos of nude women than do men.[1] They like to see how well they shape up with the model.

- Men who buy electric trains for their sons are actually buying the present for themselves. Men see the birth of a son as an opportunity to relive the magic moments of childhood.

- Forty percent more women than men remember the brand names of advertisers that use sexual content. Men tend to get distracted by such messages.

- An ad's female readers will notice blondes first; but being jealous of the blondes, they will quickly turn their attention to darker-haired models.

- Twenty-five percent of our food is consumed between meals. Even worse: if you put a TV set in your kitchen, you can expect to gain from 2 to 5 kilos the first year.

- Twenty percent of the population purchases 80% of the beer (the famous 20-80 principle).

- People spend an average of 3.2 seconds on a magazine page and 4 seconds on a daily newspaper page.[2] That's why, on average, 5% to 10% of a publication's audience reads its ads.

- People tend to read short paragraphs more often than long ones.

- Consumers look at packaging that incorporates an image.

- Round products (and particularly those targeting women) sell better than square ones.

- Consumers ignore 71% of all ads. During the first year in which ads for tobacco products were banned over the airwaves, cigarette sales climbed 3% in the United States, with advertisers saving $70 million on commercials.

1001 Advertising Tips is intended for businesspeople, advertising specialists, advertisers and entrepreneurs. It focuses on different forms of advertising that can be used in different media. Boxes provide additional information on the topics of advertising and marketing.

1001 Advertising Tips answers such key questions as: What are the secrets of effective advertising? What rules apply in creating an ad that sells? Why does one ad work, while another flops?

Society moves on, opinions evolve and styles change, but human nature is a constant. The zoologist Desmond Morris wrote: "The truth is that the human species has always possessed the same set of emotional urges and basically the same way of expressing them externally. We have always been capable of swinging from hostility to friendliness, from love to hate, from selfishness to altruism, from sadness to joy. All that has happened is that names have been changed along the way."[3]

Chapter 1

Planning your ad campaign

Preparation is the key to your ad's success. Whatever its size, an effective ad is based on the simple principle of analyzing the situation and planning your campaign. The Cossette Group says that from 10% to 90% of advertising investments are tossed down the drain due to poor preparation.

This first chapter outlines how you should plan your ad campaign.

THE 5 KEYS TO YOUR STRATEGY

Planning your advertising strategy starts by answering five key questions.

1. What's your product?

Planning a campaign starts off by knowing your product. What are its strengths? What are its weaknesses? What is your company's image? What do people think of your firm? Start by collecting all the information you can on your product before designing an ad to boost sales.

You can also boost your likelihood of success an additional notch by gathering more information about your *competitors*. What are their market shares and ad budgets? What media do they use and when do they advertise? The more you know about yourself and the competition, the more effective an ad strategy you will produce.

2. What's your promise?

Whether you like it or not, advertising is always based on the promise of satisfaction. Ads must respond to a need or to a desire.

An ad always focuses on a specific motivation. Your job is to find the right motivation—the one that will sell your product.

The Kit Kat Chocolates "Take a Break" theme is a good example of an effective sales pitch. By presenting its themes in different manners, Kit Kat has become one of North America's most popular confectionery products, with annual sales of more than $300 million.

In general, provide an original sales pitch. Rosser Reeves, of the Ted Bates agency, says that an effective ad campaign should employ a *Unique Selling Proposition* (USP). According to Reeves "Each advertisement must make a proposition to the consumer. Not just words, not just product puffery, not just show-window advertising.[1]

"Finger-lickin' good," says KFC. "It floats," claims Ivory Soap. "Eat the red ones last," suggests Smarties.

Businesses develop unique styles and pitches to survive in the fashion business. Calvin Klein alludes to sexuality, while Diesel employs irony, satire and humor.

3. What is your target audience?

Your *target audience* is the third key factor you must consider in advertising. To whom are you speaking? For whom are your ads intended? To succeed in today's world, you must define your target.

Various criteria can be applied to this definition. Advertising specialists tend to simplify their task by dividing consumers according to age and sex ("Men, 18 to 34 years old," "Women, 25 to 54 years old," etc.). Bear in mind that each such segment has its own media consumption habits. Teens, for example, are especially prone to multitasking. About 80% regularly use more than one media at a given time, according to a study by Arbitron and WPP Group's MindShare.

Brands are very important when teens are buying something they feel affects their image. Teens look to the media and celebrities to pique their interest in new brands, but they won't buy the brand just because their favorite celeb uses it. Key categories: cars, clothes, and cell phones.[2]

◆ *The 18 to 34 age bracket is a favourite of advertisers. This group likes to buy, enjoys trying out new products, and demands instant gratification.*

12 WAYS OF DEFINING A TARGET

Age group: 12-18, 18-34, 18-49, 25-54, 50+, adults

Sex: Male, female

Sexual orientation: Heterosexual, homosexual

Annual income: Under $10,000, $10,000-$14,999
                        $15,000-$19,999, $20,000-$24,999,
                        $25,000-$34,999, $35,000-$49,999,
                        $50,000-$74,999, over $75,000

Education: Secondary or less, junior college, university

Family size: 1-2, 3-4, 5+

Marital status: Single, married without children, married with a
                        child or children, separated/divorced, widowed

Occupation: White collar, business owner, property owner,
                        member of religious community, salesperson,
                        farmer, student, unemployed, other

Location: Toronto, Vancouver, Calgary, Edmonton,
                        Winnipeg, urban or rural

Buying habits: Impulsive, trendy products, environmentally
                        friendly products

Behavior: Inert, mobile, multifunctional

Motivations: Physiological and psychological needs, lifestyles,
                        etc.

4. What's your objective?

The fourth key to success for your ad is its purpose. You need to set a goal before you can build an effective plan.

The ad's purpose, which can be understood in terms of its long- and short-term goals, should be based on the featured product and its qualities. In practice, you have several options. You can get folks to try out your product, boost your popularity, change a common perception of your product, reduce competition, find new prospective users and shape a new character for your product, boost the product's sales curve, etc.

You will increase the likelihood of achieving your purpose if you set clear goals. You can define an appropriate purpose by studying the market situation and asking yourself: what are the pluses and minuses of my product?

5. What is your ad budget?

Like it or not, your leverage is largely a function of your financial resources. But a small budget does not necessarily mean corresponding results. A microbrewery with limited resources like Sleeman has shown that you can take on industry giants. But you must be realistic.

If you have $5,000 to spend on advertising, don't even consider television. You should focus your efforts instead on a weekly news-paper or a radio station. You might also put together a brochure.

In calculating how much you should spend on advertising, ask yourself the following questions:

- How much did you spend on advertising last year?
- What are your annual sales?
- What is your market share?

- What market shares do you hope to capture over the short and long term?
- How much is the competition spending on advertising?

ADVERTISING RATIOS	
(advertising budget as a % of sales)	
Food	1 to 6%
Household appliances	1 to 3%
Photo equipment	1 to 5%
Cars	1 to 6%
Aviation	1 to 3%
Alcoholic beverages	1.5 to 9%
Soft drinks	3.5%
Communication and recreation	1.5 to 7%
Cosmetics	2 to 55%
Confectionery items	4 to 10.5%
Chemical products	0.5 to 4%
Pharmaceutical products	2 to 14%
Soaps and detergents	3 to 11%
Tobacco products	1 to 4%
Telephone services	0.5 to 1%
Retail sales	2%

Source: *Advertising Age*

There are, in fact, a number of ways to determine how much you should spend on advertising.

1. *Spend what you can.* Among small businesses, this is the most popular method.

2. *Emulate the competition.* This approach will force you to keep a close eye on your rivals.

3. *Earmark a share of your revenues for advertising.* Studies show that in the food sector, for instance, 1% to 6% of your sales should be invested in advertising. For advertisers, the average figure is 4.3%. In the cosmetics sector, this ratio may surge to as much as 55%!

4. *Invest in line with your sales goals.* You might, for example, decide to put $200 in advertising money aside for every Cherokee you expect to sell in Canada over the course of the year. If you think you're likely to sell 2,500 vehicles, you should budget $500,000 for advertising

Whatever method you select, bear in mind that a company's market share is directly proportional to the advertising effort it makes. To hold on to 20% of a given market, plan to invest about 20% of your ad money in it.

Which media is best to use? In advertising, the answer to this question often depends on your creative strategy. According to media specialist John Meskill,[3] magazines are great for beauty and elegance, while radio commercials are better for creating a sense of intimacy.

Each media presents its own strengths and weaknesses:

- *Television is a multi-sensory "prestige" media.* Television is definitely the best media for product testimonials. It is also a good choice for changing the way people think or feel about a product.

- *Daily newspaper readers are better informed and have higher-than-average incomes.* Daily newspapers give you an opportunity to fully describe your product's features. Print media are best suited to comparative ads, in which you can provide such technical information as price, size, quality, defects and so forth.

- *Weekly publications are ideal for local efforts.* They provide targeted geographic coverage. Weeklies are a flexible media and ideal for small businesses.

- *Radio is an intimate and personal media that lets you reach a clearly defined target and produce a nearly immediate impact.* It is well suited to campaigns based on dreams and the imagination.

- *The billboard is a "pure" media that reaches out to a mobile audience.* Billboards provide a virtual permanent exhibition of your product in a wide variety of formats for a range of different targets.

- *Magazines communicate with a high-quality readership and let you develop a brand image.*

- *The Web is an interactive media.* It lets advertisers keep accurate track of site traffic as it reaches out to a young and well-informed audience. This specialized media also offers high potential.

Advertisers have, over time, discovered that some media are more effective than others for selling certain products. Television is widely used to sell fast food, cars and beer. Newspapers are dominated by department store and car ads. Flyers are circulated by supermarkets and drugstores.

The use of mixed media, or a combination of different outlets, is another choice for more effectively communicating with your target.

WHICH MEDIA IS MOST APPROPRIATE FOR COMMUNICATING THE FOLLOWING CHARACTERISTICS

Quality	- -	-	+	++	+++
Authority	Billboards	Radio	TV	Newspapers	Magazines
Beauty	Radio	Newspapers	Billboards	TV	Magazines
Demonstrations	Billboards	Radio	Newspapers	Magazines	TV
Entertainment	Billboards	Magazines	Newspapers	Radio	TV
Elegance	Newspapers	Radio	TV/Billboards	TV/Billboards	Magazines
Events	Billboards	Magazines	Radio	Newspapers	TV
Excitement	Newspapers	Billboards	Radio	Magazines	TV
Information	Billboards	Radio	TV	Magazines	Newspapers
Intimacy	Newspapers	Billboards	TV	Magazines	Radio
Leadership	Newspapers	Billboards	Radio	Magazines	TV
Novelty	Billboards	Magazines	Radio	TV	Newspapers
Price	Billboards	Magazines	TV	Radio	Newspapers
Quality	Newspapers	Radio	Billboards	TV	Magazines
Sex	Newspapers	Radio	Billboards	TV	Magazines
Snob appeal	Billboards	Radio	TV	Newspapers	Magazines
Surprise	Radio	Magazines	Newspapers	TV	Billboards
Tradition	Billboards	Newspapers	TV	Radio	Magazines

Source: Meskill, John J. "The Media Mix," *4A Media Letter*, January 1979, pp. 1-2.

• — F L A S H QUIZ — •

HOW MUCH SHOULD I SPEND ON ADVERTISING?

Answer the following questions and add up the points to determine how much you should set aside for winning over your market. This will give you a better idea of the percentage of your sales revenues that you should ideally earmark for advertising.

My business is located in:

- A high traffic environment   1 point
- A moderate traffic environment   2 points
- A low traffic environment   3 points

In my target market, I am:

- Well known   1 point
- Moderately known   2 points
- Little known   3 points

In terms of the competition:

- I don't have many competitors   1 point
- I have some competitors   2 points
- I have many competitors   3 points

In my business, price:

- Is of no importance   1 point
- Is of moderate importance   2 points
- Is of great importance   3 points

Add up the number of points to determine how much you should spend on advertising.

From 4 to 7 points:	3-4% of sales
From 8 to 11 points:	4-5% of sales
12 points:	5-7% of sales

REVIEW

The big challenges in effectively planning your advertising strategy are to define your product, search for a key idea, select a target, adopt a goal and set a budget. You must, however, start by selecting a tightly defined market segment, which is why we will now discuss the matter of *positioning*.

Chapter 2

55 ways of positioning your product

E ven if you work around the clock, you will not produce a great advertising campaign unless you start by properly *positioning* your product.

To succeed in today's highly competitive environment, companies must learn to carve out a specific market niche. If you want to succeed, you must position or target your product. This means determining:

- Which consumers are most likely to be interested in your product?

- Which consumers will be targeted by your ads?

- What benefits will your ads feature?

You cannot simultaneously target men, women, young and old for a particular product these days. Product positioning experts Al Ries and Jack Trout wrote: "In the communication jungle out there, the only hope to score big is to be selective, to concentrate on narrow targets, to practice segmentation. In a word, 'positioning.'"[1]

In just one decade, the number of cereal brands has climbed from 84 to 150. Over the same period, the number of different kinds of toothpaste has soared from 10 to 31. You can find up to 17,000 different products in a grocery store. Revlon now sells 2,500 different beauty products![2]

Your answers to the following questions should clearly illustrate the importance of positioning:

1. What is the difference between Crest, Ultrabrite and Topol toothpastes?

2. What is the difference between Coca-Cola, Pepsi-Cola and 7-Up sodas?

3. What is the difference between Tide, Arctic Power and Surf detergents?

Let's be honest. The difference is not in the toothpaste tube, in the soda bottle or in the detergent's strength. The difference is in the way each product has been positioned.

You can select from among dozens of different brands of toothpaste, and each brand serves a particular niche. Crest fights cavities, Ultrabrite makes your teeth white and Topol is aimed at smokers. Aim has a pleasant taste, Total fights gum disease and Aquafresh freshens your breath.

Two Canadian mega-chains are using different strategies to win over the home repair market: Home Depot emphasizes the quality of its customer service, while Rona highlights the joy of renovating. Sales of residential home-improvement products could grow from a current $360 billion into a $452 billion industry by 2008 according to the Home Improvement Research Institute, an industry trade group. Home Depot estimates that the global home-improvement market totals about $900 billion, which suggests the company has plenty of room to grow. Canadians' appetite for re-tiling the kitchen and sundry renovation projects got even bigger in 2003, a record year for home improvement retailers, whose sales increased 8.2% to $32-billion.[3]

Studies show that 80% of those who buy sports shoes use them for some purpose other than sports. This is a highly competitive market and we should be able to distinguish between such products. Nike, with its "Just do it!" slogan is the $200-a-pair shoe that uses testimonials from sports stars. Puma and Adidas take a more traditional approach by seeking to recover their past glory. New Balance, which focuses on an adult clientele, employs testimonials from happy customers.

It is obvious that people will never admit that their choices were influenced by ads, slogans, visuals or logos. Rather, they will say that they are seeking information and that their buying habits are quite reasonable. *This is not true.*

With few exceptions, people are incapable of distinguishing between one brand and the next. One study took 300 smokers of a particular brand of cigarette and had them smoke different cigarettes with hidden brand names. They were then asked to identify their usual brand. Only 2% were able to pick out their brand from among the cigarettes they had smoked.[4] Marketing experts have observed the same kinds of results among users of stereo systems,[5] shaving cream,[6] beer,[7] soft drinks[8] and champagne.[9]

More recently, researchers placed a Sanyo label on RCA equipment. They then asked 900 different people to compare the performance of that equipment with the same product bearing an RCA label. Seventy percent stated that the Sanyo product was better. However, they were comparing the same RCA device in all cases.

In marketing, we don't sell products, we sell product positions. We are in fact guided in our selection of products and brands by the desire to express our personalities. Spending money is a way of communicating our social identities, whether with respect to beer, cigarettes, toothpaste, hardware, sports shoes or cars.

DOES THIS CATEGORY HAVE THE RIGHT NUMBER OF PRODUCT CHOICES?

	Too many	Right number	Too few
Cigarettes	80%	16%	1%
Dry cereal	72%	24%	4%
Alcoholic beverages	64%	29%	2%
Cough syrups	61%	29%	4%
Soaps bars	60%	36%	4%
Beer	53%	37%	4%
Automobiles	52%	37%	10%
Soft drinks	50%	43%	6%
Toilet paper	45%	50%	4%
Razors	36%	52%	7%
Major appliances	29%	64%	6%
Canned vegetables	24%	63%	11%

In order to attract the consumer to your brand, you must strategically position it on the market. BBDO found that 40% of the people surveyed said that shopping was made more difficult by the number of products to choose from. Consumer confusion is particularly evident with cigarettes (80%) and cereals (72%).

POSITIONING YOUR MESSAGE

What counts in advertising is positioning your product. Aim holds up to 10% of the market thanks to a strategy geared to positioning the product around its pleasant taste. The company made the unfortunate mistake, however, of trying to please all consumers by creating an anti-tartar version of Aim toothpaste and a mint-flavored Aim gel.

McDonald's strived to cover all consumer bases over a dozen-year period by creating new entities, one after another, such as McHotels and McCafés. The firm also acquired five fast-food chains and planned to launch McTreat, on the model of Dairy Queen. However, it is only since McDonald's has returned to its core mission of hamburgers and French fries, and brought salad and submarine sandwiches on board, that the firm has resumed its growth. This is because its product positioning is clearer. (McDonald's was, incidentally, the first fast-food chain to provide nutritional information on its products, back in 1971.)

The moral of the story is that by trying to reach out to everyone you reach no one. This rule applies equally to small businesses as it does to marketing giants like McDonald's.

Here, then, are 55 ways of positioning your product:

1. "Authentic" product positioning

This strategy can be used by any firm that happens to be the first to develop a position for its product type. Levi's slogan *"the original jeans"* is a good example of this kind of positioning. Levi's makes it clear with its slogan that its product is the original one and exploits the public's natural tendency to perceive the first brand as more authentic, with subsequent products being no better than pale imitations.

Many other products use similar approaches, such as:

Coca-Cola: *It's the real thing*

Camel: *A real cigarette*

Speed Stick (Mennen): *The original*

Sanka: *You can't beat the original*

Absorbine Jr.: *The original*

Kellogg's Special K: *The original and best*

Popsicles: *The original brand*

Bailey's: *The original Irish cream liqueur*

Perrier: *It's original, it's Perrier*

Ex-Lax: *The original chocolate laxative*

Maille: *The real Dijon mustard*

Chiquita: *A banana by any other name is not the same*

Beemans: *The original taste*

Pabst Blue Ribbon: *The real taste of beer*

"We're the original product" positioning is generally quite profitable. Studies show that pioneers of a particular brand often win larger market shares than newer competitors over the long term.[10]

How can we recognize pioneers of a new brand? Easily. Leaders win much recognition over time. Ski-Doo has become the generic name for all snowmobiles. Kleenex refers to all types of tissue paper. Band-Aid means any kind of bandage. Jell-O refers to any gelatin-based dessert. Q-tips applies to all cotton swabs, and Saran Wrap signifies any plastic wrap.

Some firms, unfortunately, continue to underestimate the importance of positioning as the original and genuine product. In the 1980s, the new Coca-Cola formula was supposed to revolutionize the cola industry. Sweeter than the original, it was based on scientific research indicating that the new Coke would be a big hit. Instead, it bombed. Coca-Cola had underestimated the importance of its historic positioning.

HOW PIONEERS STAND OUT IN THE MARKET

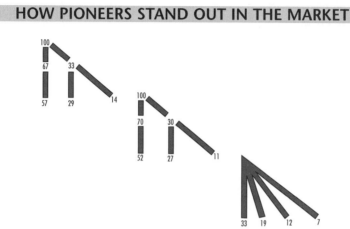

Research tends to show that natural rules apply to market evolution.

At the top of the list is the Boston Consulting Group's "3 and 4" rule, which demonstrates that the market tends to break down in a 4:2:1 ratio. In other words, the first brand in a given segment will, over the long term, hold twice the market share of the second and four times the share of the third.[11]

Next is the Hendry Corporation rule that the first brand to become established in a given sector of activity will at first capture 100% of the market. With two products in the same category, the first brand will retreat to 70% while the second brand can look forward to 30% of the market, on average, and the third to 11%, and so on, in an approximate 2.5:1 ratio.

Finally, Robert Buzzell measured the market shares of 200 Fortune 500 firms. It learned that 76% of the markets produced respective market shares of 33% for the first company in that market, 19% for the second, 12% for the third and 7% for fourth.[12]

WHAT BECAME OF 1923's LEADERS?

Product or brand leader in 1923	In 1983
Swift Premium bacon	No change
Kellogg's Corn Flakes	# 3
Eastman Kodak camera	No change
Del Monte canned fruits	No change
Hershey's chocolates	#2
Crisco shortening	#2
Carnation powdered milk	No change
Wrigley's gum	No change
Nabisco crackers	No change
Eveready batteries	No change
Gold Medal flour	No change
Life Savers candies	No change
Sherwin-Williams paint	No change
Hammermill paper	No change
Prince Albert pipe tobacco	No change
Gillette razors	No change
Singer sewing machine	No change
Manhattan shirts	Among top five
Coca-Cola beverages	No change
Campbell's soup	No change
Ivory soap	No change
Lipton tea	No change
Goodyear tires	No change
Palmolive soap	#2
Colgate toothpaste	#2

Murray Lubliner compared the market shares of 1923's top brands with those of 1983. He found that 19 of the leaders in 1923 remained in the same position for their respective products in 1983.[13]

2. Catch-up strategy

The first example of this sort of positioning that comes to mind is Avis, without a doubt. Second in the rent-a-car market, Avis launched an ad campaign in the 1960s with the slogan "Avis is only No. 2 in rent-a-cars, so why go with us? We try harder."

To the surprise of many, this strategy enabled Avis to quickly boost its market share by 6%. Better yet, the firm turned a profit for the first time in 13 years. Consumers wound up thinking that Avis was in the same league as the industry leader Hertz. At the same time, the industry's third ranking firm, National, began to lose market share through a ricochet effect.

What would explain this reaction? Psychological studies have shown that it is difficult for consumers to recall more than two brands for any particular sector of activity. For any given product family, people generally recognize the top two brands. This would be Eveready and Duracell in the world of batteries, Kodak and Fuji for film and Listerine and Scope for mouthwashes. Also, consumers are usually familiar with one generic brand.

3. Lowest price

Low price is a third positioning strategy. You can use this technique to bring customers into your store, expand your clientele, change perceptions and highlight competitive benefits.

Maybelline cosmetics, Barbasol shaving cream, Savin photocopiers, ABC detergent, Old Milwaukee beer and WestJet airlines all successfully apply low-price positioning.

Days Inn, Comfort Inn, Motel 6, Econo Lodge and Super 8 Motels all occupy the economy hotel position.

Greyhound Lines Inc. has utilized the *MoneySaver* name since 1986 to advertise its most heavily discounted bus fares.

In the late 1970s, the Japanese Fuji company made inroads against industry leader Kodak with an "equal quality at lower price" strategy.[14] The technique helped Fuji boost North American market share from 10% to 25%. Kodak's share dropped from 80% to 65% over the same period.

The new bargain-based mentality is fueling phenomenal growth of dollar stores, or small-box discount retailing. In the United States, consumers who don't want to sacrifice on price, while seeking smaller, more convenient alternatives to the big boxes, are turning to such chains as Dollar General, Save-A-Lot, Dollar Bill$, Uncle Buck's, Lots for Less and Family Dollar for basic fill-in goods, from commodities like laundry detergent to treasure-hunt items at deep discount. From 1998 to 2000, small-format value retailers grew sales at an average compounded annual growth rate of 6%. Surveys from AC Nielsen have reported that more than 66% of US households shop at dollar stores, with these numbers rising each year.[15]

In terms of superstores, the Wal-Mart chain is a good example of a leader with a "low price" position. Established in 1962 by Sam Walton, this American chain employs 1.6 million people throughout the world and now has 5,170 outlets (with 3,600 of them in the United States). Every week, 138 million customers visit a Wal-Mart, and the firm's international sales total $256.3 billion.

4. Higher price

Oddly enough, people are not always won over by the lowest price. High-price positioning applies to all types of products and particularly those that we consume in public, such as perfume, beer, watches, clothing and cars.

Many brands use high prices to attract consumers and to play on the idea of prestige. They include Mercedes-Benz, Gucci, Rolex, Rolling Rock, Beefeater, Tommy Hilfiger, Versace, Montblanc, and Häagen-Dazs. Grand Gourmet and Purina ONE dog foods, and Fancy Feast cat foods are sold at high prices. True Religion jeans go for $300 a pair. The marketing strategy for L'Oréal hair products says, "It costs a little more but I'm worth it."

Higher prices draw customers with the idea that product quality is related to its price. Many consumers are prepared to pay higher prices for prestigious brands. This kind of positioning is strongly linked to concepts of the past, of tradition, and of the price of the product in question.

During a study conducted on behalf of the Stanford Research Institute, Douglas McConnell gave people the same brand of beer in three containers at different prices.[16] He had them taste each one and then asked them to name their favorites. McConnell said they always chose the "highest priced" container.

In another study, Robert Andrews and Enzo R. Valenzi offered margarine and butter of identical appearance in containers marked with different prices. The researcher asked respondents to taste each one and then rank them by order of preference. Once again, tasters reported that the margarine and butter in the more expensive wrappers were "best."[17]

Many other studies also show that people tend to associate higher price with superior quality for foods, restaurants, clothing and automobiles. This includes research by such individuals as Harold Levitt,[18] Tibor Scitovszky,[19] James E. Stafford and Ben Enis,[20] and Donald Tull, R. A. Boring and M.H. Gonsior.[21]

5. Sturdiness

Maytag, Glad and Volvo are good examples of brands that are known to be sturdy in their respective fields.

One ad demonstrated product sturdiness by showing a child playing with a Samsonite suitcase in an amusement park. Another showed a Pittsburgh Steeler punching a case during a training session.

6. Safety

A study conducted by Roper Research revealed that safety has become the number one issue in advertising, taking over the lead from sexuality.

7. Quality

When Japanese car makers began targeting North American markets, they decided to highlight the excellence of their products. To overcome their poor reputation from the 1960s, when the term "made in Japan" was equivalent to "poor in quality", they developed manufacturing techniques that considerably reduced the risk of defects.

Although Americans return 50,000 out of every million products they buy due to manufacturing defects, the Japanese only return 200 in every million products. The Japanese are seeking to go even further in reducing errors. To do so, they must carry out additional testing and trials to ensure that their products are of outstanding quality.

8. Quantity

Certain products make their mark by playing on the idea of quantity. In the case of weight-loss products, for example, every brand is aimed at a particular type of woman. Ultra Slim-Fast targets women seeking to lose from 15 to 50 kilos.

9. More bang for the buck

Another positioning strategy is based on concentration. Gillette's Trac II razor was originally introduced in 1971 as the only razor that had two blades, based on the concept that *two blades shave better than one.* Now, Mach3, another Gillette product, offers three-blade shaves. Unilever's Surf detergent offers twice as much scent as other cleansers. One Motrin IB has the strength of two Tylenols. Tums claims that it is *twice as fast, twice as strong* as regular Rolaids. Certs offers *two mints in one.*

10. Sex appeal

In a body-worshipping culture, such products as beer, champagne, shaving cream, toothpaste, soap, chewing gum, perfume, underwear, shampoo, deodorant, bathing suits, and women's lingerie can be successfully positioned around the concept of sex appeal.

Sex appeal-based positioning is particularly effective if you are dealing with teens and young adults. "It's the only constant thing you can sell these kids on," says Ken Utech, Director, Market Research at Chattem, which produces the leading teen-age cologne.[22] "Sexy ads always do well on the college level," said Joe Venaglia, president of College Market Consultants.[23]

Calvin Klein's success clearly illustrates the importance of sex in advertising. From the very start, the firm gained notoriety for its risqué ads. In 1982 Calvin Klein posted a huge ad on a skyscraper showing a muscular man in tight-fitting underpants. It has subsequently featured long, slim and hairless pre-teen males in its images. Calvin Klein's racy ads have also helped launch the careers of such stars as Brooke Shields, Kate Moss, and Mark Wahlberg.

There are, however, some limits to the use of sex. During the impeachment of President Bill Clinton, designer Tommy Hilfiger portrayed a young woman wearing black leather slacks backed into a cor-

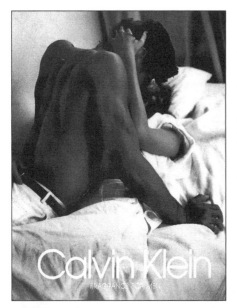

◆ These Calvin Klein ads are the best examples I have found of using sex appeal to position a product.

ner of the president's office. Another showed a girl on her knees by the presidential seal. Even before the Hilfiger ads, Calvin Klein had drawn negative attention for using pictures of young and anorexic teens photographed in basements.

11. User's sex

This is one of the oldest forms of positioning. Marlboro cigarettes, Irish Spring soap, and Lava are all male-oriented products. Secret deodorant and Virginia Slims cigarettes are similarly aimed at women.

A series of ads from General Foods International Coffees specifically targeted *women*. Those in charge of the campaign identified twenty magazines capable of efficiently reaching this market. In applying this strategy, sales soared by 15%.[24]

Advertisers have historically always paid special attention to women. This is not a matter of chance. Although women only represent half of the population, they are central to the process of acquiring goods and services. Many studies have confirmed that women make up to 80% of all household purchasing decisions. Women buy 80% of men's undergarments and 65% of their dress shirts. They are behind 75% of all home improvements and provide input on the car-buying process. In other words, women are important.

Cigarette makers have long understood the importance of positioning for each of their products. Women's cigarette brands have generally borne such names as Slims and Superslims. These products were mainly aimed at traditional-oriented women. Manufacturers have recently launched such brands as Dakota for women who are drawn to such activities as wrestling, tractor pull contests, pool, and drag racing.

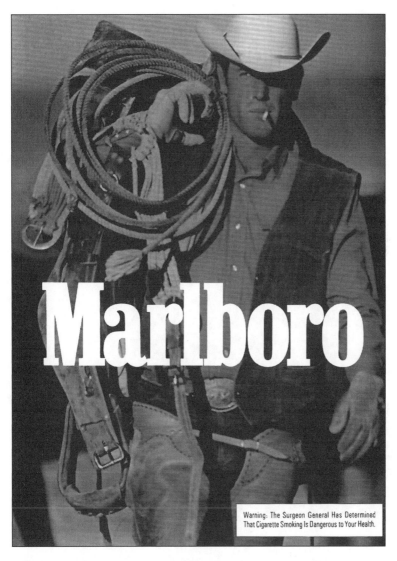

Warning: The Surgeon General Has Determined That Cigarette Smoking Is Dangerous to Your Health.

◆ *With a red filter that smokers perceived as "effeminate," Marlboro had a minuscule market share (less than 1%) when Leo Burnett won the account in 1954. Against all odds, Burnett still decided to position Marlboro as a men's cigarette. The agency did so by using a Wild West image to suggest masculinity and by only showing men—never women—in its ads. Within a few years, Marlboro had become the world's most popular cigarette.*

There used to be a lot more pressure for a woman to succeed in middle management.

YOU'VE COME
A LONG WAY, BABY.

© Philip Morris Inc. 1991

9 mg "tar," 0.7 mg nicotine av. per cigarette by FTC method.

◆ *Virginia Slims: The slogan "You've come a long way, baby," the product name, and the advertising style have served to position the brand as a women's cigarette.*

◆ *The advertising community has made big changes over the past few years in the way it presents women, who are no longer necessarily portrayed as wives or mothers. Today's ads show the modern woman to be determined and dynamic. Men are shown providing support to women, not the other way around.*

12. Marital status

This segment offers multiple opportunities. Nestlé focused attention on its brands targeting singles. Carnival Cruise Lines offers cruises for singles, an idea that was unthinkable 20 years ago. AT&T and GE base their ad campaigns on family values and home comforts. Thyme Maternity is Canada's only maternity clothing chain, with some 60 outlets.

Dreft detergent is aimed at new mothers, a specific consumer group that was targeted after research revealed that second and third-time mothers returned to their original brand after the birth of each child. Within 18 months, Dreft managed to surpass Ivory Snow as the number-one baby detergent brand.

Ronald McDonald, the famous clown who got his start in 1963 in Washington DC, has helped make McDonald's a family restaurant. In the mid-1960s, McDonald's decided to invest almost all of its $500,000 budget on the renowned clown. Some initial consideration was given to transforming Ronald into a cowboy, and then an astronaut, but the decision was finally made to stick with the status quo and retain the chain's young customers.

13. Gay

Gay-oriented advertising is gradually increasing in volume. In Canada, this market is estimated at $40 billion. American gays have some $250 to $350 billion in purchasing power. With the US gay community's population numbering anywhere from 17 to 22.5 million people, this is a highly lucrative market.

In the early 1960s, Gitanes was among the first brand of cigarettes to target the homosexual market.[25] The firm's style and status-based campaign boosted sales by 30%.

Businesses are more willing these days to advertise in gay newspapers and magazines:

- Subaru used Martina Navratilova in its car ads.

- In April 1994, IKEA launched its first TV ad campaign aimed at the homosexual community. Ads were initially shown after 10:00 p.m.

- Visa recently created the Rainbow Card, and signed up Martina Navratilova to promote it.

- Naya sponsored New York's gay games in 1994.

- Nivea launched Nivea for Men.

- In early 2003, Jaguar began to directly target the gay market. Even the very staid *New York Times* began printing news of gay unions in its wedding announcement pages.

In 2005, the Canadian Tourism Commission, a Crown corporation, launched a $300,000 campaign to give Canada a new, spicier image, and to convince American homosexuals that Canada is a great, gay place. The commission advertised in gay and lesbian magazines in the United States, and on gay websites and set up stands at gay and lesbian events.

Studies reveal that the gay community is quite open to innovation and is often considered a launch pad for new trends in fashion, interior decoration, and music. Gays have better-than-average buying power and this market is an excellent testing ground for marketing experiments. The boxer shorts launched by Calvin Klein are just one example. Gay New York men first adopted this kind of underwear, before heterosexual men jumped on the bandwagon.

14. Age

The trend of breaking customers into different age groups has become a more pronounced advertising trend over the past few years.

Ivory Snow detergent, Coppertone's Water Babies sun cream, and Gerber food products are aimed at babies. The GapKids product line and Kid Cuisine foods are aimed at kids. Teen Spirit deodorant targets 9 to 16-year-old girls. Coors targets young adults. IKEA's distinctive US market consists of young and active urban adults, from 25 to 35 years of age. Basic 4, when served with milk, contains four basic food groups and is positioned as an adult cereal. Olay facial lotion is a successful product aimed at older women.

Youth is one of the most difficult markets to target. Young people are well aware of image, but not loyal to any particular brand. They are pleased when a product's color has no bearing on its taste. Young people are also well-attuned to humor and enjoy provoking others. Naturally, there is no point in lecturing youths about a product's nutritional qualities, targeting them with traditional ads, playing it cool, or trying to oversell an item. Young people are also attracted to symbols of success, while always on the lookout for pleasure. They are delinquents and rebels at the same time. Young people from 15 to 25 years of age form the foundation of our consumer society by dictating its trends.

FLASH INFO

MARKET SEGMENTS AND MEDIA CONSUMPTION HABITS

- Teens have $15 billion in buying power in Canada. A bit more than 59% get money from their parents, 33% have casual jobs and 23% have part-time jobs.[26] In the US, teenage girls (12 to 17 years old) report spending $47 per week vs. $45 per week for boys. Teenagers get most of their spending money from their parents.[27]

- 18 to 24 year olds. The 18 to 24-year-old group is the most likely to watch movies, comedies, cop shows, and music videos.

- 18 to 34 year olds. The 18 to 34-year-old group consists of trendsetters who quickly adopt new fashions. This group is heavily influenced by the media and by image. It consists of impulse buyers. They are, however, more sensitive to price and discounts.

- Baby boomers. This postwar group (born from 1947 through 1966) is the most popular segment among advertisers. They are at the root of many demographic and commercial changes.

- Fifty and older. Consumers aged 50 and over represent a choice segment, particularly in the fields of insurance and finance. Statistics Canada says that the number of Canadians who are 50 or older grew by 1.4 million from 1976 to 1988, and now totals 6.5 million. This segment of the population controls 55% of the nation's available personal income and 80% of its personal wealth.

The 50 and over group could profoundly change the world of advertising over the next few years. In Canada, half of all luxury cars were purchased by people in the 55 and older group. This segment is also responsible for one third of all restaurant expenditures. There are 63 million mature adults in the US, and by the year 2025 that number will soar to more than 113 million. According to Donnelly Marketing, the 50-plus age group is the most affluent in the nation and accounts for 50% of consumer discretionary income, as well as 77% of all financial assets. The Bozell advertising agency indicates that this group purchases:

- 40% of all consumer products

- 80% of all luxury travel

- 43% of all new domestic cars and 48% of all luxury cars

- 37% of all spa memberships[28]

A number of industry sectors should rethink their marketing strategies in view of the aging population. The challenge is huge. Members of the "Me Generation" own their own homes. They like luxury cars and love to travel. Wilson Sporting Goods made sure it placed a line of golf clubs on the market for golfers aged 50 and over.

Seniors' market potential is now estimated at $800 billion. Pockets of resistance still remain. The automobile industry, for example, continues to refuse to portray individuals over the age of 50 using its products. As Chris Cedergren, senior auto analyst at J.D. Power & Associates, puts it: "No one wants to drive an old person's car."[29]

15. Consumer physique

Many examples come quickly to mind in this department, particularly in the clothing industry. Reitmans and Laura Canada stores have decided to cater to the plump women's market. Laura Petites specializes in clothing for women under 5'4", with waist sizes from 2 to 18. Laura Plus, on the other hand, goes after bigger ladies. In the US, Retail Forward reports that 40% of the women who responded to their latest annual shoppers' survey say they wear size 16 or larger.

Retail sales for the US women's plus-size apparel market stood at nearly US $32 billion in 2000, up US $7.8 billion from 1996, according to the 2001 report on the "US Market for Plus-Size Apparel" published by Packaged Facts, a division of MarketResearch.com. The same report forecasts that sales will rise to US$47 billion in 2005.

"Waistband Segments" shows that the top stores shopped by overweight or obese women are Lane Bryant, Fashion Bug, Dress Barn, Leggs/Hanes/Bali Outlet, Payless Shoe Source, and Ross Dress for Less.

The clothing market for big ladies is surging and now represents nearly 20% of the women's clothing market. That is why storefront mannequins are now a bit rounder. And it would seem this effort works, as sales have risen in stores that apply this tactic.

16. Consumer issues

Ecotrin is an analgesic for those suffering from arthritis. Dove is a soap for women suffering from dry skin.

In 2003, Hanes launched the first label-free T-shirt for men. This innovation caused Hanes' sales to surge. J.C. Penney, Gap and Banana Republic have since followed suit. The NPD Group reports that 10% of all clothing will bear no labels by 2007.

17. Time of day

Kit Kat is a lunchtime chocolate bar. Vicks' NyQuil is a nighttime remedy. Coast is "The eye opener."

Cora's restaurant chain specializes in breakfasts and serves 7 million customers per year. To brighten up its outlets, founder Cora Tsouflidou selected such enticing images as colored posters, hens, and a large sun. The chain also sells some of its products at supermarkets and is eyeing the US market.

18. Time of year

The Virgin Islands boosted its tourist trade by 24% by presenting itself as the ideal winter vacation spot.[30]

Quebec City's Winter Carnival has become the world's biggest festival of its kind and took third place among other major carnivals, just behind those of Rio and New Orleans.

Quebec City's first Winter Carnival took place in 1894. The city has thus effectively revived a popular tradition and established a snow festival that serves to warm the hearts of residents and visitors alike. Although the Carnival was put on hold throughout most of the two world wars and the Depression, it was revived sporadically until the early 1950s. In 1954 a group of businesspeople re-launched the event, generating economic development for the Old Capital. Bonhomme, "the living incarnation of Quebec City's snowmen," was born in 1954 and appointed host of the festivities.

The first revived Quebec City Winter Carnival took place in 1955 and immediately became a key event for all inhabitants of Quebec City, and a driving force in winter tourist activity. Bonhomme Carnaval travels throughout the world each year to promote his event. His itinerary takes him to such exotic locations as Brazil, Belgium, France, Japan, China, Cuba, the Bahamas, New York, Louisiana, and Vancouver.

19. 24/7 availability

Kinko's has 1,200 outlets offering courier service, color copies, printers, and computer rentals. FedEx took over the firm in 2004.

20. Internationalism

It is not a bad idea to position your product as being international in an increasingly multicultural world. The Visa card is an excellent example of successful products and services that employ an "international" position.

Benetton gave itself effective international positioning through its "United Colors of Benetton" slogan. Benetton's anti-racism campaigns from the 1990s featured young models from all parts of the world. The company has, at the same time, never been afraid to try something new or to shock its audiences. In addition to using condoms in its ad campaigns, Benetton sponsors a Formula 1 racing team.

21. Product continent of origin

Alberto is a European hairspray that uses its origin as part of its name. Manufacturers of natural products often make references to traditional Native American remedies.

22. Product country of origin

IKEA is a Swedish furniture store. Dior, Yoplait, and Renault are French. Ragu is an Italian sauce. Volkswagen is a German brand. Finlandia vodka is imported from Finland.

The Revlon International line includes a French formula for maximum volume, a Far Eastern formula for long and silky hair, a Scandinavian botanical formula for highlighting, a Latin American formula for curls, perms and waves, an Australian One-Step shampoo and conditioner, and a Mediterranean formula for sun, salt and chlorine protection. Harley-Davidson is an American motorcycle. During World Wars I and II, most of Harley-Davidson's production was devoted to supplying U.S. and allied troops with motorcycles, an activity that further strengthened its link to American culture.[31]

Canadian Tire has proudly stood the test of time since it was founded in 1922. Canadian Tire's name highlights its clear purpose: it is a proud Canadian family of retail, retail-related, and financial service businesses that are inter-related.

Molson Canadian's sales have stabilized ever since the company decided to adopt a pro-Canada advertising theme for the brand. In 1994, sales rose 5% following the first such message in the series. In 1995, a second TV spot won the company another 5% of the Canadian beer market. Molson oddly forgot about its positioning and featured monkeys in the brand's 1998 campaign. Sales plunged and Molson once again positioned Canadian as the Canadian beer. In July 2000, the Joe Canadian character, a proud representative of his nation, traveled the country and gave ten speeches on Canada Day.

23. City or region

La Parisienne bleach is a good example of a product name that adopts this style of positioning.

The cosmetics industry deftly exploits the world's great capitals in the positioning of its product. Perfumes often sport names including the words "Paris" and "New York."

Until the early 1970s, Coors was only sold in 11 Western states and was perceived as a cult product with special status.

That said, the ultimate symbol of a city is neither London nor Paris. The centre of the world's business is now situated in the United States, and particularly in New York, which serves as the prime image of a modern, dynamic and vigorous metropolis.

24. Ethnicity

In August 1963, Lever Bros., one of the largest advertisers in the USA, asked its agencies how it could more effectively use African-Americans and other minorities in advertising. And so ethnic advertising was born.

Ethnic positioning offers great potential. Immigration is clearly redefining the US population. The US government's 1990 census shows that America's population changed more rapidly in the 1980s than in any other decade of this century. Nearly one of every four Americans claim African, Asian, Hispanic, or Native American ancestry as compared to only one in five in the 1980 census.

The Hispanic community is in fact the fastest-growing demographic group in the United States. Personal consumption spending by Hispanics will grow at an average annual rate of 9.1% from 2002 through 2020. As of July 1, 2003, the Hispanic population of the United States was estimated at 39.9 million people, forming the country's single largest racial or ethnic minority. Hispanics constitute 13.7% of the country's population (not including the 3.9 Hispanic residents of Puerto Rico). By 2050, the Hispanic population is expected to number 102.6 million, which would make them 24% of the total population of the United States.[32]

Cigarette makers are among the businesses that have made the greatest strides to target their products to such narrowly defined segments as female blue-collar workers, Spanish speakers, inner city blacks, young smokers, and so forth.

In the early 1990s, RJ Reynolds Tobacco tried to launch Uptown, a cigarette that had been specifically designed for the black community. However, after encountering problems with the US Secretary of Health & Human Services, Reynolds dropped the plan.

Mattel carefully studied the marketplace when it decided to develop an African-American doll. Many black employees worked on the project. The company hired a psychologist specialized in the behavior of African-American children. A black PR firm was employed to officially launch this doll, dubbed "Shani."[33] A few years later, Mattel repeated the experience with a "multi-ethnic" doll named Kayla.

FLASH INFO

ETHNIC MARKETING

How fairly do you think the following groups are represented in advertising?

	Under	Over	Right
Handicapped people	57%	5%	27%
Hispanics	41%	8%	38%
The 50 and over population	37%	6%	47%
Blacks	29%	16%	45%
Housewives	29%	12%	46%
Employed women	23%	10%	52%
People in their 30s and 40s	20%	10%	59%
Teenagers & young adults	9%	35%	47%

Source: The Roper Organization.

In 1946, Pepsi hired a team of ten African Americans to promote its product among the black community. Two years later, Pepsi began broadcasting its first advertisements targeting blacks. The featured character in these ads was a 7-year-old black boy named Ron Brown, who would eventually become nothing less than Secretary of Commerce in the Clinton administration. Pepsi provided scholarship funds in the 1950s to the United Negro College Fund, and then in 1958 named a black to head its sales team. Four years later, and despite boycott threats from the Ku Klux Klan, Pepsi named a black as its vice president.

Each ethnic group has its distinctive traits. Blacks are seen as trendsetters. Hispanics are perceived as being traditional and religious. Members of the Spanish community are also seen as opinion leaders because of the popularity of Ricky Martin and Jennifer Lopez. Dorado cigarettes and Ariel detergent are specifically aimed at Hispanic-Americans.

25. Religion

Religion has become a factor in targeting advertising segments. General Electric has equipped 65 of its ovens with a "Shabbat" mode to permit observant Jews to keep warm meals that were prepared prior to the start of the sabbath, without requiring any user interaction.

26. Social

There are two approaches to social positioning: charitable publicity and social publicity.

Newman's Own salad dressing is a good example of "charitable" publicity. The actor Paul Newman and a friend launched a new brand of salad dressing in 1982. The brand was based on two principles: 1) Superior ingredients with no artificial additives, and 2) All profits would be turned over to charitable organizations. The dressing was an immediate hit. In its first year, Newman's Own turned over more than $1 million to charitable groups. Ever since, more than $125 million has been dispensed to thousands of charitable works.

To increase its stock of goodwill in Canada, International Paint became a supporter of the beluga whales, a friend of Great Lakes birds in Ontario, and a benefactor of Pacific salmon in Western Canada.

Più bella è la maglia
più bella sembrate

Così morbida, soffice, leggera leggera, in tutti i colori di
è la maglia per la bellezza e l'eleganza di ogni donna.
In "cashmere" o in "lambswool" è così comoda e calda.

Maglierie benetton - Ponzano (Treviso)

◆ Success in advertising depends on how well yo
brand is positioned. This means you must give yo
brand a distinctive personality.

Above: when Benetton first started spending money o
advertising, its visual message failed to make t
sweater maker stand out from the crowd. At the tin
Benetton had no brand image.

Below: Benetton's image underwent a sea change ov
the years. Toscani's various campaigns not or
shocked their audiences, but set Benetton clearly ape
from the competition.

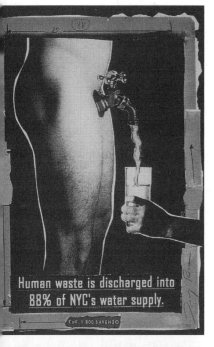

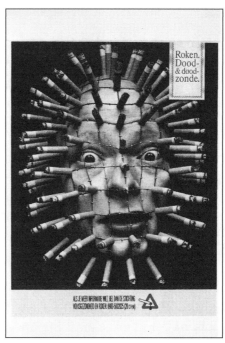

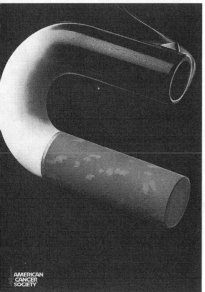

◆ *Social marketing campaigns often rely on pro-voking visual shocks. The more surprising the image, the better it should work.*

27. Size

Doyle Dane Bernbach produced a landmark campaign that positioned Volkswagen's Beetle as a small car. And little looks like the next big thing in plastic, with the Minicard, a half-pint version of popular credit cards, appearing nationwide throughout the US.

By humorously presenting the various problems that could be caused by the length of their cigarettes (popping a balloon, burning a newspaper, being caught in an elevator door, setting a beard alight, etc.), Benson & Hedges successfully positioned this product according to its *large* size.

28. Shape

Everyone is familiar with Wendy's square hamburgers. In England, meanwhile, Tetley's has begun to market round tea bags.[34] Perceived by the public as being more amusing and providing a better taste than the tea contained in square bags, the round format has helped Tetley boost sales by 20% since 1989. In Canada, these strange little Tetley bags have worked miracles by enabling the firm to stand out from the competition.

SURGEON GENERAL'S WARNING: QUITTING SMOKING NOW GREATLY REDUCES SERIOUS HEALTH RISKS.

◆ *This kind of image serves to position Benson & Hedges as long cigarettes.*

29. Color

One marketing technique involved the use of different colors to boost sales. Within one year, Nuprin managed to substantially increase its market share with its yellow analgesic tablets.

Kellogg's launched Mickey's Magic cereals, featuring blue milk. Cheer is a detergent that claims to make colors brighter. General Mills created Pop Qwiz, a popcorn for use in microwave ovens which bursts open in six different colors: blue, orange, green, purple, red, and yellow.

Green, yellow, and red sodas have recently appeared on super-market shelves. After testing over 100 concepts and working nine months on the project, Pepsi launched a blue version of its famous drink. By increasing the number of colors, Pepsi thinks it will attract a young-adult crowd. Studies show that two thirds of all teens confirmed that they would buy Pepsi Blue. Furthermore, 80% of all consumers who have sipped Pepsi Blue say that it was as good as or better than they had imagined.

In 2000, Heinz placed a green "kids'" ketchup on the market. When green proved a hit, Heinz introduced a purple, and then blue ketchup. The company also redid its ketchup bottle to make it easier to handle.

If you plan to use color in positioning your products, make sure that you take style into account. Some years ago, Pepsi-Cola launched Pepsi Crystal, a clear drink. Amoco also sold a clear gasoline. Studies at the time suggested that people perceived clear products as being more *natural*. These products have subsequently vanished from the market.

30. Fragrance

After color, marketing specialists say that fragrance is the best means of boosting sales.

Many studies have shown that fragrance affects the ways consumers think and feel. Research conducted by Jean-Charles Chebat, a professor at the Université de Montréal business school, revealed that dispersing a citrus scent at one shopping centre boosted average per-customer sales from $55 to $90.

Studies by Renault have shown that drivers don't like the plastic scent to be completely eliminated. If they smell nothing, prospective buyers think a car is used.

Many product sales strategies are primarily based on fragrance. These include Johnson's baby power, Coppertone sun cream, Crayola crayons, and Play-Doh modeling clay.

31. Taste

Taste is another profitable strategy. Coca-Cola and Pepsi-Cola respectively launched Lemon Coke and Pepsi Twist. 7-Up Tropical and Vanilla Coke followed. Coca-Cola and Pepsi had previously produced cherry-flavored versions of their sodas.

32. Softness

Puffs Ultra tissues are so soft they claim to provide comfort even to sore noses.

In Canada, Cottonelle toilet paper sells its softness. In 1992, Cottonelle took a new approach by marketing toilet paper containing 50% more tissue. To be sure to attract attention a few years later, the company distributed free rolls of its product to every spectator attending a Montreal tennis match.

Scott Paper Ltd., Canada's leading tissue manufacturer, will see its licence to the brand name Cottonelle expire in 2007. So, to retain market share, Scott has set out to "revitalize, differentiate and elevate" its premium product by rebranding the product as Cashmere. The two-ply and three-ply ("Ultra") versions will *be* Cottonelle, but with a quilted look, slick packaging and a fresh uptown attitude.

33. Temperature

Some products are positioned on the basis of temperature. Slogans such as *nothing works better in cold water* and *the clean winner in cold water* position Arctic Power as a cold-water detergent.

One ad agency selected a very simple strategy to draw tourists to New Brunswick: *its waters are hot.* This New Brunswick tourist campaign won awards for creativity.

For some time now, certain websites have been using the idea of temperature to boost the effectiveness of their advertising. They do so by marketing different products to different audiences from their sites. Users from the Miami region will see an ad for a fan, while in Milwaukee they will read an ad for winter tires.

Home Depot and Wal-Mart know that temperature has an effect on consumers. The Weather Channel has for many years tailored its ads to the weather. Campbell's has observed that people buy more hot soup when it's cold or rainy outside.

34. Time

Minute Rice is a long-grain rice that is ready to serve in just *five minutes.* Western Union is *the fastest way to send money.* According to the ads, *your glasses are ready in about an hour at LensCrafters.* Polaroid offers *a finished picture in ten seconds.* Federal Express: *When it absolutely, positively has to be there overnight.* Extra chewing gum *lasts an extra long time.*

35. Supply channels

Domino's Pizza in the United States focuses all of its efforts on home delivery. Founded by Tom Monaghan, the chain now has 7,400 establishments in 50 countries. During the 2002 Super Bowl, Domino's sold nearly 1.2 million pizzas in a single day. (The average American eats 46 slices a year).

Tupperware sells its products through group get-togethers. The firm achieved sales of $2.7 million per day in 2002 through this system. Statistics show that, somewhere in the world, a new Tupperware meeting begins every 10 seconds.

Avon distributes its products through a network of 500,000 North American representatives. The 118-year-old company operates in 143 nations and sells $6 billion in beauty products each year.

Dell has set up its own mini-empire by selling computers straight from the manufacturer. Created in 1984 by Michael Dell, the company posted sales of some $49.2 billion in 2004. The firm has 55,200 representatives in 81 nations and uses 28 languages or dialects.

Dell's advertising strategy is a model of efficiency. The company initially spent almost its entire budget on computing magazines. It quickly became the dominant advertiser in IT magazines read by industry trend makers.

Dell has long reserved one fourth of its advertising budget for PC World, in which it buys up to 10 pages of space in a single issue. During the same period, IBM and Compaq spent colossal sums on general interest magazines, such as *Time, Business Week,* and *Fortune.*

36. Use

New Quaker State 4x4 motor oil is a lubricant designed specifically for light trucks, sport-utility vehicles, and minivans.

In the chewing gum market, Cristal proclaims that it does not stick to dentures, Trident is the sweet sugarless gum, and Dentyne makes teeth brighter and breath fresher.

- *Are you advertising a food product?* You can position it as a sugarless product, with low carbohydrates, no caffeine, no additives, no salt, low cholesterol, low calories, or for use in the microwave.

- *Are you producing cigarette ads?* You can present your brand as a mentholated, mild, extra mild, ultra-soft, smoke-free, nicotinefree, or odorless product.

- *Are you producing hotel ads?* You can aim your ads at travelers seeking a good night's sleep and a quick breakfast. Or you can target those longing for a good quality-price ratio. Another segment seeks to impress a spouse or friends. And then there are those who are merely looking for comfort.

The effectiveness of all these approaches naturally depends on whether or not a niche for your product type exists. And only research can answer that question.

Half a century ago, Gleem toothpaste was aimed at "people who can't brush their teeth after every meal." This seemed like a great idea on paper. But the campaign flopped. Why? The targeted segment was not viable. Studies showed that most people do not brush after each meal. But who would openly admit it?

◆ *This ad positioned 7Up as the "Uncola," a concept that reappeared in the ad's headline and in its visual components.*

●————— **FLASH** INFO —————●

THE IMPORTANCE OF RESEARCH
IN MARKETING AND ADVERTISING

What do all those shoppers tell P&G?

"P&G SPENDS BIG on consumer research every year and gets a great deal of feedback from consumers. Aside from the insight about tastes and behavior, it allows the company to determine just how many people are squeezing the Charmin.

Nearly 70% of primary grocery shoppers are women.

P&G spends more than $100 million annually on consumer research.

P&G got more than 3.5 million consumer contacts in 2004 via its email and phone center, up from 1,000 letters in 1940 and 800,000 calls when toll-free lines opened in 1974.

P&G was the first consumer-products company to print toll-free numbers on its packages.

P&G's consumer-contact volume is up 75% in only the past five years, driven largely by the addition of Clairol, which in itself accounts for about 1 million calls and emails annually.

P&G contacts another 1 million consumers annually through its outbound research efforts.

More than 50 million households in North America squeeze—or otherwise come into contact with—Charmin tissues every day.

People eat 275 million Pringles every day. The chips' curved shape inspired the design of the Olympic stadium in Sydney, Australia.

Tide does more than 32 million loads of laundry globally each day.

Consumers buy enough Bounty towels each year to soak up more than 3 million Olympic-size pools.

P&G conducts roughly 10,000 formal consumer research projects each year.

Crest.com set a P&G record for hits to a brand website in a day with 3 million visits following the appearance of Crest Vanilla Mint on "Apprentice 2" in September.

Each of P&G's top 50 managers is required to visit with consumers, either in their homes or on a shopping trip, at least once each quarter."

Source: P&G in Neff, Jack. "P&G Kisses Up To The Boss: Consumers," *Advertising Age,* May 2, 2005, p. 18.

37. Big consumers

Researcher Dik Warren Twedt revealed that certain consumers buy large quantities of products that are of little interest to the public at large.[35] For example, 39% of all households drink 90% of all colas, and 37% of these households consume 85% of all cake mixes. In economics, this principle is called *Pareto's Law* and finds many applications in marketing. If 80% of a company's sales come from 20% of its operations, 80% of its profits are generated by 20% of its customers. This law applies to big and small business alike.

The slogan *if you take aspirin more than once a week* served to position Bufferin as an analgesic for *heavy users* of aspirin.

Be careful, though, about basing your entire strategy on big users, who often form a fickle community. Such users won't hesitate to switch brands if a competitor offers a better price.

38. *In products*

Absolut became the best-selling brand of vodka thanks to a series of campaigns that defined the brand as an "in" product. Company president Michel Roux started out by asking artist Andy Warhol to paint a bottle of Absolut for an ad. Following the positive reaction triggered by Warhol's work, Roux hired artists Keith Haring, Kenny Scharf, and Ed Ruscha to produce their versions of the brand image. Roux received two unexpected boosts during the campaign: the Russian invasion of Afghanistan and the Soviet attack on a Korean airliner. Both events led to the boycott of competing vodkas from the USSR.

Roux said: "The key to successful marketing is starting with a good product [by] developing positioning, then making sure all subsequent events and programs reflect that positioning. The impression you make in ads, sponsorships, point of purchase, the way the brand is handled at retail, all of these impressions have to integrate to produce a powerful, focused brand image."[36]

Krispy Kreme is famous throughout North America for its hot donuts. The company acquired its renown through the simple strategy of distributing thousands of free donuts every time it enters a new market.

Buzz marketing is a technique that took off with the advent of the Internet. Krispy Kreme generated this kind of buzz by passing out its donuts for free. This effort allowed the firm to reach out to opinion leaders and to benefit from their impact. Research conducted by McKinsey & Company in 2001 revealed that 67% of all sales are influenced by word of mouth.

Word of mouth is in fact a very old phenomenon. It has been studied by sociologists, ad experts and rumor specialists. We know that nearly 80% of all consumer purchasing decisions are influenced by word of mouth. Hotmail's free email service and the *Blair Witch Project* owe their respective successes to buzz.

39. Not tested on animals

Revlon exploited the nonviolence niche by launching a line of cosmetics that had not been tested on animals. Studies showed that 60% of all women preferred to buy beauty products that had not been used in such tests.[37]

To boost the profiles of *cruelty-free* products, lobbyists created the icon of a small rabbit, which appears on products not tested on animals. Hundreds of firms, such as the Body Shop International and John Paul Mitchell Systems have, since the logo's creation, placed this mark on their products.

40. Eco-friendliness

Procter & Gamble has recently adopted an environmentally friendly strategy. The firm launched the Downy refill, a concentrate that appears next to Downy softener on supermarket shelves. This new product already accounts for 40% of all Downy sales. Procter & Gamble now spends one third of its budget on the research and development of environmentally friendly products.

41. Health products

West Lake Village plans to launch a product called Nico Water, which contains a nicotine supplement. The product aims to serve as an alternative to gums and patches for individuals who wish to quit smoking.

42. Disposable products

It is difficult to imagine a society without disposable products, no matter how much they may contribute to pollution. Launched in 1961, Pampers diapers rapidly replaced their cotton counterparts. Studies have shown that the typical child goes through 6,000 such diapers before being toilet trained.

Fujifilm invented the first disposal cameras in 1986. Kodak followed suit in 1987 and they proved a big hit. In 1992, 9.3 million such cameras were sold in the United States. Studies show that 50% of the pictures taken with such equipment would not have been taken if they did not exist.[38]

Disposable contact lenses also benefit from this strategy. Launched by Vistakon in 1995, they were designed to be worn and disposed of the same day. They had required research and development expenditures of more than $200 million.

43. Sports

You could also present your product as sports-related. Right Guard took this approach with its personal deodorant, Wheaties with cereals, Gatorade with soft drinks, Vogue with bras, and ESPN and TSN with the special-segment TV market. Schering-Plough launched Coppertone Sport for players of tennis, golf, and other outdoor sports.

44. Clubs

When it was established in 1970 by Sol and Robert Price, Price Club became the first private North American warehouse club that worked on the "pay and take it away" principle. The firm merged with Costco in 1993. Today, 43 million people are Costco members and use its 450 warehouses worldwide.

45. Personal property

Apple didn't take on IBM by directly challenging the industry leader. Rather, it focused on being known as the "personal computer" company. This strategy enabled Apple to carve out a respectable market share. Apple continues to focus on "personal" positioning in computing (iMac) and entertainment (iPod).

Black & Decker launched DirtBuster in 2002. This small vacuum cleaner was designed to clean townhouses, apartments and dorm rooms.

46. Mix ingredient

Post Grape-Nuts are intended to be mixed with yogurt or rolled oats. Schweppes sodas are mixed with rum, bourbon, gin, or vodka.

47. Substitute products

Kraft's Parkay margarine is sold as a butter substitute. Coffee-Mate is a milk replacement that can be kept on the shelf. Equal is used in place of sugar and contains fewer calories. And the Wrigley's gum ad markets this product with the message: "When you can't smoke, chew!"

48. Taking on preconceived notions

The Chiat/Day/Mojo agency helped launch the Nissan Maxima in 1989 by underscoring how it stood apart from others of its class with the "four-door sports car" slogan. This formula helped generate sales of 106,000 vehicles, a 43% rise over the previous year, despite a hike in the sales price during the year.

Heinz recently introduced the "upside-down" ketchup bottle that's always ready for serving. Gone are the days of shaking: ketchup flows when the container is squeezed.

49. Two-for-one

Little Caesars has become one of the highest money-making home-delivery pizza chains by offering "two pizzas for the price of one" at all times.

Pearle always offers two pairs of eyeglasses for the price of one. The advertisement offer states: "Buy a pair of glasses, get the second one free."

50. Two-in-one

Considered to be on the verge of discontinuation only a few years ago, Pert Plus has become the world's number-one selling shampoo after its relaunch as a two-in-one product that combines shampoo and conditioner. Ultra Care by Vidal Sassoon has since become the first three-in-one product, combining a shampoo, a conditioner and a finishing rinse.

51. House brand

The concept of house (or generic) brand first made waves in the United States, like many other marketing phenomena.

In Canada, house brands began to soar in popularity beginning in the 1980s, following the lead of Loblaw's President's Choice. Steinberg had adopted the same approach some time before, but in the case of Loblaw's, "house brand" began to mean more than just "discount."

Loblaw's would go on to create other brands with their own names and personalities. Packaging was improved. The products were of the same or better quality than their competitors, but always sold at lower prices.

Drug stores, superstores, and hardware stores soon climbed aboard the bandwagon to launch their own brands. Wal-Mart now has a house brand called Equate.

This process explains why many popular brands have revamped their familiar packaging to look either more contemporary or more classic, in other words to look like a leading brand. "They've been hurt very badly by private-label competition. As a result, many brands have lost market share and are strengthened to reinvent themselves," said Tony Pearson, managing partner at Peterson Blyth Pearson, a New York-based packaging consultancy.[39]

In the food market, generic products represent up to 20% of total sales. In Canada, Cott makes more than 90% of the generic products in the soda sector. Cott also has agreements with Wal-Mart and Safeway in the United States.

The success enjoyed by house brands clearly illustrates the chronic lack of consumer loyalty. A recent study shows that brand name is a factor only among 18% of all consumers who buy frozen pizza. When asked why they switch brands, 78% of those interviewed said "price." Three product families maintain high loyalty rates: cat food, soft drinks, and ketchup.[40]

52. Nostalgia

With an aging population and the first baby boomers already retiring, nostalgia is the keyword on radio, TV, and in clothing.

Some companies are already exploiting this phenomenon, with Volkswagen's remodeled Beetle and Chrysler's PT Cruiser providing two examples.

53. Social class

Socioeconomic factors are useful in distinguishing between the social classes. In 1948, Lloyd Warner, of the University of Chicago, published a book called *Social Class in America.*[41] In this work, Warner showed for the first time that people's motivations and desires depend on their social class. In his study, Prof. Warner said that the behavior of each social class is fairly uniform and predictable.

Warner identified six social classes:

1. *Upper upper class:* aristocrats whose families have long been established in their communities.

2. *Lower upper class:* the "nouveaux riches" or newly rich.

3. *Upper middle class:* members of the liberal professions, executives, owners of large businesses.

4. *Lower middle class:* office workers, tradesmen, and some specialized laborers.

5. *Upper lower class:* mainly specialized or semi-specialized workers.

6. *Lower lower class:* laborers and unassimilated immigrant groups.

Perrier positioned itself as a non-alcoholic beverage for the upper classes when it was launched in the United States.[42] The brand was originally sold in America's most prestigious retail outlets and price was set accordingly, with six 6-oz. bottles retailing for $2.39 and three 11-ounce bottles for $1.49 in 1978. Perrier ads appeared in prestigious magazines, and the TV commercials were narrated by Orson Welles.

Grey Poupon mustard targeted high-class clients in 1986. Product advertisements feature British lords riding around in Rolls Royces. The campaign served to boost the manufacturer's market share by several points.

The typical BMW buyer is described as a college-educated 40 year-old male with a household income of $130,000. Wendy's positioning strategy involves targeting white-collar professionals. The idea is to offer a superior-quality product at a premium price in attractive surroundings.

The Bay modified its positioning in 2002, from high- to medium-line. To take on Wal-Mart, the chain decided to promote private brands and to cut its stocks of sophisticated clothing.

54. Lifestyle

Lifestyle positioning targets specific consumer activities, interests, and opinions. It is important because two individuals with similar demographic profiles (same nationality, age, sex, and income) may have very different lifestyles. One may be extroverted, the other introverted. One a follower, the other a leader. One may be sensitive and the other concerned with his or her health.

Many companies have large research budgets to study lifestyle. They try to determine consumer habits within their sectors of activity.

For example, a study by *Self* magazine maintains that women can be grouped into seven major lifestyle categories[43]:

- *Searchers:* usually young and married, these women want children and careers but aren't quite sure in which direction to proceed.

- *Traditionalists:* home- and family-oriented women. Some work outside the home, but family is still the main focus of their lives.

- *Strivers:* work-oriented or career women.

- *Copers:* self-sufficient single or divorced women who are forced to work but enjoy working.

- *Undecideds:* mostly younger, single, career-oriented women looking to marry but not ready for children.

- *Dreamers:* women who work because they have to. Usually trapped between feminist and traditionalist roles.

- *Day-to-dayers:* usually younger women who haven't decided on their future career or family plans.

Adidas believes there are many sports shoe customer categories. Some require very high performance shoes. Others shun cool styles. Many want trendy sports shoes.

Perfume ads are aimed at four major consumer categories: the sensual woman, the prestigious type, the romantic type, and the eccentric type. In the perfume industry, advertising for Charlie is aimed at women who are independently adventurous and modern. Anaïs Anaïs appeals to romantics, Joy to the middle-class, and Chanel No. 5 to the woman of classical taste.

Other research shows that drinkers of Pepsi-Cola and Coca-Cola are more extroverted than are drinkers of Dr. Pepper. In contrast, typical Dr. Pepper drinkers believe they should live life in accordance with their own personal values and not try to meet other people's expectations. They view themselves as original, even a little crazy, and they search for interesting experiences (add reference).

Volkswagen's Golf, in the world of marketing, is economical and attractive. Jell-O is the happy family's dessert. Studies reveal that buyers of Jaguars tend to be more adventuresome and less conservative than those of Mercedes-Benzes or BMWs.

In Canada, Krispy Kernels, which sells more than 200 products, including its famous peanuts, is in the business of providing pleasure and happiness.

US-based Fox News beat the ratings of its competitor CNN through its anti-snob and openly conservative positioning. While CNN is still the more credible station, according to the polls, Fox News is in the process of establishing a new tone and identity in the market through the strong personalities of its broadcasters.

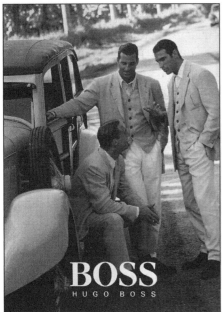
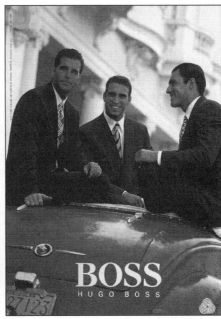

◆ *To endow its products with high social standing, Hugo Boss drew on the past and a conservative system of education. Established in 1923, this brand has succeeded with its campaigns in giving this product an envious position at the high end of its market.*

Pillsbury's analysis of data from more than 3,000 respondents over a period of fifteen years identified five distinct groups of consumers.[44] The five groups are:

1. *The Chase and Grabbits*: young urbanites who eat on the run or out of a sense of opportunity.

2. *The Functional Feeders*: early middle-aged people who rely heavily on convenience foods to prepare their traditional meals.

3. *The Down Home Stokers*: people of all ages and varying geographic regions who appreciate the value of regional culture along with a meal's nutrients.

4. *The Careful Cooks*: typically older people whose diets are based on both medical advice and nutritional knowledge.

5. *The Happy Cookers*: career homemakers (both grandmothers and young mothers) who value traditional sit-down meals as a way to nurture their families.

Even leisure travelers can be segmented into three broad but distinct psycho-graphical groups. These three segments include travelers seeking experience, sun-and-fun travelers, and non-risk travelers.

55. Against the competition

Medacid coated caplets are positioned against liquid medications and chewable tablets. They are easy to swallow, quick to dissolve, and have no aftertaste.

Contrary to Coke and Pepsi, 7-Up is the "Uncola." In fact, less than a year after Leo Burnett resurrected 7-Up's uncola positioning (first introduced in the late 1960s), the brand achieved its first market share rise in a decade.

HOW TO DETERMINE PRODUCT POSITIONING?

A product's position is built over a long period. Positioning a product means selecting a niche for it.

Back in 1930, Procter & Gamble realized that every product must be distinctively positioned. Tide, Crest, Pampers, and Secret are all made by the same company. However, each is differently *positioned* in consumer minds.

Cake-mix maker Betty Crocker once unsuccessfully tried to launch a line of cereals. Cereal maker Kellogg's has had just as little success marketing fudge mixes. Both multinationals failed because their new products fell outside the scope of their respective market positions. Consumers perceive Betty Crocker as selling cake mixes and Kellogg's as selling cereals.

Many factors determine a product's position. *Name* is one of the most important. Success requires a name that properly positions your item in people's minds. Some examples of names that have effectively positioned a product include Arctic Power for a cold-water detergent, Honey Nut for a honey-flavored cereal, Visa for a credit card with global use, Price Chopper for low-priced supermarkets, and Häagen-Dazs for a super-premium ice cream.

Make sure that consumers can pronounce the name of your product with ease. Take Raid, Zest, and Tide for example. These names are all easy to pronounce. When Seagram launched the leading Japanese spirit Sochu in the United States, the company dropped the 'h' for easier pronunciation.

Easy-to-remember names are short, easy to pronounce, and easy to write. Try to include in the name some of the letters from this group: b, c, d, g, k, p and t. Linguists refer to such letters as "explosive consonants" because they release entrapped air when they are pronounced.

A professor at Michigan State University, Bruce Van den Bergh conducted research on the letters used in brand names.[45] He discovered that 172 out of 200 of the best-selling brand names in the United States use at least one explosive consonant. These include Bic, Buick, Burger King, Cadillac, Coca-Cola, Colgate, Crest, Crisco, Delta, Kmart, Kentucky Fried Chicken, Kodak, Kraft, Pampers, Pepsi-Cola, Pizza Hut, Polaroid, Pontiac, Tide, and Toyota.

● —— FLASH INFO —— ●

FACTORS THAT DETERMINE POSITIONING FOR A PRODUCT OR SERVICE

- Your product and its history
- Your brand name
- Your packaging: its shape, texture, fragrance, and color
- Your logo
- Your price
- The place your product was made and its shelf life
- Your sales outlets
- The style of your advertising, of your public relations, of your sponsorships, and of your promotions
- Your sales pitch (communications angle, image, layout, copy, etc.)
- Your spokespersons
- Your slogan
- Your selection of media
- Your forms of payment
- Your firm's social commitment to the community
- The competition

The sound of your name will influence the perception people have of your product. Lexicon Branding, which develops new brand names, found that those beginning with the letters V, F, S and Z evoke a sense of speed, while the letter X represents precision (Timex, Lexus, Xerox).[46]

Try not to choose a brand name similar to one from the competition. The Fonorola company had to change its name in 1998 because it sounded too much like Motorola.

If you are active in such fields as fashion or the restaurant industry, a French name, which evokes high social standing and excellent taste, could position you well in consumer minds. One example of this phenomenon is Cirque du Soleil. The exotic and international flair of its name sets this organization apart from other circuses.

In the mid-1980s, when Cirque du Soleil began performing outside Quebec, management decided to translate its name to Sun Circus. That was a mistake. A record number of people demanded refunds. They were disappointed not to see elephants and dog tricks. After chalking up a deficit of $750,000, Cirque du Soleil resumed using its French name. Cirque du Soleil now has nearly 3,000 employees, more than 600 of whom are performers. It has drawn tens of millions of spectators in over 100 cities around the world.

In some cases, a product name makes all the difference. It is not uncommon to see a company switch its name in mid-stream:

- Tilden-National became Kangouroute.
- EuroDisney in France was redubbed as Disneyland Paris.
- US cigarette maker Philip Morris selected the new name of Altria, to dodge adverse publicity pertaining to its main product.
- KFC resumed using the name Kentucky Fried Chicken in 2005. Research showed that the KFC name failed to effectively position the restaurant chain in consumers' minds.

In 1971, economics professor Ralph Anspach designed and launched a game called 'Bust the Trust' to a tepid reception. It was only after the professor relaunched the product under the new name of Anti-Monopoly that the product took off. In three years, he sold 419,000 games.

Name changes can prove costly. In 1971, Esso, Enco, Standard, and Jersey spent more than $100 million to be reborn as Exxon. In the airline sector, Allegheny paid $3 million to become US Airways.

FLASH INFO

SELECT A NAME

Corporate names were long a matter of chance. When George Eastman invented the word Kodak, he instinctively chose the letter K, the first letter of his mother's name. He decided to add another K to the end of this name. He also wanted to make sure the name was short and easy to pronounce. Before registering this name, he checked that it had no adverse meaning in another language.

Today there are companies that deal exclusively in name creation. Many options are open in selecting a new product name.

- Initials: IBM, A&W, CNN, CBC, ESPN, TSN
- Invented names: Kleenex, Kodak
- Numbers: Boeing 747, Century 21, Remax 2001
- Mythological characters: Atlas tires, Samsonite suitcases
- Proper names: Ford, Labatt, Molson
- Geographic names: Texas Instruments, Southwest, Air Canada
- Dictionary words: Close-Up, Tide
- Foreign words: Nestlé, Lux
- A combination of words: General Foods, Head & Shoulders

Make sure when you choose a name that there is nothing pejorative about it. Recently, Hormel Foods, makers of the well-known Spam canned pork products, was faced with an unusual dilemma. The firm's core product had acquired a new popular meaning of "unwanted email." Hormel decided to file a complaint with the United States Patent and Trademark Office to contest the use of the word spam in the computer world.

If you have a good product and a good name for it, make sure to register it with the trademark office. Coca-Cola and Heinz took the precaution of registering the shapes of their respective bottles. Toblerone Chocolates registered its triangular packaging. The silhouette of Stephen Spielberg's character E.T. has been trademarked. Even the roar of the Metro Goldwyn Mayer (MGM) lion that begins each of the studio's films is registered.

Your product's *logo* is the second most important factor in its successful positioning. A logo represents your brand. It must be simple, provide a positive image of your product, and convey a message. It must also be original and ideally capable of weathering at least 10 to 15 years of use.

Corporate and brand logos are the most visible traits of a marketer's image. Alvin Schechter of the Schechter Group in New York has said, "A corporate or brand logo is the single most pervasive element in corporate and brand communications. It represents a continuing, cumulative investment that influences the perceived value of everything that it touches."

When Nike took over Canstar in 1995, the firm carefully planned how its logo would be used. Hockey equipment maker Canstar's different product families (Lange, Micron, Cooper, and Bauer) were initially brought together under the single hat of the Bauer brand. Nike subsequently forged a link between itself and hockey gear by adding its name and logo to hockey skates. To further build on its presence in this market, Nike became the official supplier of National Hockey League jerseys, and the official sponsor of the US hockey team during the subsequent World Cup.

The *outlets* in which your product is sold represents the third key element in its successful positioning. Consider, for example, that you have two perfumes from the same manufacturer. Let us also assume that they were both developed in the same lab, give off the same fragrance, and are shipped in similar bottles. It might be impossible to distinguish one from the next. But let us imagine that one of the two perfumes is sold in a supermarket, while the other is distributed in chic stores. All the evidence would suggest that these perfumes are no longer identical. They have been differently positioned.

Packaging is the fourth key to successful positioning. In Canada, Molson Dry Beer changed its appearance in 2000 by using a different typeface and labeling, combined with silver tints added to the beverage's usual blue, to reach out to a new generation of drinkers. Studies had shown that these changes could boost new-customer sales. They also gave the beer the image of being easier to drink and of a better quality.

Packaging often makes people want to buy your product. The Coca-Cola bottle, for example, was designed by Alex Samuelson and T. Clyde Edwards, and first appeared on store shelves in 1915. Nowadays, Coca-Cola claims that 90% of the human population recognizes the characteristic shape of its bottle, which was eventually redone by designer Raymond Loewy.[47]

Why do cereals come in boxes? Why do consumers prefer yogurt in plastic containers? Why do Canadians prefer to drink beer out of bottles? Advertising and packaging may make all the difference in the world.

Your product *slogan* is the fifth key to its success. As André Gide put it, "slogans are war cries that bring people together." A good slogan should motivate them to act.

Many slogans have failed because they are too general. They fail to position the product. Here are some examples:

- *Nothing moves you like a Mercury*   Mercury
- *Sometimes you've gotta break the rules*   Burger King
- *I love what you do for me Toyota*   Toyota
- *The new spirit of Dodge*   Dodge
- *Built for the human race*   Nissan
- *Get to know Geo*   Geo
- *It just feels right*   Mazda
- *The art of travel*   Louis Vuitton
- *The art of writing*   Mont Blanc
- *The art of being unique*   Cartier
- *The art of perfect timing*   Ballantine's scotch
- *The art of engineering*   Audi
- *Bringing the future to you*   Ameritrust
- *Performance that counts*   Kodak
- *A passion for perfection*   Lufthansa
- *Where imagination becomes reality*   Ricoh
- *Because today isn't yesterday*   Bankers Trust Co.
- *The image of the future*   Anacomp

Slogans help sell inexpensive products that involve little risk and are bought on impulse. Slogans sum up the company's mission in a few words and implant a simple idea in consumers' minds. Slogans also create a sense of unity when you use different media. They are crucial in the political arena.

Slogans that work well must be repeated, which means they must be short, easy to memorize, and pleasant to repeat. In the words of Kevin Clancy, president and CEO of Copernicus Marketing Consulting: "A slogan means coming up with two or three words or possibly two or three brief phrases and implanting them in people's minds. If you succeed, people will unconsciously want to use your brand and will begin to talk about it among themselves."

A good slogan can propel a product toward success. When the manufacturers of Wisk introduced the slogan *Ring around the collar* for the first time, sales tripled with a significant increase in advertising.

Intel revolutionized the computer world by investing six percent of its sales in a fund earmarked for slogan promotion. The company's ad strategy was originally based on the name of the x386 processor. The company subsequently began emphasizing the slogan "Intel. The Computer inside." This eventually became "Intel inside." At virtually the same time, IBM was the first computer maker to use the Intel logo on its products. From the time of its launch, the Intel campaign and its famous logo have benefited from an advertising budget estimated at some $11 billion.

And while we are on the subject of slogans, I should add that a successful advertising campaign keeps the same slogan, the same look, and the same personality of the brand consistent for many years, even decades. For Ron Kovas, president of J. Walter Thompson, "The most valuable advertising strategy is the one that doesn't significantly change, but continues to build and reinforce brand attribution and perceptions year after year." DuPont's campaign theme *better things for better living* ran for 55 years. *Pepsi Generation* was launched in 1963 and is still used today. Hallmark's slogan *When you care enough to send the very best* had already been employed in 1956.

On the topic of slogans, it might be noted that a successful ad involves reuse of the same slogan and product personality for years, if not decades.

Experts generally agree that Winston cigarettes lost their market position to Marlboro because of unnecessarily frequent changes in their advertising format. Winston modified its slogan five times over the last 10 years, while Marlboro concentrated on its preferred target, men, and focused their slogan on the expression *Marlboro Country*.

1954: Winston tastes good like a cigarette should

1971: Winston and me

1971: How good it is

1974: If it wasn't for Winston, I wouldn't smoke

1974: There's a lot of good...between Winston and should

1974: I smoke for taste

1979: Big red

1979: America's best

1985: Men on America

1985: Real taste. Real people

1989: Winning taste

Marlboro is now the best selling cigarette brand in the world, and Winston just keeps on losing market share.

Larry Light, vice president of McDonald's, said, "The biggest mistake marketers make is to change the personality of their advertising year after year. They end up with a schizophrenic personality at worst, or no personality at best."[48]

BEST SLOGANS OF ALL TIME

Be all you can be.	US Army
Friends don't let friends drink and drive.	US Department of Transportation
Good to the last drop!	Maxwell House
Got Milk?	American Dairy Association
Tastes great…Less filling.	Miller Brewing Company
Have it your way.	Burger King
I LOVE NEW YORK.	New York State Division of Tourism
Imagination at work.	General Electric Co.
It's everywhere you want to be.	Visa
It takes a lickin' and keeps on tickin!	Timex
Just do it.	Nike
Look ma, no cavities!	Crest
Raising the bar.	Cingular
They're Gr-r-reat!	Kellogg's Frosted Flakes
We deliver for you!	United States Postal Service
We try harder.	Avis
What happens here, stays here.	Las Vegas Convention & Visitors Authority
When you care enough to send the very best.	Hallmark
You can do it. We can help.	Home Depot, Inc.
You're in good hands.	Allstate

Source: *Advertising Age,* 2005.

REVIEW

Experience shows that the best way to succeed in today's supersaturated market is to position your product and to maintain this position as long as possible.

"More and more, to be successful, you have to focus on a target group. In pure numbers, that might not be as much [as the whole], but it's significant if you make yourself pretty special to that group," says Barry Crossland, Nestlé's marketing director.[49]

It may be difficult to position a product, but changing an existing position will prove even more of a challenge. It is very hard to improve a negative product image. Sears tried to boost its image—and profit margin—in 1974 by boosting ladies' garment prices. Sales plummeted 28% and Sears dropped the project.

Another example is the case of Black & Decker. Despite success with new products, the company continues to wrestle with its image. Typical focus group comments include: "You'll hear power tool users say 'You used to be good. Now you're making popcorn poppers and toasters,'" says Ellen Foreman, Black & Decker power tool advertising and communications manager.[50] Of course, the success of any positioning is often a matter of timing. In 1988, Procter & Gamble successfully introduced Luvs diapers, with specific boy and girl designs. Yet, the idea of gender-distinguished diapers had already been tried in the early 1970s by Scott Paper with only limited success.

It is usually wise to avoid trendy positioning, which is all too often based on passing fads. In 1988, transparent products such as beer, deodorant, shampoo, dishwashing liquids and soft drinks were taking the market by storm. Consumers had begun to associate a product's quality of clarity or transparency with environmental consciousness, purity, and mildness. Four years later, interest in clear products had already begun to wane: "Consumers began to balk at paying higher prices for products that actually claimed to have fewer ingredients," writes Kathleen Deveny of *The Wall Street Journal*.[51] The *clear* concept was dead.

If you decide to shift your product's positioning, do so gradually. And start by changing the packaging.

Tim Hortons outlets suffered from a positioning problem a few years back. Consumers believed the chain sold mostly donuts (although it also sold soup and sandwiches). To correct the problem, the word "donuts" was taken out of its name to give a higher profile to its other products.

To learn more about positioning, I suggest you read *Positioning: The Battle for Your Mind*, by Al Ries and Jack Trout.

Chapter 3

What kinds of images attract the most attention?

Image is largely responsible for the big changes over the past two decades in the world of advertising.

Like it or not, we live in a world that is dominated by appearances. Image plays a key role in politics, economics, sports, and marketing.

In deft hands, ad images can prove to be powerful tools of persuasion. Research shows that image-heavy advertisements are recalled by 41% more readers than those dominated by text. It is, in other words, important to speak with images.

The image is often the only element consumers will notice in your ads. A compilation of Starch studies confirms the power of images: 44% of all readers notice an ad, 35% can name the advertiser, but only 9% read more than half of the text.[1]

Claude Cossette says that images offer two advantages over ad copy: "To begin with, an image's meaning travels at the speed of light, while words are only understood at the speed of sound. Images also bring together symbolic elements that transfer their meaning to the objects with which they are associated. Ladies put on Obsession to obtain the seductive powers suggested by the ad image. People drive the new Beetle to enjoy the second youth evoked by its poster's colors."[2]

Advertisers have long been aware of the fact that consumers buy images. As far back as 1917, adman Walter Dill Scott was aware of the fact that advertising was not aimed at convincing people, but offering them suggestions by using images.

Napoleon once said, "If you want to mesmerize crowds, speak to their eyes." The same rule applies in advertising.

Curiously, the political and social aspects of the European Community are likely to accelerate the trend of communicating with images, since the EC has twelve different national languages. "What it means for advertising," said Ronald Beatson, director general of the European Association of Advertising Agencies, "is a greater emphasis on non-verbal communication: the big visual idea, and the use of visual symbols to transcend national frontiers and national languages."[3]

This chapter will feature the more effective advertising images, and show how you can use them in successful ad campaigns.

◆ *Illustrations can command far more attention that the written word in a society suffering from an overload of information. Unlike text, images get your message across with the speed of lightning.*

• ——— MEDIA ADVISORY ——— •

THE IMAGE'S ROLE...

ON TV

The visual is the key element in TV commercials. While sound may also play an essential role in understanding your message, its function is generally limited to that of support.

Television was not designed for long speeches. The first five seconds of your ad can make or break it.

To test how well your TV concepts work, put together a focus group. Have this group view your messages with the TV sound off. If they don't get the picture without sound, your commercial should be redesigned.

RADIO

Certain ad experts will tell you that radio spots are less effective because they lack visuals. They fail, however, to mention that there is nothing better to create the illusion of a hot southern beach than the roar of a breaking wave.

Radio is the media of dreams. It uses words, music, and silence to generate different ambiances and locations. Listeners are constantly enticed over the radio to envision different scenes. It is not their ears that are at work, but their imagination.

BILLBOARDS

Readers of print ads can take the time to stop and read your ad. That is not the case with billboards, which may only have a fraction of a second to attract viewers. This means publicity posters must be spectacular.

Publicity posters depend more than any other media on the quality of the message.

MAGAZINES

Magazines let advertisers build a brand image. This is the media that conveys the greatest sense of refinement and esthetics.

Magazines are perceived as a prestige media. They are also a credible source of information.

DAILIES AND WEEKLIES

Your image must take up as great a percentage as possible of your layout. Some years ago, you could advertise in print media without using pictures. But that is no longer possible under present circumstances.

INTERNET

The Internet is a spectacular media. It offers unlimited visual means for attracting attention. Some software can produce animated sequences, such as an aircraft flying across a banner ad, or a group of dancers.

CATCHING THE EYE

Speak with images to draw attention to your ads. If you have five hours to put into an ad, spend four on selecting your image.

I share the opinion of Robert Plisken, vice-president in charge of art for Benson and Bowles: "Eventually, print ads will be all picture, like TV, the bigger and brighter the better. And, maybe at the bottom somewhere, there will be a small line of type."[4]

Here are 10 tips for boosting the effectiveness of your image.

1. Show the product

Whenever possible, make your product the focus of your image. In his book *Tested Advertising Methods*, John Caples notes that other kinds of images also work well: "1) Pictures of the product; 2) Pictures of the product in use; 3) Pictures of people who use the product; 4) Pictures showing the rewards of using the product."[5]

When launching a new product onto the market, an ad's main objective is to bring about the public's awareness of your product. Thus, you should show the product's packaging in your image.

2. Include the human factor

Show people using your product. Advertisements containing pictures of people command twice the attention and retention, on average, as those without people.

Faces attract the most reader attention. Ad research expert Pierre Martineau explains this fascination: "Identification is an extremely important avenue for persuasion and teaching in advertising. If the reader or viewer can identify with the users of the product, if he can see himself in the situation, then his feelings become involved and the process works toward conviction and believability. 1) The model person has to be someone like me or ourselves, so that I can see myself in the same setting. 2) Someone I admire or someone I wish I were. Without it, the entire burden is placed on the buyer to imagine without assistance the role that the product will play in his life."[6]

Oddly enough, men and women tend to pay more attention to pictures of members of their own sex. Typically, 33% more women than men look at photos of females. On the other hand, 50% more men look at pictures of other males than do women.[7]

FLASH INFO

COMING UP WITH EMPATHETIC IMAGES

The word "empathy" became the rage in advertising, starting in the early 1950s. Stephen Baker says an effective image is one that affects people personally. He offers six recipes for cooking up an empathetic image:

1. It represents an activity familiar to the reader and one with which they can identify.

2. Readers can identify with the models: friendly looking and generally younger folks.

3. The ad does not evoke any unpleasant situations.

4. Nothing in the ad conflicts with the reader's moral sensibilities.

5. Nothing in the ad suggests a complicated, difficult, or tedious effort.

6. The ad promises that the product or service it features will fulfill the reader's wishes.

7. The ad features a hero or a heroine that the reader has always dreamed of resembling.

◆ *Images that portray well known personalities generally command twice as much attention and retention as those that do not. To see how Jockey took this picture, rotate the ad 90 degrees to the right.*

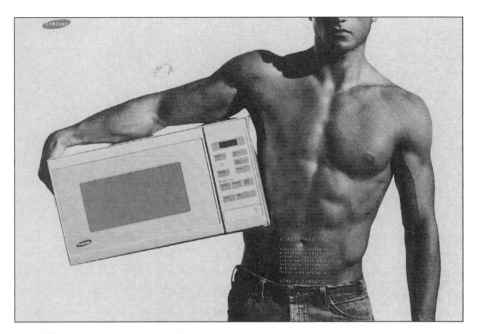

◆ *Ads confirm, repeat, and hammer in an idea. It's masculine, it's virile. Men are men of action in ads. Men have also recently assumed the more subliminal role of sex objects.*

Research on advertising suggests that more people look at ads featuring young people than those with old ones. Furthermore, people of one sex prefer to look at older members of the same sex or younger members of the opposite one.[8]

If your message is aimed at children, avoid projecting a childish image. Use characters a few (two or three) years older than your target audience. If you are not sure whether to use a boy or girl, McCollum/Spielman says that boys tend to yield better results.[9] However, if your product is aimed at an older crowd, select a figure who is 10 or 15 years younger than your targets. Research shows that most elderly people perceive themselves as thinking and feeling younger than they actually are, so it is always a good idea to avoid stereotypes. Show older consumers jogging and gardening, rather than baking or knitting.

Why are so few visible minorities featured in ads (just 9% according to a 1980 Amherst College study)? Does this fact demonstrate that advertisers are racist, or even that companies refuse to give certain positions to people of identifiable ethnic minorities?

Only a few major advertisers, such as Benetton, get involved in exploring the subject of race relations. When relations in the Cold War improved, Benetton was the first to show a "Russian" child and an "American" child together. The visual contrast of an Israeli and a Palestinian together puts two different nations into perspective.

Ad experts have long been aware that consumer behavior is a function of culture, which can be summed up as specific values, standards, and languages. Gearing your ads to specific cultures should boost your sales and profits. Use pictures of members of visible minorities to encourage cultural identification. Studies show that whites react more favorably to white models in ads, while blacks have a more positive attitude about black models.[10]

◆ *Give a touch of "humanity"
to your visuals, whenever possible.*

◆ *Use ethnic minorities in your images
to promote identification with your product.*

◆ *If your ad is going to appear in different countries, make sure to properly localize it to the markets of each country.*

Certain stars, however, transcend culture altogether. This has been the case with Bill Cosby (Jell-O), Ray Charles (Pepsi-Cola), and Magic Johnson (Gatorade).

Just because the visual for your ad has worked in one market doesn't mean that it will work in another. Some years ago, a Diet Coke TV commercial showed the Grand Canyon and typical US images. Consumers in France felt that these pictures were too "American." The advertisers thus decided to change some pictures and add some others.

Australia's rugby star Jacko helped Eveready boost its battery sales. The campaign struck out, though, in the USA, since consumers thought Jacko was too aggressive.

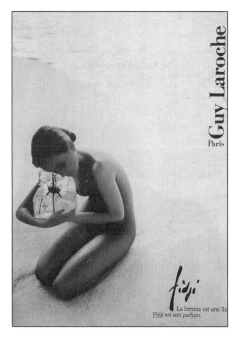

◆ *Pictures comprise their own special language, in which a range of symbols can express and define a particular idea.*
Left: Concept as developed in Europe. Right: Canadian version. The pose is similar, but the model is clothed.

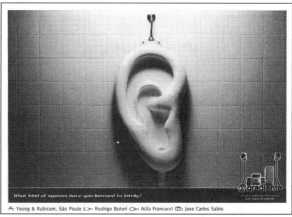

A: Young & Rubicam, São Paulo ▭: Rodrigo Butori ▭: Atila Francucci ▭: Jose Carlos Sabio

◆ *Optical effects are always good ways of giving your image more impact.*

● ─── **FLASH** INFO ───●

ADVERTISING IS EVERYWHERE

TV	Movie Theaters	T-shirts
Radio	Elevators	Movies & videogames
Newspapers	Cabs	Coffee cups
Magazines	Subways	Blimps*
Billboards	Trains	Pizza boxes
Websites	Planes	Tattoos
Stadiums	Phones	Football fields, hockey
Buses	Parking meters	rinks, and baseball bases**
Bars	Postcards	
Bathrooms	Grocery bags	

---

* The Goodyear blimp, for instance, has been around since 1925 and attends more than 55 events a year.

** In 2004, major league baseball canceled a co-promotion with Sony after a media-fueled fan outcry. Less than 48 hours after MLB announced plans to put logos for the upcoming film Spider-Man 2 on the bases at 15 parks, the league reversed itself and scaled-back the co-promotion.[11]

● ─────────────── ●

3. Use photos

If your printing quality is adequate, I suggest that you place photos rather than drawings in your ads. "On the average," write Jane Mass and Kenneth Roman, "ads illustrated with photos are remembered by 26% more readers than ads with drawings."[12] You should, however, use drawings in the following cases:

- To create the impression of a sensational living environment.

- To reveal a facial expression or emotion.

- If your message is aimed at young consumers and you want to employ humor.

Whether the visual element of your ad is a photo or a drawing, it should be properly showcased. In today's maze of information, people tend to leap from one picture to the next.

4. Use fictional characters

Images that use characters or animals to represent a particular product get results that are clearly better than the average. Claude Hopkins said that "By making a character famous, you make the product that character represents famous as well. People are not interested in corporations. They are interested in people and in their achievements."[13]

Fictitious characters that have brought fame to their products abound in the world of advertising. They include the Pillsbury Doughboy, the Marlboro cowboy, Tony the Tiger, Mr. Clean, the Man from Glad, Aunt Jemima, Betty Crocker, the Maytag repairman, the Jolly Green Giant, and so forth.

These characters are very effective. In polls conducted in 1985, 93% of American women shoppers could name the familiar bald-headed Mr. Clean, the man who cleans kitchen floors "to a shine," while only 56% could identify then Vice-President George Bush Sr.[14]

Ronald McDonald is one of the world's best known fictional characters. This famous clown got off to a stunning start in Washington in 1963. By the mid-1960s, McDonald's had invested a significant share of its advertising budget on Ronald McDonald. For some time, the company entertained the idea of turning Ronald into a cowboy, and later into an astronaut to symbolize the future. However, the decision was finally made to keep Ronald as a clown and to preserve the company's young customer group. Ronald's face is recognized by some 96% of American children, and he sells Big Macs in more than 25 languages.

Studies undertaken by McDonald's research department have shown that the more a child likes Ronald McDonald the clown, the more he or she will be likely to identify McDonald's as his or her favorite restaurant.[15]

Several years ago, Kraft successfully reversed the decline of its Kool-Aid crystals with the creation of an effervescent and energetic character, the Kool-Aid Pitcher. A few years earlier, Antonio Gentile, a Suffolk, Virginia schoolboy, drew a character that would achieve great renown: Mr. Peanut. He was paid $5 as a thank you.

More recently, Camel's Joe Camel character did a great job by turning an old-fashioned cigarette brand into one appealing to today's smokers. But Joe Camel also drew criticism from the US Surgeon General and the American Medical Association—both saying that studies showed the cartoon encouraged youngsters to smoke. The Joe Camel character was first drawn in 1974 by a British illustrator for a French Camel campaign, and imported in 1987 to the US for use in a 75th anniversary ad for Camel cigarettes.[16]

Colonel Sanders is one of the most famous characters in the history of advertising. In 1955, Colonel Sanders ran a little fried chicken restaurant by the highway. Forced to shut down, he asked a number of other restaurants to try out his new chicken recipe. Three years later, Colonel Sanders began selling franchises. He rented out pots and pans and let his clients have paper, napkins, and paper cups at cost. He sold his enterprise for $2 million in 1964.

Betty Crocker was created in 1921 after an ad campaign for Gold Medal flour resulted in a flood of baking questions to the Washburn Crosby Company. The firm decided to answer customers in a more personal manner by creating a fictitious kitchen expert. Her last name "Crocker" was taken from that of a recently retired company director and her first name "Betty" was added because it sounded

◆ *A drawing may help you portray a particular physical appearance, an emotion or a sense of nostalgia.*

◆ *Did you know that the Santa Claus we have come to know and love was first created by Coca Cola? The company was searching in 1931 for a means of popularizing its soft drink during the winter. It asked the Swedish firm Haddon Sundblom to help boost Christmas sales with an image of Santa sipping a Coke. Sundblom went about making some changes to the original St. Nick. He added some weight and had the character don a red and white (the product colors) costume—rather than his traditional blue, yellow and green garb. Sundblom used a Coke delivery man as his model for Santa. When the delivery man died, Sundblom had to search for a new face. Not finding anyone else, he eventually decided to build a Father Christmas around his own appearance!*

friendly. Betty's image was refined over the years to reflect the changing status of women. Betty has had eight different "looks," so far, from the original stern grey-haired, older woman of 1936 to today's olive-skinned, dark-haired Betty, a product of computer morphing.

Recently, the Brawny man has gotten an extreme makeover. After 30 years of sitting on top of Brawny paper towels, the silver-haired muscleman was replaced with a dark-haired younger character who might be labeled a metrosexual.[17]

●——— **FLASH** INFO ———●

NUMEROUS CHARACTERS HAVE MADE
THEIR PRODUCTS FAMOUS

Colonel Sanders	Morris the Cat	Honeycomb cowboy
Marlboro Man	Victor the RCA dog	White Swan swan
One-eyed Baron Hathaway	Spuds MacKenzie	Spot for 7UP
Tony the Tiger	Elsie the Cow	Domino's Pizza Noid
California Raisins	Miss Clairol	Quaker Man
Mr. Clean	Merrill Lynch bull	Campbell's Soup Kids
Aunt Jemina	Dreyfus lion	Jack the Lego Maniac
Man from Glad	McGruff the Crime Dog	Snuggle Bear
Betty Crocker	Smokey the Bear	Uncle Ben
Maytag Repairman	Mr. Bib	Taster's Choice couple
Captain Crunch	Kellogg's Corn Flakes rooster	Speedy Alka-Seltzer
Orville Redenbacher		Fruit of the Loom guys
Frank Bartles and Ed Jaymes	Punchy for Hawaiian Punch	Mr. Peanut
Juan Valdez		Old Spice Mariner
The Esso Tiger	Dutch Boy	Yellow duck for Duck Bathroom and Toilet
Fido Dido	Raid Bugs	
Jolly Green Giant	Morton Salt Girl	Madge the Manicurist
Energizer Bunny	Kool-Aid Pitcher man	Sailor Jack and his dog for Cracker Jack
Joe Camel	Sam the Toucan	
Chef Boyardee	Charlie the Tuna	Bud Man
Pillsbury Doughboy	Kool cigarettes penguin	Mac Tonight
Mr. Bubble	Mr. Pringles	Snap, Crackle and Pop
Mr. Whipple	Sugar Crisp Bear	

●————————————————●

Herb the Nerd is one of the rare examples of a fictive character that had no success breaking into the market. In 1986, Burger King created the annoying Herb with his big glasses and featured him in a $40-million campaign that flopped. That was because consumers associated crabby old Herb with Burger King's typical customer.

TOP 10 AD ICONS

1. The Marlboro Man—Marlboro cigarettes

2. Ronald McDonald—McDonald's restaurants

3. The Green Giant—Green Giant vegetables

4. Betty Crocker—Betty Crocker food products

5. The Energizer Bunny—Eveready Energizer batteries

6. The Pillsbury Doughboy—Assorted Pillsbury foods

7. Aunt Jemima—Aunt Jemima pancake mixes and syrup

8. The Michelin Man—Michelin tires

9. Tony the Tiger—Kellogg's Sugar Frosted Flakes

10. Elsie the Cow—Borden dairy products

Source: *Advertising Age*

---

5. Show the character head-on

Before deciding on your character's position in the ad, you should know that each choice is filled with meaning.

Georges Péninou distinguishes between ways of presenting a character: head-on, profile, and a three-quarter view.

- *Head-on.* The character speaks, talks, or solicits. He or she appeals directly to the reader. The head-on character is the most effective means of attracting attention.

- *Profile.* The reader becomes a spectator to an event taking place in front of him or her.

- *Three-quarter.* This character expresses all of the nuances of the character's psychology. This character exists in a world of mystery, temptation, narcissism, introversion, introspection, dreaming, uncertainty, and delicacy, as well as awareness.

Milk ads in the United States have for many years used the simple and striking images of head-on photos of film, sports, and music stars bearing milky "mustaches."

6. Suggest motion

Give the sense of movement to your illustration. Moving objects attract more reader attention than do still ones.

It may seem that a photo is better at freezing motion than portraying it. But you can suggest motion with the following three techniques:

- Use a set of pictures, each illustrating an action's key moments.

- Blur part of the image through movement of the subject—or camera. You can blur the background and focus on the foreground, or vice versa.

- Use a sharp photo taken at a key moment in the action that readers will see and enhance in their minds.

People will instinctively look at anything that moves. Our eyes are involuntarily attracted to movement like a moth to light.

◆ *Images that suggest motion always attract attention.*

7. Use regular-sized pictures

People tend to look at shapes with clear geometric contours. Research shows that rectangular pictures draw more attention than those with irregular shapes. Rectangular pictures also tend to be perceived as more credible.

Many studies have shown that people refuse to consider the surrounding environment as being in a state of disorder. We are constantly seeking familiar and geometrically simple shapes such as the triangle, square, and circle.

8. Tight framing

Framing lets you emphasize certain details in your pictures. There are seven ways to frame a photo:

- *Long shot.* Includes a vast landscape, such as a desert or an area inhabited by one or more persons who appear minuscule in scale.

- *Medium long shot.* Places your character within the appropriate setting and thus presents the character against a much more limited background (a room, the wall of a small house, etc.).

- *Medium shot.* Reveals your character from head to toe to emphasize his or her general body language.

- *Close medium shot.* Close shot of your character, giving the reader a better idea of that person's activities.

- *Medium close shot.* Head and shoulders shot of one or two characters. Another variation is the medium close shot from the waist up.

- *Close-up.* Draws the reader's attention to a face.

- *Big close-up.* Features details. With tight framing, you exclude everything from the picture that is inconsistent with the message you wish to convey, thus increasing the likelihood that it will be transmitted.

Starch has noted that many of the highest-scoring advertisements use contrasting elements. One example of this technique is an American Express ad featuring the slight Willie Shoemaker and a towering Wilt Chamberlain standing side by side.

Open for inspection.

McDonald's® invites you to break off a corner of our Filet-O-Fish™ and take a peek inside. See that sparkling-white, flaky filet? That's North Atlantic Filet. Not a fishcake—but a real filet portion.
Our fish are pulled gleaming fresh from the icy ocean depths. Then fileted and flash-frozen at their plumpest and juiciest. And they're continuously inspected throughout processing. Not just by us, but by the U.S. government too.
So come on in and give our Filet-O-Fish its final inspection. Then take a bite. We think you just might be hooked.

Nobody can do it like McDonald's can **McDonald's**

◆ *Close-up or establishing shot? It all depends on your goal. If you want to emphasize a product feature, the close-up is best.*

9. Don't let your readers get sidetracked

Keep your ads simple. Make sure your photograph repeats exactly the same message as the text. If you write, "This beer refreshes you well," make sure to also picture a cold beer. Repetition facilitates learning and retention.

A study conducted by Ogilvy & Mather shows that one third of all advertising is poorly understood.[18] More than 40% of those tested during a study thought that a Cointreau ad was promoting a bath oil. Even worse, 45% felt that a bank ad was actually trying to sell a suitcase.

Following the attacks of September 11, 2001, Kmart used a simple image that would strike the imagination and be easily understood by all: an American flag on a full-page color ad in the *New York Times* and the *Washington Post*. The ad also said: "Remove from newspaper. Place in window. Embrace freedom." Kmart's signature appeared in small characters on the lower left. Thousands of New Yorkers put this ad in their windows.

FLASH INFO

BE HONEST

Retouched and trick photos have been responsible for a number of embarrassing incidents over the years. Here are a few examples:

- Volvo used a special chassis reinforcement so the car would better withstand impacts during photo shoots.
- Campbell placed marbles at the bottom of a bowl to give the soup a more consistent appearance.[19]
- Bermuda's Tourist Ministry acquired an image bank to use in its ads. Unfortunately, it turned out that the pictures had not been taken in Bermuda. The first photo used showed a woman on a beach in Hawaii. Two others showed a swimmer and diver in Florida.

Even before that incident and in an attempt to save a few thousand dollars, an advertising agency used photographs taken in Hawaii to promote Australia. Unfortunately, several vacationers recognized the famous sand dunes of the 50th American state. A few months later, the advertising agency lost the airline's account.

Just don't expect it to roar.

Under pressure to be swifter, stronger and more agile, some organizations may be tempted to seek superficial solutions.

But in this era of unrelenting change, the true character of every enterprise will be tested.

So rather than shallow, short-term fixes, Andersen Consulting can help you achieve lasting improvements by aligning all of your essential components: strategy, technology, process and people.

Because these days, you either

transform the whole organization. Or risk becoming a paper tiger.

ANDERSEN
CONSULTING
ARTHUR ANDERSEN & CO., S.C.

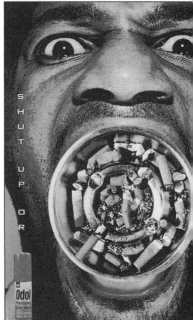

◆ *Images that shock are the most effective means of commanding attention.*

10. Be original

Ads are everywhere, for better or worse. To get attention in today's advertising environment, you have to hit home. In 1968, Harvard Business School Professor Augustine Bauer and Strathclyde Business School Professor of Marketing Stephen A. Greyser estimated that the North American consumer sees hundreds of ads each day.[20] Twenty-five years later, Regis McKenna, president and CEO of the McKenna Group consulting firm, said that all people are exposed to as many as 3,000 ads each day. This is a tall order for ad specialists.

Adman William Bernbach once said, "Why should anyone look at your ad? The reader doesn't buy his magazine or tune in his radio and TV to see and hear what you have to say…What is the use of saying all the right things in the world if nobody is going to read them? And, believe me, nobody is going to read them if they are not said with freshness, originality and imagination…If they are not…different."[21]

Most ad writers usually generate original ideas through *brainstorming* sessions. This method, originally created by Alex F. Osborn, produces a variety of ideas. It is based on the simple idea that group work stimulates competition. Brainstorming also enables each contributor to come up with a larger number of ideas, particularly if the issue is posed in a simple and concrete manner.

Brainstorming sessions must comply with a few basic rules. First of all, participants should not criticize each other's ideas. As many ideas as possible should be sought and free rein given to unbridled imagination. Ideas should also be linked in a search for other ideas. Brainstorming is by definition a team activity.

The challenge faced by ad designers is even greater. They must attract consumer attention and be universally understood. And that is no easy task.

◆ *Show your readers something new if you want them to notice you!*

WHAT TOPICS GET THE MOST ATTENTION?

If you want your ads to really sell, people have to stop and look at them first. As Victor Schwab said: "It can't make sales if it isn't read; it can't be read if it isn't seen; and it won't be seen unless it gets attention."[22] Readers prefer 11 types of photos:[23]

1. Newly married couples

2. Babies

3. Animals

4. Celebrities

5. People decked out in unusual costumes

6. Strange-looking characters

7. Photos that tell a story

8. Romantic scenes

9. Disasters

10. Headline issues

11. Photos pertaining to key moments in life

Men like pictures of animals, and particularly of big dogs. Women pay more attention to pictures of babies and young children. Both sexes like pictures of celebrities.

When you want attention in advertising, it has long been known that you should show a baby, a child, or a sexy woman. Whether for Michelin, McDonald's, or Saturn, babies have shown that they can capture attention and significantly boost sales.

Just because people look at your picture, however, does not mean that it will sell your product. First there must be a link between the product and your concept. Pictures of babies will sell no more computers than pictures of animals will sell detergent.

Pictures of young children are, however, great for selling candy, chewing gum, ice cream, cake, cereals, and soft drinks. But such images perform poorly in promoting financial services, farm equipment, and garden products.

DO PRETTY MODELS HELP?

The choice of model depends on the type of product you are advertising. Baker and Churchill say that attractive women do not work as well for products that have nothing to do with seduction (such as coffee).[24] However, if you are selling products related to sex appeal (such as perfume), pretty women give excellent results.

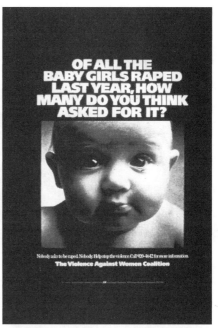

◆ *Ad experts know that the public loves pictures of babies, young children, and newly married couples.*

◆ *Two ads that employ sensuality to command interest.*

128

The presence of a pretty lady has an odd effect on how your product is perceived. Smith and Engel demonstrated during a study that a car shown along with a pretty woman is perceived as being more attractive, younger, faster, costlier, more powerful, and safer than a vehicle surrounded by more neutral images.[25]

Studies have shown that we attribute such qualities as talent, kindness, honesty, and intelligence to beautiful people. We also perceive such individuals as being sexually active, more cordial, and more outgoing than less attractive persons.

Advertisers like Dior, Valentino, Ungaro, and Vuitton often employ images of a sexual nature. That is not always a good idea. American adman Major Steadman showed a set of men some photos containing sexual references, and others with none.[26] After a while, Steadman observed that people were less likely to remember brand names shown in the company of pretty and scantily dressed young women than they were those illustrated with more neutral images. Wayne Alexander and Ben Judd studied the same subject with similar results.[27]

"Sex in advertising definitely catches people's attention," commented Daniel Howard, Ph.D., who teaches consumer behavior at Southern Methodist University. "But sex only works in selling a product when it is relevant. In fact, it can have a negative effect. Catching the consumer's attention doesn't always translate into sales."[28]

A recent Starch study indicates that advertisers who market their products on the basis of sexual stereotyping may be missing an opportunity, because many products once considered the domain of one sex are increasingly drawing the other.

◆ *Images that use sex merely to get attention achieve lower-than-average results.*

FLASH INFO

IMAGES THAT BOOST SALES

You can count on the fingers of both hands the types of images likely to boost sales:

- *A certain portion of your product.* This lets your audience focus on a specific aspect of your product. This kind of image can work if your product stands out from the competition.
- *Your product's use.* This helps generate interest in your product. Such pictures also promote viewer identification with the item. Make sure, however, to design a straightforward image that always features the product.
- *Using your product.* Use this kind of image if your product is new to the market or if consumers are under the mistaken impression that it is hard to use.

- *The satisfaction you get using your product.* All ads should ideally give a sense of the pleasure that will result from using your product. Such an image lets you show what the product can do for the consumer.
- *Your product.* This is the simplest image. It can work if your product has flair and style. It is ideal if your product is at the top of its line, like a performance or luxury car.
- *Your packaging.* This is important if you have your product's packaging, or if the idea is new or little known.

TESTIMONIALS FROM STARS

Ads that use testimonials from stars tend to give good results. Stars generally boost sympathy for and credibility of a product. A study by Video Storyboard Tests that was conducted among 30,000 consumers showed that 1986's 10 to 25 best-liked TV advertisers used celebrities.[29]

One out of five commercials broadcast in the United States uses a star[30] and there is a good reason why. Studies by Starch have shown that ads with celebrities scored 13% higher than non-celebrity versions. Not only do such ads promote attention and identification, but stars generally command large reserves of affection among viewers.

Nike's international growth has been exceptional from the moment the firm signed an advertising contract with Michael Jordan in 1985.

Even major cosmetics producers have replaced famous models with film stars. When Brooke Shields said in one ad that she wouldn't let anything come between her and her Calvin Klein jeans, sales shot up 300%. Nuprin's ad campaign using tennis star Jimmy Connors boosted sales for this pain-relief product by 23%.[31]

Here are 10 good reasons to use a celebrity:

1. If your product only exists because of a star

This is the case, for example, with Jennifer Lopez's Glow perfume and Bugs Bunny vitamins.

2. If the celebrity strongly communicates your product's personality

Make sure that there is a link between any star you might use, the product, and the target audience. If the link is obvious, your campaign should be a success, as was the case with Catherine Deneuve and Chanel No. 5, and Hank Aaron and Wheaties.

"Out of place" testimonials from stars will only yield mediocre results. Examples of such failures are legion and include, most recently, Grace Jones for Honda motorcycles, David Copperfield for Kodak, Jack Klugman for Canon copiers, Burt Lancaster for MCI, Kirk Douglas for Sperry, and Peter Sellers for TWA.

When Bic Disposable Razors signed up John McEnroe, enthusiasm ran high. McEnroe was a star player and the crowds loved his wild style. But the star failed to sell the product. In reviewing what had happened, Bic realized that McEnroe had the lamentable habit of not shaving when he participated in big tournaments. So he appeared on TV with three- or four-day stubble.

When the makers of an analgesic known as Datril finally managed to persuade John Wayne to pitch their product, they thought their ship had come in. But consumers didn't buy Wayne's sales arguments. Subsequent studies showed the public simply found it impossible to see the famous cowboy with a headache.

A few years ago, Sears tried to boost its fashion image with Cheryl Tiegs, but the approach did not deliver the desired results. Alvin Achenbaum recalls that "Tiegs was neither a widely known personality to the ordinary consumer nor associated with the apparel field; her reputation was with inexpensive supermarket cosmetics."

On the other hand, the combination of Wilford Brimley and Quaker Oatmeal was an instant success. The spokesperson enabled the company to build a solid and wholesome image for the product.

Bert Lahr for Lay's and Avery Schreiber for Doritos delivered excellent results, because snack foods are products that lend themselves to a humorous approach.

Many other stars have helped their products: Karl Malden for American Express, Catherine Deneuve for Chanel No. 5, Jaclyn Smith for Wella Balsam, Orson Welles for Paul Masson, Hank Aaron for Wheaties, and Joe Namath for Brut and Noxzema Shaving Cream.

3. If your spokesperson is perceived as being an expert in the field

Specialists tend to win more consumers over to a product than can the average citizen.[32] The many examples include Andre Agassi for Nike, Wayne Gretzky for Daoust skates, Steffi Graf and Stefan Edberg for Adidas in Europe, and Michael Jordan for Nike.

4. If you are seeking notoriety at any price

Friedman and Friedman have shown that celebrity is a quick way for a firm to achieve acceptable levels of notoriety.[33] The presence of a well-known personality like Paul Newman for American Express assures the visibility of your ad.

"We used Garfield for star power, to get people to notice the ads and build awareness for Embassy Suites, and Garfield has done that very well," said Diego Garrido, VP-marketing.[34]

What a star actually guarantees is that people will look at your ad. In this regard, female stars generate better results than do their male counterparts.

Pepsi produced what quickly became at the time America's best-remembered TV commercial by making Madonna its star.

Research has shown, however, that while many consumers may notice a star in an ad, they have trouble remembering the product it presents. A study by McCollum/Spielman, a New York communications research company, found that only about 41% of celebrity commercials scored above average when measured for their contribution to brand awareness and to attitude shift.[35]

5. If you want to break into a new market

A local star is often a must for breaking into a new market. Basketball player Yao Ming gave a big boost to American multinationals seeking entry into the Chinese market. Apple, Visa, Gatorade, Coca-Cola, and Nike each signed contracts with this Houston Rockets player. In 2003, Ming earned $10 million in sponsorship income.

6. If you are reaching out to young people

In 1983, Charles Atkin and Martin Block studied the impact that celebrities have on consumers.[36] In particular, they noted that stars worked very well for selling alcohol to teens. They concluded that "the use of famous people to endorse alcohol products is highly effective with teenagers, while the impact on older persons is limited. For teenagers, the impact of the celebrity ratings extends to the message and product."

When Steven Spielberg had E.T. snack on Reese's Pieces, sales of the peanut butter candy soared 70% in just two months.[37]

7. If you want an agreeable, lively and modern ad

The best crowd-pleasers are singers and actors, as has certainly been the case with Michael Landon for Kodak, Bill Cosby for Jell-O, Whitney Houston for Coke, and Tina Turner for Pepsi.

Cartoon hero Bart Simpson helped boost sales of Butterfinger chocolate bars. According to Bob Sperry, Nestlé's marketing director, "Butterfinger was perceived at that time as old and out-dated and had no personality. So we tried to link the brand personality with Bart's irreverent, mischievous personality."[38]

Charlie Chaplin's Little Tramp character was the key to one of IBM's most effective and entertaining ad campaigns. This campaign, which was aimed at demystifying IBM technology, served to reposition a company not particularly well known for having a sense of humor.

8. If you are promoting services or important causes

Jerry Lewis used to host the annual 24-hour muscular dystrophy telethon, which raised millions of dollars each year for many years.

9. If there is little interest in your product or it is perceived as risky

A star can help calm consumer nerves and arouse their curiosity. The mere fact that Christie Brinkley drinks Anheuser-Busch's Natural Light is enough reason for some people to try the product.

By portraying pop singer Marky Mark in suggestive poses, Calvin Klein boosted sales of underwear, a product that usually generates little interest, by 40%.[39]

Jockey has long used former baseball star Jim Palmer. Fruit of the Loom ads feature former "Hill Street Blues" actor Ed Marinaro and "Dallas" star Patrick Duffy. Hanes' stable of endorsers includes former San Francisco 49[ers] quarterback Joe Montana, and Michael Jordan, then of the Chicago Bulls.

For financial firms or services, a powerful and unwavering personality can inspire trust. This is the case of advertisements for services, institutions, and charity organizations. For example, Dallas Cowboys coach Tom Landry, surrounded by Washington Redskins football players in an Old West saloon for American Express, or Jerry Lewis for the Jerry Lewis Labor Day Telethon.

10. If your target is too broad or too narrowly focused

A product spokesperson can deliver a strong and consistent message to ads aimed at the millions, as well as for products designed for finely targeted groups.

However, there is also a flip side to the coin. The credibility and sales impact of celebrities who endorse an excessive number of brands (such as John Madden, coach of the Oakland Raiders, and Mike Ditka of the Chicago Bears) begins to fade.[40] When John Houseman did ads for Smith-Barney, Puritan cooking oil, Plymouth cars, and McDonald's, these companies sacrificed their credibility. In such repeat appearances, the star fails to trigger associations with a specific sponsor. "Such over-exposure may confuse people about which brands the celebrity endorsed," says Barry Day, vice-chairman of McCann-Erickson Worldwide.[41] Such overexposure creates confusion in the minds of con-sumers and ends up hurting all of the brands endorsed by that star.

FLASH INFO

A FEW PRODUCT SPOKESPERSONS

Christina Aguilera	Virgin Mobile
Beyoncé	Pepsi-Cola
David Bowie	Volkswagen
Kobe Bryant	Nike
Sean Combs	McDonald's
Snoop Dogg	Nokia
LeBron James	Nike
Jessica Simpson	Pizza Hut
Britney Spears	Mazda
Sting	American Express
Justin Timberlake	McDonald's
Serena Williams	Nike

If you have no choice but to share your star with other advertisers, you should repeat your message more often and for a longer period. Despite such notable exceptions as Michael Jordan (who has represented up to 14 companies, including Coke, McDonald's, Nike, and Gatorade) and Tiger Woods (Buick, American Express, Nike, Disney, etc.), celebrities who endorse too many products end up by diluting the impact of their message.

Specific markets that use too many stars tend to create confusion. In 1989, Coke, Diet Coke, Pepsi, and Diet Pepsi used nearly three dozen movie stars, athletes, musicians, and television personalities to persuade consumers to buy more cola. However, most consumers couldn't remember whether Joe Montana and Don Johnson drank Coke or Pepsi—or both. According to Dave Vedhera, editor of Video Storyboard Tests' newsletter *Commercial Break*, the ads were so filled with celebrities that recall studies showed consumers remembered the celebrities, but not the message.[42] Ultimately, people do not remember which star supported which product.

Celebrities may occasionally lose their selling abilities without warning. For many years, Fabio, a long-haired he-man, was a star of the romance novel industry. His picture on the front cover of a book could, in and of itself, boost sales by 40%. But when Fabio decided to do a margarine ad, sales didn't budge. Fabio's star had dimmed.

Sports stars are less favorably perceived in advertising these days. A study by Consumer Network showed that most respondents had negative feelings toward such stars.[43] More than 74% of them did not like to see sports stars in ads. They perceived such individuals as self-centered and spoiled.

No star can be guaranteed to stay clear of sports, sexual, or political scandals. Many stars have been involved in incidents that could tarnish the products they represent, as with:

- 7-Up, when Flip Wilson was arrested for cocaine dealing.

- Mazda, when the scandal broke out over steroids and Ben Johnson at the Seoul Olympics.

- Gillette, when Vanessa Williams' nude photos appeared in *Penthouse*.

- Ace Hardware, when Suzanne Somers' nude photos appeared in *Playboy*.

- Pepsi, when Mike Tyson was accused of rape.

- Seagram, when Bruce Willis was admitted to a rehab centre.

- The beef industry, when Cybill Shepherd told a reporter she never eats red meat.

- Ivory Snow, when Marilyn Brigg became the porn star Marilyn Chambers.

When Mike Tyson was reported to have beaten his wife actress Robin Givens, and given away a luxury automobile after he had driven it into a parked car, companies like Diet Pepsi, RJR Nabisco, and 3M all decided to drop the famous boxer as an endorser.

To protect yourself from recurring negative publicity due to scandals, opt for a multi-celebrity approach. Have the celebrities sign contracts that will allow you to dissolve your association quickly in case of any difficulty. Here is a model draft:

"We shall have the right to terminate this agreement upon immediate written notice in the event that our client is of the belief that the artist's actual or alleged conduct occurring or reported subsequent to execution of the agreement, and the client's and the public's perception thereof create the result that the public association of the artist with our client may be injurious to or embarrassing to our client or inconsistent with the best interests, reputation or marketing position of the product."[44]

In rare cases, scandals may boost returns on advertising. The incident that would prove so costly to Michael Jackson gave Pepsi millions of dollars in free advertising in the world's media.

The decline of athlete endorsements reflects a growing backlash against athletes perceived as "too self-centered or mercenary." According to Joe Mandese, such a perception was reinforced by the unsportsmanlike behavior of US athletes, and particularly the basketball team, during the 1992 Olympics.[45]

Baseball stars seem to be in a particular lull. "Look at the major stars in baseball—Jose Canseco, Wade Boggs, Rickey Henderson, Roger Clemens. Need I say more? They are not advertisers' dream people," says Nova Lanktree, director of Burns Sports Celebrity Service.[46]

"Advertisers are very cautious now about all athletes. They worry about spending massive amounts of dollars on a player who one day is selling their product—and the next day, fined for spitting on an 8-year-old girl," adds Bob Dorfman, senior copywriter for Foote, Cone and Belding, San Francisco.[47]

Whatever the reason, many companies prefer to showcase their products using deceased stars or fictional characters like Bugs Bunny and Mickey Mouse. Like deceased celebrities, cartoon heroes are usually immune to negative advertising.

F L A S H I N F O

DEAD CELEBRITIES

"Dead celebrities have caught on big in advertising since a 1991 Diet Coke commercial featuring Elton John performing with James Cagney, Louis Armstrong, and Humphrey Bogart was such a success that Coca-Cola created a sequel featuring footage of other famous celebrities. Since then, technological advances have allowed advertisers to seamlessly incorporate footage into ads of deceased celebrities such as John Wayne for a Coors campaign. One of the most memorable examples of this kind was the use of a Fred Astaire dance in a Dirt Devil commercial.

Forbes' annual ranking of the Top-Earning Dead Celebrities proves that these familiar faces are still money-makers long after they're gone. The magazine's fourth-annual list, released in late 2004, listed 22 deceased celebrities who earned at least $5 million over the past year.

Elvis Presley's estate topped the list with $40 million in earnings that Forbes attributes not to his music sales, but to Elvis Presley Enterprises' extensive use of licensing and marketing to sell Elvis-sponsored products and admissions to Graceland. According to Forbes, the singer's estate has more than 100 licensees who use Elvis' image to sell products ranging from Zippo lighters to cards by American Greetings.

In its latest 2005 Dead Q tallies, Lucille Ball, Bob Hope, and John Wayne top the list of the public's favorite dead celebrities. Although Elvis was Forbes' top-earning dead celebrity, he ranks at No. 12 on the Dead Q list. Also among the top 15 are Jimmy Stewart, Katharine Hepburn, and the Three Stooges.

Two recent deaths made this year's Dead Q list: Johnny Carson, who is ranked No. 7, died Jan. 23, and John Ritter, who is ranked No. 8, died Sept. 11, 2003."

Source: Heinemann, Anna. "In search of the right dead celebrity: How Do You Find the Best One for Your Ad Campaign?" *Advertising Age,* July 18, 2005.

INTERPRETING IMAGES

Studies on perception have highlighted certain principles on how people read images. Researchers know, for example, that rather than continuously scanning a page, readers' eyes hop around, alighting here and there for a few moments, as it suits them. A reader will linger on an item for such reasons as the facts that:

- Our eyes tend to focus on four points in turn. These points are the intersection of the straight lines parallel to the sides of the page and traced at one-third and two-thirds of the length and width of the page.

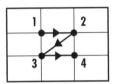

- The eyes tend to track in a clockwise pattern.

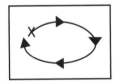

- The eyes tend to spend more time looking at the upper-left portion of an image.

- The eyes tend to look first at human beings, then at moving objects, like clouds and cars, and finally immoveable objects.

Since people now typically look at all shapes from left to right and from top to bottom, it would be worthwhile to design your pictures based on this scan pattern.

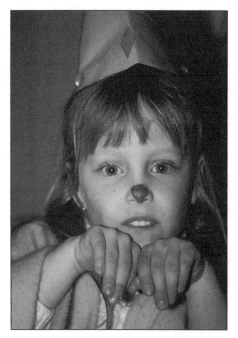 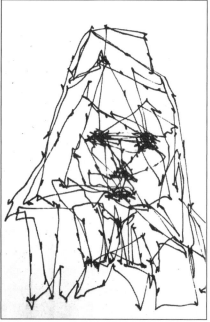

◆ *Studies on human perception have revealed certain principles that govern the manner in which people assimilate images. Scientists have, for example, discovered that people do not continuously scan a page, but hop about, pausing here and there, as illustrated in the diagram on the right. People also pay particular attention to a character's nose, mouth, and eyes. (Collection: Claude Cossette.)*

9 TIPS FOR SUCCESSFUL PHOTOS

1. Only show one product at a time.

2. Limit your photo to six or seven graphic elements.

3. Be straightforward.

4. Simplify the background.

5. Show a key subject.

6. Keep the subject off-centre.

7. Use different angles.

8. Shoot small objects from above and big ones from below.

9. Make sure your photos have a professional look.

Since consumers tend to look and see what a picture offers them, I strongly recommend that you include a visual in your ads.

Henri Joannis once said there are three cases in which you might prefer not to use a picture:

- For a very serious announcement.

- If providing a picture of your subject would prove a breach of etiquette or of morals.

- If your message is so original that text alone will carry the point home.

The fact of the matter is, though, 9 times out of 10 you must use a picture. Jay Chiat, one of the twentieth century's most influential and creative admen, said, "The reality is that as products mature and people understand what the product is, there is probably more reason for imagery than information. You wanna get away from sheer written data. You want more visual messages to come."[48]

"As the need for quicker and more global communications increases," said Keith Reinhard, chairman, CEO and creative head of DDB Needham, "we need creative people who understand the power of visuals and symbols—people with a high sense of visual acuity. In time, that will be a bonus hiring requirement."[49]

The image holds the big advantage over writing: *it delivers the message instantaneously.*

Chapter 4

Writing catchy headlines

The headline is the most important factor in ad copy. Albert Lasker, the father of modern advertising, once said: "The headline counts for 90% of an ad's effectiveness."[1]

When you produce print ads, the big difference often resides in the headline. One title may catch the eye of 15% of all readers, while another hooks 25%, 30%, or even 50%. Consider the following headlines:

1. Half price

2. Buy one, get one free

3. 50% discount

Each of these ideas is ultimately the same. But number two regularly generates bigger results than one or three.

Many factors play a role in the effectiveness of your headline: the number of words, the number of lines on which the title is printed, the size of the characters, and the use of plays on words.

A successful headline must attract the attention of prospective customers, elicit interest, stimulate desire and, ultimately, get people to buy.

Headline writing is a science. To paraphrase John Caples, your headlines are critical to your success or failure.

In this chapter, we will review eight headlines that tend to produce superior results. We will then provide a list of some "miracle" words in advertising, and discuss whether long or short headlines would better suit your ad.

◆ *The headline must deliver a clear, straightforward, and precise message. This Pirelli ad promises to deliver tires that really grip the road.*

●────**MEDIA** ADVISORY────●

THE HEADLINE'S ROLE...

Most ads contain headlines. They often sit at the top of the ad in dailies, weeklies, and magazines. On billboards, titles accompany and enhance the image. A title will also serve as the lead-in to a television or radio commercial.

ON TV

Make an impact. Present your key argument from the outset to get viewers interested. In an age of zapping, you have just a few seconds to make a good impression. If you don't manage to elicit the viewer's interest quickly and intensively, the game is lost from the start.

ON RADIO

Radio is an intimate and personal media. It lets you get close to people. It communicates with the public in a direct and instantaneous manner.

ON BILLBOARDS

To capture the attention of passers-by and drivers, focus on one issue and boil it down to its core ingredient. Get consumers' attention by making your ad posters short and sweet. Present the essence of your message and drop the rest.

Ideally, use just one word and one image. The shorter your headline, the better the likelihood that it will be read. Strike swiftly and effectively: long, technical pitches are not for billboards. Tense and distracted drivers speed on by. You have little time to grab their attention.

IN MAGAZINES, DAILIES AND WEEKLIES

Headlines make all the difference when you advertise in daily newspapers or magazines. Short headlines sell best and generally promise consumers some kind of benefit.

OVER THE WEB

Focus your ad campaign. What is your target customer base? What sites do they visit? Set up your campaign, for example, based on the day and time your ad will be shown. If you want to contact the business community, buy space from 6:00 a.m. to 9:00 a.m. To reach children, obtain space from 2:00 p.m. to 6:00 p.m. Those are the times each group is most likely to be surfing the Web.

●────────────────────────────●

BETTER THAN AVERAGE HEADLINES

Eight kinds of headlines give superior results in advertising.

1. Headlines that promise some kind of benefit to consumers

Such titles typically sell the best. People always want to buy products that are advertised to be simple to use, to save energy, to make them successful in love, and to enhance their social standing.

Consumers don't buy cars. They buy speed, safety, or social standing. Cosmetics makers don't sell a water and oil-based cream. They sell beauty, seduction and youth. *And you should never forget it!*

Effective advertising is based on clear positioning and an implicit promise. Samuel Johnson once said: "Promise, large promise, is the soul of an advertisement." Calvin Klein does not sell perfume. *It sells sex.*

Always use positive arguments.[2] Never cause your readers to feel that they are in the wrong. Never upset them, never blame them. Ads that promote fear rarely generate great sales. There are more effective ways of getting people to brush their teeth than showing them images of dirty teeth filled with cavities.

Starch Readership Service indicates that ads with positive headlines were found to outperform those with "non-positive" headlines—50% versus 37% of the respondents "noted" the ad, while 16% versus 4% "read most" of the ad.[3]

It is always easier to sell a product by showing its good rather than its bad side, except in ads for medications, detergents, insurance, and financial services. People seek benefits, not punishments.

Some years back, Gillette launched a shampoo for people with oily hair. The product was called: FOR OILY HAIR ONLY shampoo. No surprise that the product quickly disappeared from store shelves. People refused to buy a product that reminded them of their oily hair. Gillette quickly learned from that mistake and soon after launched a disposable razor called Good News.

Some campaigns still promise multiple benefits—and often more than three. That's a mistake. You create confusion in the reader's mind by offering too many product advantages. The ad campaigns that generally achieve the best retention rates focus all of their energies on a specific benefit.

It is sometimes difficult to determine which argument is most likely to sway consumers. Take diapers, for example. Pampers disposable diapers originally emphasized their practical aspects. This argument was interesting, but the response was only lukewarm. Pampers subsequently refocused its efforts to say that the diapers would keep your baby happy and dry. Sales soared. Rosser Reeves, from the Ted Bates agency, claimed that a good ad campaign will employ a Unique Selling Proposition or USP: "Each advertisement must say to each reader 'Buy this product, and you will get this specific benefit.' The proposition must be one that the competition either cannot, or does not, offer. It must be unique: either a uniqueness of the brand or a claim not otherwise made in that particular field of advertising."[4]

Always make sure your offer is believable and don't exaggerate. If the satisfaction consumers get from using your product is less than they expect, they may not buy it again.[5]

Prodigy used an aggressive campaign that quickly succeeded in signing up 860,000 customers. But there was one problem: the best technology was being offered by America Online, which then only had 181,000 customers. Within four years, things had changed. Prodigy was fighting for its life and America Online had 8 million users.

●——— **FLASH** INFO ———●

PROMISES THAT SELL

Beauty, slimness, charm, sex appeal, seduction

Youth, love, passion, sensuality, charm

Good health, long life, strength, virility, aggressiveness

Relief of a physical or emotional pain

Discretion, sympathy, intimacy

Cleanliness, purity, freshness, naturalness

Good price:quality ratio, savings

Security, savings, protection

Modernism, progress, renewal

Happiness, joy, entertainment, wonder

Nutritional value, good taste

Self-confidence, self-assurance, satisfaction

Convenience, well-being, a sense of belonging

Good cheer, popularity, pleasure, admiration

Vitality, enthusiasm, energy, strength

Adventure, escape, freedom, the unexpected, the forbidden

Dreaming, the imagination, magic, curiosity

Rest, relaxation, creativity

Warmth, intimacy, friendship, stability, reliability

Conformity, nonconformity, patriotism, tradition

Comfort, lightness, daintiness, gentleness

Distinction, refinement, class

Perfection, excellence, a guarantee, better quality

Quantity, choice, facility, simplicity, sturdiness, speed

The essential, the novel, the exclusive, the rare

Experience, ability, knowledge, professionalism

The original, the first, the authentic, the real

The brand, the product, the logo

Performance, effectiveness, knowledge

Success, esteem, prosperity, success, superiority

Power, authority, domination, influence, power

Prestige, style, elegance, luxury, wealth, social standing

2. Headlines that offer practical advice

Such headlines systematically yield excellent results. People are fascinated by headlines that teach them how to do something.

- How to get rich
- How to make friends
- How to fall in love
- How to succeed in life
- How to lose weight

When they can select from among different types of communication, people prefer reading messages that contain useful information.[6]

The legendary David Ogilvy said that ads offering practical advice typically have a readership that is 75% larger than those that do not.[7]

A study by Brock, Albert and Becker shows that people, when given a choice between different types of messages, prefer those that present useful information.

When Shell started giving helpful consumer tips (how to save money at the gas pump, how to keep your car in good running order, how to care for tires, etc.), their ad campaign proved a big success. In the first three years, 600 million pamphlets were distributed and the company's renown grew.

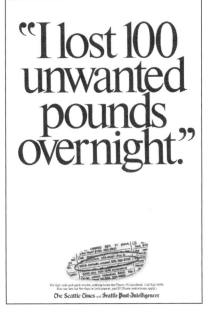

◆ *Headlines that arouse curiosity always get better-than-average results.*

3. Headlines that announce something new

These kinds of headlines work very well. Consumers are attracted to and potentially interested in anything out of the ordinary.

People feel revitalized by newness. It has an immediate and seductive effect. Fascination with novelty is based on the misguided, but well-rooted, notion that new things are better than old ones.

Each year, marketers launch more than 10,000 new food and non-food items, at a cost of $15 to $20 million per full-scale launch. Not surprisingly, Kathryn Newton, General Mills' public relations supervisor, once said that, "We are always looking at new products and new ingredient combinations."

Since its launch, Tide detergent powder has undergone 55 significant changes. Alecia Swasy said in *Soap Opera: The Inside Story of Procter & Gamble*, "Each time it's improved, P&G runs extensive tests. For instance, more than 30,000 socks were washed as part of the Tide with Bleach research."[8]

Behavioral researcher Daniel Berlyne said that human beings prefer new over familiar stimuli.[9] A study conducted by David Sears and Jonathan Freedman shows that the public prefers to be presented with new arguments.

In the shampoo industry, 90% of consumers will try a new shampoo every year.[10] A perfume's average lifespan is 18 months.

Find new ways of using a product to boost sales. Arm & Hammer baking soda sales shot up from $15.6 million to $150 million over the course of a decade.[11] The company achieved this extraordinary accomplishment by telling the public to use baking soda to deodorize refrigerators. The number of households using this product climbed from 1% in February 1972 to 57% in March 1973, and then subsequently to 90%. Other campaigns subsequently suggested using the product as a toothpaste, and as a kitty litter and dog deodorant.

Consider the case of the breakfast cereal Cheerios. Joseph Plummer, executive vice-president at D'Arcy Masius Benton & Bowles, said, "The brand has been around forever, but it is boosting its market share by pressing today's nutritional hot button—oat bran. Cheerios has always had oat bran. But to the consumer, it is new information— new, relevant information".[12]

Kleenex tissues were originally used to remove makeup from the face. When the company learned that people preferred to use them to blow their noses, it decided to refocus its ads accordingly—and Kleenex became the number one brand of paper tissues.

If you want to boost sales of an existing product, try to come up with some way of *reformulating* it. The Marketing Intelligence Service says that 77% of new products appearing on supermarket and drugstore shelves in 1995 involved new formulations, formats, or ways of packaging existing products.

It costs an average of $100 million to launch a new soap. A new cigarette brand comes to almost three times that price. Of 100 products on the market, 90% don't make it. In the fast food trade, only 1 product in 100 is a hit. The ratio is 1 in 1,000 in the pharmaceutical sector. A few notable recent failures include Pizza Hut's light pizza, Pepsi Crystal, Bic perfume, New Coke, Premier smokeless cigarettes, high-caffeine Buzz coffee, and super-sweet Kaboom cereal.

According to Kevin Clancy and Robert Shulman, new products fail for five reasons. The first involves a weak and poorly articulated targeting and positioning strategy. Three out of ten failures fall into this category. The second pertains to dissatisfaction with the product or service, or its failure to meet and exceed consumer expectations and competitive offerings. This accounts for another three out of ten failures. The third is an insufficient level of new product awareness, which is caused by weak or inadequate advertising (20% of all such failures). The fourth and fifth reasons involve inadequate promotion and distribution (10% each).[13]

●——— F L A S H INFO ———●

15 WAYS OF ANNOUNCING A NEW PRODUCT OR SERVICE

New information

New idea

New formula

New packaging

New container

New price

New format

New color

New product

New ingredient(s)

New taste

New fragrance

New technology

New way of using an existing product

New improvement to a former product

4. Headlines that directly solicit prospective customers

These headlines achieve better-than-average rates of success. Claude Hopkins, the father of advertising, claims that "a headline is intended to salute the people you desire to reach. It is just like a bell-boy in a hotel calling for Mr. Jones. Here is a message for him."[14]

You have to go out and grab your customers in today's advertising jungle. Stan Rapp and Tom Collins, of the Rapp and Collins agency, agree: "Failure to visualize who the advertising is attempting to reach and to *call out* to bonus prospects as they turn the page is the single greatest and most wasteful fault in print advertising today."[15]

Bernard Berelson and Gary Steiner have shown that ads aimed at special groups work better than those targeting the general public.[16]

Select your audience by directly identifying the prospective client, or communicate a common interest in the intended market sector. Use words like "hair loss" in your title to grab the attention of men who are going bald.

Keith Kimball, vice-president of BBDO, says, "A good advertisement is a believable promise to the right audience." That is why major companies prefer to orient their messages toward small market segments.

GM's ad execs set up a bold campaign in 2003 targeting people who had no intention of buying a GM vehicle. The ads highlighted improvements that GM had made to its fleet over the previous four years.

5. Testimonial headlines

Such headlines often generate better-than-average results. Make sure to put quotation marks around any testimonial you include in a title. And use everyday language.

6. Headlines that announce discounts

This is an excellent way to attract consumers, who are always looking for ways to save money. Price is almost always the key to good marketing.

Make sure to use clear figures if you offer a discount. List quantities, percentages, distances, durations, money saved, numbers, and specific dates. Doing so will make you more credible and give you greater impact.

WORDS THAT WORK	
Good	**Better**
Batteries that last longer	Batteries that last 30% longer
Quick long grain rice	5-minute long-grain rice
Add a few spoonfuls	Add three teaspoons
Very light	Just 6.5 lbs.
Illustrated	With 42 illustrations
Great mileage	78 miles per gallon
Save a lot	Save $100
Contains lots of nuts	Contains 64 nuts

William Strunk and E.B. White said that "the surest way to arouse and hold the attention of the reader is by being specific, definite, and concrete."[17]

During a study for a hypothetical new brand of imported beer, it was noted that statements such as "Bavaria's No. 1 selling beer for the last 10 years," "winner of five out of five taste tests in the US against all major American beers and leading imports," and "affordably priced at $1.79 per six-pack of 12 oz. bottles", generated twice as many favorable responses as abstract phrases such as "Bavaria's finest beer," "great taste," and "affordably priced."[18]

◆ *Headlines containing specific figures always get better than average results.*

7. Headlines that arouse curiosity

Quizzes, questions, and incomplete sentences generally work very well.

There is, however, a risk. You're taking a big chance by trying to hook your readers with a question. Just getting their attention isn't enough. You have to communicate a concept or prepare the reader for a promise, a tip, or something new. You have to make the reader more receptive. Your audience must be able to draw a connection between your headline and your ad copy. If you don't, your ad will flop.

8. Headlines that employ popular expressions

Experts will generally recommend that you avoid gratuitous word plays and headlines with dual meanings. Pierre Martineau of the *Chicago Tribune* wrote: "Brought up on an intellectual diet of Grade B movies, comic books and sports pages, the average individual is not equipped to cope with the professional communicator."[19]

When asked for the secret of his success, best-selling writer James Clavell said: "Putting the action ahead of word plays." There is good reason to believe this rule generally applies, but campaigns by Revlon ("Does she or doesn't she?") have shown that word plays can work.

THE MAGIC WORDS

In advertising, you not only have to pay a lot of attention to what you say but to the way you say it. Some words work particularly well for selling products. They are:

1. Words that arouse curiosity

Riddle, miracle, magic, mystery, prodigy, secret, truth, real-life experience, confidence, confession, bewitching.

2. Words with a sexual connotation

Night, love, heart, desire, sex, dear, flower, kiss, dream, seduction.

3. Words that trigger a desire to preserve and protect

Grow younger, life, death, fear, war, adventure, crime, progress, freedom, youth, beauty, security.

4. Words that pertain to key moments in life

Baby, child, fiancé, engagement, female, spouse, husband, marriage, family, father, mother, friend, people.

5. Words that correspond to an ideal

Happiness, good fortune, new, special, exceptional, spectacular, discovered, invention, unique, exclusive, hope, happy, comfortable, proud, entertaining, easy.

6. Words that trigger a desire to dominate

Money, gold, dollars, million, millionaire, rich, fortune, success, celebrity, power, achievement, glory, victory, honor, triumph.

7. Words that suggest practical tips

Why, how, here, what is (what are), tool, foundation, stage, innovation, factor, lesson, idea, reason, method, quality, key, objective, strategy, benefit, question, way, solution, tip, connection, tactic, advice, manner, rule, recipe, principle, means, technique, example.

8. Words that imply novelty

New, now, discover, today, first run, latest, warning, important, urgent, opening, progress, improvement, soon, back to school.

THIS AD IS FULL OF LIES.

LIE #1: ADVERTISING MAKES YOU BUY THINGS YOU DON'T WANT.
Advertising is often accused of inducing people to buy things against their will.
But when was the last time you returned home from the local shopping mall with a bag full of things you had absolutely no use for? The truth is, nothing short of a pointed gun can get *anybody* to spend money on something he or she doesn't want.
No matter how effective an ad is, you and millions of other American consumers make your own decisions. If you don't believe it, ask someone who knows firsthand about the limits of advertising. Like your local Edsel dealer.

LIE #2: ADVERTISING MAKES THINGS COST MORE. Since advertising costs money, it's natural to assume it costs *you* money. But the truth is that advertising often brings prices down.
Consider the electronic calculator, for example. In the late 1960's, advertising created a mass market for calculators. That meant more of them needed to be produced, which brought the price of producing each calculator down. Competition spurred by advertising brought the price down still further.
As a result, the same product that used to cost hundreds of dollars now costs as little as five dollars.

LIE #3: ADVERTISING HELPS BAD PRODUCTS SELL.
Some people worry that good advertising sometimes covers up for bad products.
But nothing can make you like a bad product. So, while advertising can help convince you to try something once, it can't make you buy it twice. If you don't like what you've bought, you won't buy it again. And if enough people feel the same way, the product dies on the shelf.
In other words, the only thing advertising can do for a bad product is help you find out it's a bad product. And you take it from there.

LIE #4: ADVERTISING IS A WASTE OF MONEY. Some people wonder why we don't just put all the money spent on advertising directly into our national economy.
The answer is, we already do.
Advertising helps products sell, which holds down prices, which helps sales even more. It creates jobs. It informs you about all the products available and helps you compare them. And it stimulates the competition that produces new and better products at reasonable prices.
If all that doesn't convince you that advertising is important to our economy, you might as well stop reading.
Because on top of everything else, advertising has paid for a large part of the newspaper you're now holding.
And that's the truth.

ADVERTISING.
ANOTHER WORD FOR FREEDOM OF CHOICE.
American Association of Advertising Agencies

◆ *Words such as LIES give your headlines a greater impact. They intrigue readers and encourage them to read your copy to learn more.*

9. Words that imply discounts or special offers

Free, bonus, half price, 20% off, end-of-season sale, competition, sale, clearance, save, economize, bargains, reduction, bonus, price special, win, guarantee.

10. Words that prompt consumers to act *now*

For a limited time, last chance, until stocks are exhausted, while supplies last, last week, Saturday only, three days only, just four days, until tomorrow, price good until, last two days, for the last time at this price, offer ends...

In 1979, the Psychology Department at Yale University revealed that the 12 most influential words in advertising are: Discovery, Love, Results, Free, Money, Safety, Guarantee, New, Save, Health, Proven, and You.[20]

These magic words are *powerful*. They have produced better-than-average results for decades. Use them to boost the effectiveness of your advertising. They make people want to read your copy.

By the same token, you should avoid certain other words—ones that make customers turn and run in the other direction—at all costs:

• BAD	• FAIL	• RECESSION
• BUY	• FAILURE	• SCANDAL
• CONTRACT	• FEAR	• SELL
• COST	• HARD	• WAR
• DEAL	• LIABILITY	• WORRY
• DEATH	• LOSS	• WRONG[21]
• DECISION	• OBLIGATION	
• DIFFICULT	• ORDER	

The ad world has been in love with the word "ULTRA" for some time now. Procter & Gamble used it well with Ultra Tide and Ultra Pampers.[22] The adjective "EXTRA-STRENGTH," which was once limited to the pain relief sector, has now made inroads among cleaners, insecticides, and condoms.[23]

One word will often make the difference between success and failure. Gablinger's introduced the first low-calorie beer in 1967. The copywriter described Gablinger's as a *diet* beer and the campaign flopped. Beer drinkers weren't convinced that a diet beer could taste good. Five years later, Miller also launched a low-calorie brew but portrayed it as a *light* beer. It was an instant hit.

Advertising is, in short, a contest of words and images. That is why companies are perfectly ready to sue their competitors to ensure exclusive use of a word or phrase. America Online claims the exclusive right to use the expression *"You've got mail"* and sued AT&T, whose slogan was *"You have mail."*

FLASH INFO

THE WORD FREE

Wal-Mart says no, Walgreens says yes; marketers caught in middle

"A battle over the word "free" could cost packaged-goods marketers millions of dollars.

The nation's leading drug retailer, Walgreens, is bucking a two-year-old edict by Wal-Mart Stores against using the word "free" on packages. Packaged-goods suppliers bowed to pressure from Wal-Mart two years ago to stop using the word "free" on special packs with extra product at no extra cost. Since Wal-Mart accounts for 35% or more of sales in many non-food categories, most marketers ditched "free" for all retailers in the name of efficiency. Packs that were once "20% More Free!" became "20% Bonus!" or "20% More!"

That may not seem like much difference. Packaged-goods executives reported, however, that Walgreens, citing research that "free" carries more weight with consumers than the alternatives, began pushing marketers late last year to restore this term to their vocabulary.

Sales and marketing executives said Wal-Mart made the change because it felt the word "free" is misleading after receiving consumer complaints that product marked "free" really should be free of charge, not just a bigger size at the same price. The policy applies to increasingly common shrink-wrapped two-for-the-price-of one packs, too."

Source: Neff, Jack. "Free Becomes Fighting Words", *Advertising Age,* January 24, 2004, p. 14.

LONG OR SHORT HEADLINES?

Most of your sentences should top out at seven words. The shorter your headline:

- *The better the chance that people will read the rest of your ad.* Harold Rudolph, who was research director at J. Stirling Getchell, said that titles of seven words or less are more frequently read than longer headlines.[24]

- *The more likely it is that consumers will remember your ad.* Harvard psychologist George A. Miller said that our memories can process up to seven items at a time.[25] That's why the most common lists consist of seven units: seven days in the week, seven digits in a phone number, Seven Wonders of the World, Snow White and the Seven Dwarfs, the seven deadly sins, etc.

Ad experts know that short headlines work better than long ones. Research shows that the average American title is 6.62 words long.

However, don't compress your headline just to make it shorter. Renowned copywriter John Caples said: "Brevity in headlines may be an excellent quality, but it is not so important that all else should be sacrificed for it. It is more important to say what you want to say—to express your complete thought even if it takes twenty words to do so."[26]

Gallup and Robinson state that "advertising success depends more on an idea than on the mechanics of execution; more on substance than on form."[27]

If your headline contains more than a dozen words, your likelihood of success will be greater if you also use a kicker or a subtitle. This rule is particularly important in direct marketing and for retail advertising.

Try to include the name of the brand you are advertising in the headline whenever possible. A study conducted by McGraw-Hill in industrial advertising indicates that advertisements with headlines that give the advertiser's name are read on average by 20% more people than those that fail to do so.[28]

FLASH INFO

HOW TO WRITE A SHORT HEADLINE

Use the imperative and second person plural in short titles.

The imperative serves, in advertisements, to guide, to advise, and to recommend. Browse through a few newspapers and magazines. You will quickly see that copywriters always use the imperative forms of certain verbs. These include: subscribe, economize, dare, participate, write, improve, call, send, learn, save, increase, try, benefit, drink, watch, win, check, indicate, order, taste, play, call, read, discover, use, become, vote, and obtain.

REVIEW

In tribute to a pseudo-modern style, some copywriters produce ads with no headlines. In doing so, however, they fail to recognize that readers are bombarded by ads in a typical newspaper.

Consumers decide what they want to read based on headlines. If you don't use a headline, there is little likelihood that your ad will be read. An advertising association once said, "The headline is the most important element in print ads." Perception Research Services has also said, "Headline readership often exceeds six or seven times the readership level of body copy."[29]

Chapter 5

Writing ad copy that sells

While you may have previously heard that consumers don't read ad copy, it's time to set the record straight. In fact, magazine ads enjoy an average readership rate of 10%.[1]

You may think that just 10% of a publication's readers is not worth the effort involved, *but you're wrong*. Most of the time, this small group of readers includes a certain number of prospective customers who want to know more about your type of product before making a final decision. Your copy should be designed to persuade them to buy your product rather than those of your competitors.

Steve Cosmopulos, Chairman of the Board of Cosmopulos, Crowley & Daly, has claimed that words make the difference: "Words can make you laugh, make you cry and make you buy. Designers who think words are just another design element miss the point."[2]

Steve Hayden, Chairman and chief creative officer of BBDO West, said, "Print copy can be the most powerful selling tool imaginable. It's the best way to communicate information. And great copy can touch both the heart *and* the head."[3]

Some years ago, the "father of modern advertising," Albert Lasker, said, "People won't be able to remember if they haven't even read your ads. If they don't remember your ad, they certainly won't buy your product." That principle is still just as sound today.

MEDIA ADVISORY

THE ROLE OF COPY...

ON TV

Visuals play the key role in TV commercials more than in any other media. The copy may be essential to understanding your ad, but it generally plays a role in supporting your sales pitch.

ON RADIO

Over time, radio is the media we have learned to listen to while doing something else. Because consumers cannot see your product or logo on the radio, make sure they remember you. Mention your product's name at the very start of the spot and then repeat it at least three times.

IN BILLBOARDS

Make brief and clear billboards to catch the consumer's eye. Boil your message down to the essentials. Make sure the picture and words work together.

IN PRINT AND ON THE WEB

The shorter your text, the more people will read it. Using a general index of 100, Starch studies show that ads of 25 words or less achieve average reading rates of 284, while those of more than 500 words only get a rate of 86, with 100 representing an average rate.[4] The percentage of readers drops dramatically for ads longer than 50 words.

WRITING COPY THAT WORKS

It takes time to write good copy. To begin with, writing is a difficult art. And special, simple but strict rules apply to ad copy.

Words that have been effectively arranged by a skilled copywriter will serve to motivate and to persuade consumers. Generally speaking, the less you say, the better your audience will retain it.

Twenty rules apply to the writing of texts that sell.

1. Be direct

Get right to the point. Eliminate any unnecessary words. The longer the drum roll, the more likely you will lose the reader.

Most TV and radio commercials last 30 seconds. Most print ads favor image over text. You have little time to run on in great detail about your product or service.

Remember what Kenneth Roman and Joel Raphaelson once said: "Your reader does not have much time. If you want to hold the attention of busy people, your writing must cut through to the heart of the matter and should only require a minimum of time and effort on the reader's part."[5]

Thomas Jefferson said, "The most valuable of all talents is that of never using two words when one will do."

In *Hard Times*, Charles Dickens wrote: "Now, what I want is, Facts. Teach these boys and girls nothing but Facts. Facts alone are wanted in Life. Plant nothing else, and root out everything else. You can only form the minds of reasoning animals upon Facts: nothing else will ever be of any service to them. This is the principle on which I bring up my own children, and this is the principle on which I bring up these children. Stick to Facts, Sir!" This rule is also true in advertising.

2. Use the lead argument to kick off your ad

Give strong impact to your first paragraph. Offer some kind of benefit.

All famous copywriters—including Bly, Caples, Hodgson, Lewis, Ogilvy, Sackheim, Schwab, Stone—recommend generating a surprise impact from the start.

Once you have drafted your first paragraph, build on your description of the product's key advantage. Tell readers what they should know about your product and repeat it often.

To learn more about writing your lead paragraph, read the chapter "How to Write the First Paragraph," in *Tested Advertising Methods*, and the chapter "Ten Ways to Write the First Paragraph," in *Making Ads Pay*, both by copywriter John Caples.

3. Be straightforward

Anyone who writes ad copy has to deal with the problem of being understood by everyone.

Ordinary mortals may not fathom your meaning if you fail to use simple language. Market analyst Alfred Politz, president of Alfred Politz Research Inc., writes: "Efficiency in advertising seems to depend on the use of simple language—simple, direct presentation of sales arguments—and the avoidance of tricky attention-getting devices unrelated to the product itself."[6]

Al Ries and Jack Trout, of the Trout & Ries agency, go further: "One means of success for many people today involves observing what the competition does and then getting rid of the poetic or imaginative elements that stand in the way of effective transmission of the message. A simple and straightforward message will let you speak directly to your prospective customers."

Remember, 25 million Americans read below fifth-grade level, and 35 to 40 million read between the fifth- and eighth-grade levels.

And this is your problem. If your style is too elementary, you may alienate your audience. If your style is overly original, you may put your readers on the defensive and cast doubts among them. You should, in short, be simple. But don't take the reader for an idiot.

4. Speak directly to your audience

Some copywriters tend to write as if they were communicating with an inanimate mass. That is not a good approach. Make sure to keep the reader in mind. Speak—and listen to—your audience. Treat your readers the same way you treat people in your daily life.

Here are four ways of making your writing more personal:

- *Speak directly to your readers,* addressing them as "you." Don't say: "The new Warner system permits a 10% reduction in heating costs." You would be better phrasing your message as: "The new Warner system will let you save 10% on your heating costs."

- *Use "personal" phrases,* direct questions, or requests of readers, exclamations, imperative sentences, and unfinished, chatty, sentences.

- *Tell a story about using your product.* Rather than giving specific arguments for purchasing it, get your readers involved in a human-interest account of its use.

- *Include the names of relatively well-known celebrities* in your ad and employ first names, personal pronouns, and personal words like *people* and *mom.*

Advertising research shows that personalized texts work very well. In a study of 50 ads that achieved very high rates of readership, and of 50 ads that proved total flops, Daniel Starch showed that successful ads always gave humans an important role.[7]

According to Dr. Rudolf Flesch, the more personalized and human a text, the more likely that it will interest a larger number of readers.[8] One thing that interests everybody is other humans. *People are more interested in fellow men and women than they are in objects or ideas.*

5. Use the present tense

The present lets you express the idea in your copy that this is what's happening and this is what you should do. It can also be used to express a future incident that is sure to occur.

You might consider employing other tenses as well. The future expresses the seller's commitment to satisfying the buyer. Use it often, because, as noted above, all good ads contain a promise. The present participle is very useful because it lets you avoid using a relative clause that would further complicate your sentences.

Avoid the infinitive, which is the most impersonal form of communication. A manufacturer may enjoy such turns of phrase as "To try it is to use it!" but such language is likely to fall flat with your target audience. The infinitive could, however, prove useful in recipes, instruction manuals, demonstrations, and different turns of phrase.

6. Use logic and emotion

Your ad should not only inform readers about a *specific advantage,* such as "Our product makes your teeth whiter," but about an emotional benefit as well, such as "See how much the ladies like your smile when you use our toothpaste."

Logically structured print ads can work well. But William McGuire, an expert in changing attitudes, has observed that the typical reader is less interested in strictly rational messages.[9]

7. Keep your paragraphs short and sweet

Readability studies by Gallup and Flesch are quite clear on this topic: the longer your paragraphs, the fewer people will read them.

8. Use short and commonly used words

Studies show that short words should always be favored over long ones. Commonly used words are, similarly, much more effective than obscure ones.

These two rules are in fact simply two aspects of a more general principle. In his book *Human Behavior and the Principle of Least Effort: an Introduction to Human Ecology*, American researcher George Kingsley Zipf showed that the most commonly used words are also short. Both short and commonly used words share the quality of being simple.

Short and commonly used words are more understood, more quickly, and more thoroughly. They are, accordingly, better retained.

USE SIMPLE WORDS	
WRITE	**RATHER THAN**
sad	chagrined
agreement	consensus
study	investigation

Statements and concrete terms are better for your ads than abstract terms. Concrete terms are not only more easily understood than abstract words, they are more likely to be retained.

The use of slang, technical terms, foreign words, dialectical expressions, archaic forms, abbreviations, and new words should be totally avoided or prudently exercised. Otherwise, your readers will understand little of your ad copy.

In an internal memo to his agency, Leo Burnett wrote: "Don't print anything addressed to a mass audience which you couldn't clearly explain to a bright 16-year-old child. Great advertising writing, either in print or TV, is always deceptively and disarmingly simple. It has the common touch without being or sounding patronizing."[10] This rule is all the more true today.

Naturally, you can talk about RAM and software when advertising in computer magazines. But I doubt that a discussion on internal and external computer memory systems will go over quite as well in a tabloid.

Bear in mind that the average North American's vocabulary consists of about 500 words, plus some specialized language based on an individual's trade, area of residence, typical activities, culture, and lifestyle. But you can only use such special expressions with confidence if your target audience is well defined.

9. Write short sentences

US reading retention studies have shown that people remember short sentences better than long ones. You should use no more than 12 words in English if you want people to properly recall what you say.

10. Be positive

If you say, "Zombo chips don't contain preservatives," most readers will subsequently only recall the idea that your product *does* contain preservatives. This is because negation is easily forgotten. When heard together, the ideas of "Zombo chips" and "preservatives" are stored in adjacent memory slots, and will subsequently be associated with each other.

Some years ago, after Philip Morris began advertising that one of its cigarette brands was less irritating than another, sales slumped. Individuals interviewed on this issue by Weiss and Geller said: "When I think of Philip Morris, I think of irritation."[11]

If you absolutely must use a negative phrase, draw the reader's attention to the negation by underlining it or printing it in italics.

11. Observing the subject-verb-object structure

The frequent use of multiple offers, each nested within the other, requires considerable effort from your readers. A high nesting rate can make it harder for readers to understand your text.

If you really want to be understood—and thus better remembered—keep the key words for the end of the sentence. People generally have less recollection of words that start a sentence than those that end it.

12. Imply a cause-effect relationship

A sentence as a whole tends to be better retained if it starts with an expression such as: *that's why, as a result, for example, it's quite clear that, because, however,* and *nonetheless*. Such a sentence implies a well defined structure containing linguistic continuity, and thus makes it likelier that the sentence will make an accurate prediction.

13. Don't get carried away with ellipses

Excessive use of ellipses tends to block the thought process and be tiring to readers.

14. Don't get carried away with exclamation marks

Exclamation marks often serve as a refuge for writers who lack emotion in their style.

15. Repeat your product's name

It is a good idea to repeat your product's name as often as possible in ads. Consider ads for Eveready batteries. They have won multiple advertising awards and were ranked among the top ads of 1990. However, 40% of those questioned thought that these ads were in fact produced by the company's competitor Duracell, which benefited from increased sales at Eveready's expense.

16. Avoid stating the obvious

Stay far, far away from platitudes and clichés like "best in the world," "the first," "everybody's favorite," "the ideal," "the most economical," "the least expensive," "the cheapest," "the most effective," "the most reliable," "the sturdiest," "the inimitable," "the incomparable," and "the unique."

Avoid at all costs overworked generalities and superlatives such as:

Best for half a century, better than ever today	Admiration cigar
Everybody loves Admiration	Admiration cigar
Always first, always fair	Indianapolis Star
Nothing reduces fever faster	Children's Panadol
Nothing sparks like Champion spark plugs	Champion
Nobody beats Midas. Nobody	Midas
Nobody treats America like Brachs	Brachs
No one reports the news like Newsweek reports the news	Newsweek
Nobody does as much as Extra Maalox Plus	Extra Maalox Plus
Nothing eliminates spots like Sunlight	Sunlight
The world supreme experience	American President *Lines*
The difference makes the difference	Anne Alt brassiere
From freezer to microwave, nothing protects food better	Saran Wrap
Who else competes like Chrysler? Nobody	Chrysler
Nobody, but nobody, sells for less than Highland	Highland
As new as tomorrow	Dictaphone Corp.
A step ahead of tomorrow	Zurn Industries

Very few ad campaigns have succeeded by using this strategy. Naturally, there are some exceptions, but such exaggerations have lost all of their selling power over time.

Randy Zanatta, vice-president of Marketing for Best Buy, said that, "customers are not as naive as they once were. They know what they want, they know the model they want, they know where the values are. They aren't going to be fooled by the old frantic sell."[12]

17. Totally leave yourself out of it

Don't use expressions like: "Demand this brand," "Buy my brand," "Refuse imitations", and "Beware of imitations." Consumers may be receptive to such advice if they agree with it. But they will steer clear of your product if they sense you are twisting their arm and looking out for their money rather than their best interests.

18. Be cordial

According to James D. Woolf, author of a column that appeared in the magazine *Advertising Age* in the 1950s and 1960s, people who are warm, sincere and amiable are more likely to write successful ads.[13]

19. Use subheads every 25 lines

The most effective subheads keep the reader interested, and let him get the gist of your pitch without having to read it from start to finish.

20. Provide a conclusion

Messages that contain a clear conclusion work twice as well as those that don't.[14]

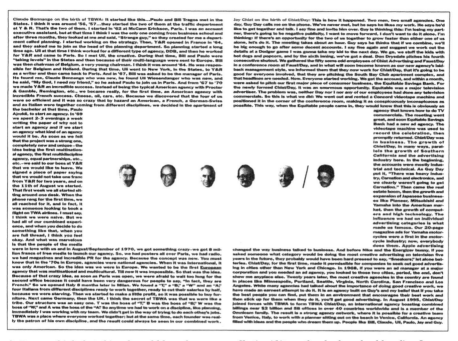

◆ *Do you think that this ad would have been more effective if its author had used subheadings?*

Use your conclusion to try to get your prospective customer to take some kind of action. Your readers are in the process of leafing through the newspaper in which your ad appears. They have read the sports news and checked the lotto numbers. They suddenly see your ad and begin reading it. Then, after a few seconds, they resume reading their papers as if nothing had happened. That's no good. Don't let yourself lose thousands of customers that way. Employ techniques that can get your reader to respond positively to your offer.

You can start by reformulating the manner in which you offer a product's key benefits. The more such benefits are uppermost in your readers' minds, the more likely they will justify the decision you want them to make.

179

Follow through by getting readers to take action. Make them understand that such action must be performed immediately. Set a deadline and remind them that quantities are limited.

Reassure consumers by offering full guarantees. A guarantee is essential for selling products and services. People are often nervous about the idea of purchasing a new product. They want to be able to trust it. A satisfaction guarantee reduces tension and stimulates sales.

Conclude your copy by indicating your *terms of sale, address, and telephone number*. Jaguar automobiles have successfully employed a 1-800 telephone number in their magazine ads. Research has shown that 35% to 40% of all those who called the 1-800 number later went to a Jaguar dealership, and that 10% even bought a car.

The launch of Saturn's print advertising campaign generated 22,000 calls to 1-800 number. "About one third of the callers agreed to be contacted by a dealership in their area, and 93% of the callers asked for literature," says Mr. Shaver, Saturn's director of marketing services.

Every Gerber Products ad encourages parents to call the company's 1-800 number for more information about the care and feeding of babies. Gerber's receives about 1,200 such calls a day.

To help customers remember their 1-800 numbers, some companies translate these numbers into words, such as 1-800 FLOWERS. Although this can be a shrewd strategy, some firms have learned at great expense that they shouldn't rely on such easy solutions. This was the case for AT&T, which created 1-800 OPERATOR to get people to use its services for collect calls. Unfortunately, AT&T failed to anticipate that many people don't know how to spell OPERATOR, and would end up calling 1-800 OPERATER. One of AT&T's competitors, MCI, saw an open door. With MCI's 1-800 OPERATER number, unsuspecting customers sent a whopping $500,000 worth of business to a firm with which they had had no intention of doing business.

Include your signature and your logo. Be aware, however, that logos can backfire. A study conducted by the Schechter Group found that Borden's "Elsie the cow" helped the company's image, but that Oldsmobile has been hurt by its rocket logo. Among all of the logos tested, the images of IBM Corp. and Mercedes-Benz were most enhanced by their logos.

LONG OR SHORT TEXTS?

Studies generally show that the length of your copy should be based on the following three factors:

1. *The media you plan to use to conduct your campaign.* In direct marketing, for example, copywriter John Caples has argued that short texts don't sell. He wrote: "Long texts always sell better than comparable short ones."[15] In his book *Direct Mail and Mail Order Handbook*, Richard Hodgson reported that one 11-page letter to 500 prospective customers elicited 161 positive responses, and a 45:1 revenue-to-cost ratio.[16]

2. *Your targets.* Unfortunately, certain sectors of the population categorically refuse to ever read more than a few words at a time. According to Joseph Newman and Richard Staelin, the better informed a product's prospective customers, the more

likely they are to seek information before buying.[17] People 50 and older tend to read more and to demand more information as well. Take this factor into account.

3. *The product or service that you are advertising.* A long text sells better than a short one, particularly if you are advertising something new, if you are speaking to technically minded people, if you want to realign your product's position, or if you are asking people to spend large sums of money. According to Perception Research Services, long copy implies a good reputation, and people are more willing to try out the product of a company with such credentials. This process ultimately leads to increased market share.

However, tighten your copy if you are advertising soft drinks, clothing, candy, potato chips, beer, wine, jewelry, lingerie, perfume, soap, beauty products, or shampoo. These products, which are purchased for emotional reasons, require virtually no sales pitch.

•——— **FLASH** INFO ———•

4 REASONS TO WRITE LENGTHY COPY

1. If you are advertising a new product
Whenever you launch a new product on the market, your copy should contain specific information on the product such as its shape, dimensions, weight, colors, price, overall size, performance, qualities, and so forth.

2. If you are speaking to technically minded people who are buying products for their businesses
Such items are generally for industrial, agricultural, commercial, or household use and include equipment and tools, construction materials, industrial supplies, and any other general groups of products aimed at a specific class of buyers and which, by their nature, correspond with technical sales arguments.

3. If you are realigning your market position

To put a crisis behind you, explain the issues to customers. When Chrysler was suspected of having disconnected the odometers in some of its cars, the company responded by publishing an approximately 350-word ad in all of America's leading daily newspapers to clear the air. The ad was signed by Chrysler chairman Lee Iacocca himself.

4. If you ask the reader to spend large sums of money on a computer, a car, a mutual fund, or a seminar, lengthy copy is required.

Consumers can expect to make long use of such products, and need adequate information before deciding to buy. Your copy is in all cases designed to help justify your product's price for reasons of quality, performance, social standing, and prestige.

●━━━━━━━━━━━━━━━━━━━━━━━●

HOW TO BOOST THE CREDIBILITY OF YOUR ADVERTISING

Make sure to back up all of the claims in your ad. Most folks tend to be skeptical of advertising. A Gallup poll revealed that two out of three Canadians believe that most TV commercials are not true, and that one out of four believes that all ads are dishonest.

According to a survey done by Market Facts Inc. for *Advertising Age* magazine, 43% of the respondents chose advertising as the profession with "the lowest ethical standards."[18] A Harris survey asked the public how much confidence they had in the people who ran various institutions. Ad agencies ranked last. Here are 11 ways of making your claims more believable:

1. Studies and tests

Studies and surveys conducted by independent research firms achieve better than average results in persuading consumers to buy a particular product.

2. Reports of outstanding use

Maytag once published an ad to demonstrate the sturdiness of its machines that said:

> "Our Maytag has been doing the wash for our entire community since 1969 ... and there are 35 of us!
>
> "Our Maytag has served us incredibly well for all these years and we cannot praise it too highly.
>
> "We bought our Maytag washer for the convent 10 years ago [...].

"Ever since, it has been doing an average of 50 to 60 washes per week. It required little in the way of repair throughout this period. This clearly demonstrates that Maytag washers are made to last longer, and that you will save through fewer repairs."

3. The satisfaction guarantee

A study by William Bearden and Terence Shimp showed that a comprehensive refund guarantee has become a vital sales argument.[19]

When Scotch offered a life-long guarantee on its all-purpose videocassettes, and free replacement should a defect ever appear in the product, the brand took over the market lead.

Holiday Inn was surprised to learn that its offer of a free stay to dissatisfied customers also served to boost the quality of customer service.

Guarantees can occasionally have a negative impact. After offering its customers guaranteed 30-minute delivery, Domino's Pizza was forced to rethink this policy because of the hazardous driving performed by some of its delivery people.

◆ *By offering a guarantee for Prestone antifreeze, the manufacturer draws consumer attention to product quality and value. At the same time, the manufacturer helps overcome any consumer resistance to the product.*

4. Endorsement by an official organization

Obtaining a credible endorsement from an outside consumer organization, educational institution, trade association, or government agency is a proven means of winning over customers.

Dr. Ballard's cat food bears the seal of the Canadian Veterinary Medical Association. Dunlop tennis balls are approved by the United States Tennis Association. When Procter & Gamble received the American Dental Association's backing for its Crest toothpaste, sales shot up 23% within a few months.[20]

After receiving the recommendation of America's National Fraternal Order of Police, sales of The Club, an anti-theft device, topped $100 million, a 75% rise over the previous year.[21]

5. Awards and medals

Keep records of any trophies or prizes that your product wins. The public believes that products that win awards and medals are of superior quality.

In a saturated market, like the auto trade, many companies rely on support from independent organizations to boost their credibility. General Motors' Pontiac division uses its car's selection as "best domestic sedan" by *Motor Week,* and Jeep Cherokee's selection by *4 Wheel & Off-Road,* to boost sales.

"We found out that endorsements by third-party, independent organizations actually carry a lot of weight in influencing people," said Mark Gjovik, senior VP-management supervisor of the Pontiac account at D'Arcy. "Our research told us that in this cluttered field of alternatives, if one vehicle stands out as having gotten special recognition, it meant something to people as one of the better options they could shop for."[22]

Bozell and its client, Taylor California Cellars, set up a wine competition in San Francisco to boost product credibility. Based on a very positive outcome for Taylor, Bozell created a successful campaign that quickly established the superior quality of these wines in consumers' minds.

6. Product history

Consumers tend to assume that long-lived products are of better quality.

Ivory Soap has been in existence for 126 years, Welch's grape juice for 136 years, Pennzoil for 116 years, and Weston bread for 123 years. Crayola crayons have been with us for 102 years, Hershey's chocolate for 111 years, and Jell-O for 108 years. Molson's beer has been marketed for 219 years, Cow Brand baking soda for 158 years, and Hellmann's mayonnaise for 100 years. All of these products are successes.

When Tylenol suffered problems during the cyanide scandal, the company invested $1 million for several one-minute spots over four consecutive days. The company's medical director, Dr. Thomas Gates, spoke to the viewers and reminded them that the brand had been in existence for 20 years.

7. Number of customers served

The number of satisfied customers may sway prospective customers, as, for example, when McDonald's claimed to have served more than 70 billion burgers.

Many consumer trends are directly influenced by fads. Parents massed to buy Cabbage Patch dolls for their kids one Christmas, while they lined up to get them Nintendo video games the next. Everyone wanted sailboards one year, while they asked for mountain bikes the following one. One season, women prefer Anaïs Anaïs perfume, while they use Obsession the next. Here are three ways of benefiting from such popular enthusiasm:

- You can advertise percentages, as in: "90% of all Canadians choose Anacin."

- You can refer to sales: "More than 12,000 cars sold last year."

- You can mention satisfied customers: "9 out of 10 prefer 7-Up."

Whatever approach you select, your ads will be well served by projecting the image of a product everyone wants to have. Claude Hopkins, of the Lord & Thomas agency, writes: "People are like sheep. They cannot judge values, nor can you and I. We judge things largely by others' impressions, by popular favor. We go with the crowd. So the most effective thing I have ever found in advertising is the trend of the crowd. That is a factor not to be overlooked. People follow styles and preferences. We rarely decide for ourselves, because we don't know the facts. But when we see the crowds taking any certain direction, we are much inclined to go with them."[23]

If a product loses its public allure, the consequences can be disastrous. When Martha Stewart was accused of insider trading, public opinion was slow to express itself. Initially, 17.8% of all people said that this situation would make them less inclined to buy Martha Stewart products. One year later, that percentage had soared to 28.6%. Shortly thereafter, Ms. Stewart's face vanished from magazine covers.

8. Famous customers

At the start of his term, Bill Clinton took to winding up his morning jog with a stop at McDonald's. It goes without saying that his regular presence helped boost the hamburger giant's profile.

According to Thomas Harris, former director of public relations for McDonald's, "It legitimizes their menu and gives permission to have a hamburger. It makes McDonald's in and trendy, even for people who wouldn't normally go there."[24]

9. Number of stores

McDonald's has 30,000 fast-food outlets in more than 100 countries. It serves more than 46 million customers each day.

Subway boosted its product strength by boasting that it has 21,629 restaurants in 76 nations.

10. Loyal customer testimonials

Testimonials from loyal customers still represent one of the most effective means of selling such common consumer products as coffee, detergent and shampoo.

If you have loyal customers ready to attest to the quality of your products, use just one testimonial at a time. And don't improve on their styles. Robert Bly, a copywriter and author of some 50 books on direct marketing, said, "A natural, conversational tone adds believability to the testimonial."[25]

McCollum/Spielman advise that you avoid selecting people who appear too stilted, regional, or unattractive. They generally call more attention to themselves than to the product. Also note that testimonials by a single individual will in most cases yield better results than will a group testimonial.

11. Testimonials from senior executives

Ad campaigns by Remington, Chrysler, Sleeman, Perdue Farms, H&R Block, Prudential, and K-Mart have used highly placed company spokespersons to boost credibility, along with product sales.

After Victor Kiam appeared in his company's ads, Remington electric razor sales climbed from an annual $43 million to over $100 million. While the commercial did not win any awards or popularity contests, it did persuade many people to buy Remington razors, as noted by Edward F. Cone.[26]

Wendy's founding president Dave Thomas appeared for many years in the well-known fast-food chain's ads. During his life, he was featured in more than 800 Wendy's ads. Although he passed away some time ago, Thomas will long remain linked to the company's image. In fact, Wendy's purchased the image of its former president just prior to his passing.

Lee Iacocca's presence in Chrysler's national ads had a remarkable impact, and made Iacocca a hero for an entire generation of Americans.

Stephen Baker wrote: "Though reluctant at first to appear on television, it soon became apparent that his was just the right personality to embody all that his company stood for. A scrappy, second-generation American, the 'car guy' executive had become a genuine folk hero...Sensing his immense popular appeal, agency Kenyon & Eckhard insisted that he return to the television screen again and again, even after Chrysler's miraculous recovery from near bankruptcy. No one else would be able to duplicate the impact of his appearances; his was an impossible act to follow."

Three days after "Black Friday" on Wall Street in 1987, Merrill Lynch chief executive officer William Schreyer appeared in a television commercial to offer reassurance and present a positive attitude about the future.

Testimonials from senior executives can obviously prove a double-edged sword. If that executive becomes involved in a scandal, as was the case with Martha Stewart, the entire company will be tarred with the same brush.

DOES HUMOR SELL?

Humor is quite popular in advertising. In the US, humor finds its way into 24.4% of all TV commercials.[27]

Some writers always use humor in their ads. Heineken has been employing humor and music to boost sales for many years. More than 55% of all professional researchers believe that humorous ads get better results than serious ones.[28] Famous admen like Claude Hopkins, Rosser Reeves, and David Ogilvy have, however, tried to point out to advertisers that advertising is not aimed at amusing or entertaining the public, but at selling the product.

It is clear that humor has a positive influence on the *amount of attention people give to an ad*. A study by McCollum Spielman showed that 75% of all ads containing humor received average or better-than-average attention.[29] Humor generates better attention rates in magazine ads,[30] in TV commercials[31] and in radio commercials.[32]

Humor can work when there is a link between the concept and the product.[33] This approach produces good results if you have an apology to make. Humor is also typically employed by a challenger seeking to acquire the leader's crown. Humor can also be used to play down product or service issues.

Humor is a better tool than fear for persuading people and for increasing goodwill toward a product. Funny ads are particularly effective among young men,[34] and for selling such common consumer items as beer, cookies, chocolate bars, soft drinks, and chewing gum.[35]

FLASH INFO

HUMOR AND THE MEDIA

TELEVISION

It provides full stories with a beginning, a plot, and a finale.

RADIO

Funny stories that take the form of brief dialogues between different characters are common. Sketches are often prepared by professional comedy writers to maximize results.

PRINT

Humor is a challenge in this media and must be subtle. Visuals must have a strong impact in this media.

BILLBOARDS

Word plays are most common on billboards, which have little time to deliver their messages. Such displays often refer to a commercial previously aired on television.

Advertising studies offer a range of conclusions on how humor *affects* consumer behavior. McCollum/Spielman discovered that only 31% of humorous ads were more persuasive than serious ones. It seems that humor makes it harder for people to understand—or remember—an ad.[36] Humorous ads also lose their effect more quickly. Companies that plan to use humor should accordingly plan to provide a variety of ads.

Prudential Insurance dropped the use of humor when research showed a more traditional approach generated superior results. To stand out from the competition, American Motors employed a funny approach. Unfortunately, it did not sell. In the 1960s, everyone enjoyed and laughed at an Alka-Seltzer spot, but the client's market share kept dwindling.

Stan Freberg remarked: "Humor in advertising is like gum in the hands of a child...It can blow up on you."

On the other hand, Federal Express, Wendy's, Chivas Regal, Miller Lite, and Bartles & Jaymes have shown that humor sometimes sells. But the risks are significant: ethnic humor, making fun of the product, making fun of the consumer, or making fun of advertising in general poses a threat to the advertiser.

Humorous messages generally yield poorer than average results for the sale of new products and medications, alcohol, cosmetics, perfumes, luxury cars, insurance, financial services, and new products.

Studies have shown that funny ads work better on radio and TV[37] than in print. Other research has shown that radio, followed by television, is best suited to humor.

PLUSES AND MINUSES OF PROMOTIONAL CAMPAIGNS

Promotional campaigns are aimed at quickly boosting revenues, and are generally publicized through posters at the store, mass mailings, newspaper ads, and flyers.

Sales have grown in importance over the past two decades at the expense of advertising. In 1969, 53% of marketing budgets were invested in advertising. Twenty years later, Donnelley Marketing reported that 70% of such budgets went instead to promotional campaigns.[38] Here are 10 ways of making such campaigns more effective:

1. Discount coupons

Discount coupons are one of the most widely used promotional tools. According to NCH Promotional Services, Canadian companies distributed 2.32 billion coupons in 2002. Of this number, 110 million were used. Such coupons offer numerous benefits:

- They can help relaunch a declining brand.

- They can boost market share over the short term.

- They generate interest in your product.

- They let you contact a multitude of consumers within a short time frame.

- They cut down on customer disloyalty. ACNielsen says that coupon users stay faithful to a brand longer than do customers who get discounts straight from the store.

- They can be used to get consumers interested in a new taste or presentation.

- They make people want to try your product. It has been estimated that 65% of all coupons that are used enable you to communicate with new clients (50% for established brands).

Information Resources Inc. reported that 25% or more of the sales of popular brands such as Scope mouthwash, Bayer aspirin, Kraft barbecue sauce, Kellogg's cereals, and Wisk powder detergent come with coupons. By the late 1980s, it was estimated that 20.8% of fast-food sales were being bought at discounts through coupons or specials.

Nielsen reported that 58% of all American families used discount coupons in 1971, 65% used them in 1975, and 76% used them in 1980.[39] The biggest users of such coupons were middle-class families.

FLASH INFO

HOW TO PRODUCE A GOOD COUPON

The offer
Must be clear, visible, specific, and precise with respect to quantity, presentation, color, etc.

The value
Your coupon must be worth at least 50 cents.

Expiration date
Should appear in the centre of the upper portion of the coupon.

The product
Clearly give your product's name. Present it and include a logo to avoid any confusion.

The title
Refer to savings. Emphasize savings of money. Be short and sweet. Use words like "Save" or "Discount."

Location
The coupon should appear in the lower part of your ad and ideally to the right.

Bar codes
Should be in the lower right-hand side of the coupon.

Format
Use a standard 6" x 2" format.

Discount coupons are more widely used in some countries than others. The rate in Canada during 2004 was about 4%,[40] while it was 56% in Belgium,[41] 16% in Italy and Spain, and 7.5% in the UK.

Coupons present two disadvantages. First of all, more than 20% are used fraudulently, which poses an increasing number of headaches for businesses.[42] They also fail to boost loyalty to a particular brand or to boost mid- or long-term sales. In fact, only 1 out of 10 campaigns generates more than a 10% rise in sales.[43]

FLASH INFO

FACTS AND FIGURES ON COUPONS

- Coupons that were used in 2002 had an average value of $1.25.

- Food discount coupons were worth less on average: 75 cents.

- Coupons for household maintenance products, children's food, and pet food made up 30% of the coupons distributed each year.

- Food coupons, representing 50% of the total, were those most widely used.

Source: AC Nielsen, 2003.

2. Special events

Such events let you reach out to a captive—and interested—audience. Even lower profile special events represent an important tool in your marketing efforts.

GM organizes exclusive open-air shows for Saturn owners. Molson invests some 30% to 40% of its annual communications and marketing budget on hosting events and product launches.

3. Samples

Distributing free samples is a powerful means of boosting sales for an existing product, or for launching a new one. Even without any other advertising or promotional effort for the product, 33% of those who receive a free sample of a new brand of coffee will mention it to friends and family.[44]

In the food industry, tasting events can generate impulse sales 8 times out of 10.

In the perfume industry, samples, and not advertising, often make the difference. "Advertising will still be needed to establish an image, but we've found the most important thing we can do for a fragrance is to get it into the hands of the consumer," declares Sharon LeVan, senior vice-president of Max Factor.[45]

4. Gifts

Gifts represent another means of bringing customers into your shop. McDonald's gives away 1.5 billion toys throughout the world each year. McDonald's and its competitors, in fact, give away nearly one third of all the toys distributed each year in the United States.[46]

If you give away a gift as a bonus, make sure it's a surprise.[47] Curiosity is one of the most powerful forces in human nature. If you say precisely what you are giving away, some people will still want it, but an even greater number will decide they don't need it. But everyone loves a surprise.

5. Price reductions

Product price is now more than ever a key to marketing. Price is a factor that will make consumers purchase or avoid your product. A study by *Cahners Advertising Research Report* revealed that 98.7% of all consumers are influenced by price when they purchase a product.[48]

There is a complex science involved in setting a product's price. Most research reveals that prices ending in odd numbers achieve better sales than those ending in even ones. Some 80% of all product prices end in the digits 9 or 5.

Jo Marney, a Toronto-based advertising/media consultant, says, "Pricing is a complex science and the situation differs from product to product, and from market to market. Many basic marketing textbooks assume that prices ending with an odd number (e.g. 1, 3, 5, 7, 9), or just under a round number (e.g. 99, 98), increase consumer sensitivity. In 1969, it was suggested by Lawrence Friedman (*Psychological Pricing in the Food Industry*) that certain psychological prices may have their roots in tradition, since he found that prices ending in "9" or "5" account for as much as 80% of retail food prices. Nearly 50% of all special off-priced promotions were in multiples of 5, but even-number discounts were more predominant."[49]

Research findings by Edward Blair and Laird Landon, published in the spring 1981 *Journal of Marketing,* reveal that consumers feel they have saved more with advertised prices when compared against some benchmark. However, this benchmark is not always accepted as a true comparison for calculating savings. In one study, consumers consistently discounted such benchmarks by about 25%.

Brian Wansink made an interesting discovery when playing around with prices and formats. If consumers are offered canned soup at 79 cents per can with no purchasing limit, they generally buy three or four items. However, if a limit of 12 cans per customer is imposed, they will buy an average of 7, for a 112% increase. In the same vein, a poster that offers four items for $4 will sell more than one offering one for $1.[50]

In any case, proofread your promotion carefully before sending it off for final printing. In 1993, an ad for Continental Airlines, printed in the *Boston Globe,* offered flights from Boston to Los Angeles for $48 instead of $148. Dropping the 1 cost the airline $4 million.

6. Special packaging

Use packaging to promote your product whenever possible. During the 1990 holiday season, Coca-Cola sold commemorative six-packs of 6 1/2-ounce Coke bottles with images of Santa Claus. During Christmas, Anheuser-Busch changed its usual packaging design on 12-packs and 24-packs of Budweiser to present teams of Clydesdale horses in the snow. But "it takes a product with a secure identity to be able to play around with its trademarked look," said Howard Alport of Lipson-Alport-Glass & Associates.[51]

This rule may seem obvious, but test your packaging before launching it on the market. The Magic Summer '90 promotion, which was one of Coca-Cola's biggest-ever campaigns, came to an abrupt halt when devices on some of the 750,000 cans of carbonated beverage in question failed.[52] The device was supposed to pop up with prizes ranging from $5 to $200 when cans were opened, but it fizzled on several occasions. At least one child drank the liquid that had been used to replace Coke in the winning cans. Other children were surprised to see rolls of dollars tumbling out of their cans. Finally, Coca-Cola was lambasted for sending winning cans to journalists on a promotional basis. The entire effort resulted in a stinging financial disaster.

Taco Bell recalled 300,000 plastic bottles after learning that a child had successfully taken the bottle top apart, and attempted to swallow the mouthpiece. Hardee's Food Systems voluntarily recalled 2.8 million promotional toys after several children had tried to swallow the toy's batteries.

7. Free offers and bonuses

In a world in which customer disloyalty has become the norm, ads that announce free offers ("Buy three bars of soap and get one free") and special offers ("conditioner included free, along with shampoo") are sure hits.

8. Customer loyalty programs

Savings stamps were among the first customer loyalty programs. Sperry & Hutchinson introduced S&H Green Stamps in Jackson, Mississippi in 1896 with the simple premise of rewarding customers for their loyalty. General Mills introduced Betty Crocker points in the 1920s. In the 1950s, cigarette companies started loyalty programs with coupons in the packs.[53]

Customer loyalty programs began to proliferate in the 1980s. Airlines were the first businesses to recognize the potential of this strategy.

Loyalty programs were also set up in the mid-1980s by numerous hotel chains, such as Marriott, Holiday Inn, Radisson, and Hyatt. A study by Radisson revealed that 70% of all travelers surveyed were influenced by this kind of promotional program.

These days we estimate that 60% of all Canadians hold loyalty cards, while nearly 75% of US shoppers belong to at least one loyalty program. Loyalty programs are based on the simple premise that 80%

of the revenues are generated by 20% of the customers in any sector of activity. A company can be sure to meet its financial needs by attracting that 20%.

Such loyalty programs as Air Miles, Optimum, and Aeroplan in Canada, not only boost a company's earnings, they let it get to know its customers better. Zellers has maintained a loyalty program for some 15 years. Club Z has nearly 10 million members, 7.6 million of whom make purchases on a monthly basis.

The Canadian Tire loyalty program with its Canadian Tire money is another example of an original and effective scheme. Created in 1958, customers come back to spend about 80% of this store-printed cash. An estimated $200 million of Canadian Tire money is currently in circulation. Dollars can also be replaced by stamps. In either case, the idea is the same: bring customers back to the store or product. Viagra recently introduced its Value Card. For every six prescriptions of Viagra purchased, the seventh is free.

9. Mail-in rebates

This has become an increasingly popular technique, particularly in the computer sector. Mail-in rebates offer an important benefit to companies, as their internal figures reveal that a significant percentage of buyers fail to ask for their money.

10. Competitions

Competitions are the most stimulating tool to use with consumers. Competitions get people to try out a product and promote enthusiasm. Over the years, businesses have handed out every conceivable kind of prize, including jewelry, travel, money, cards, boats, and so forth.

If you set up a promotional campaign, don't make the same mistake as Kraft, Anheuser-Busch, and Maytag did by printing up too many lucky tickets. In 1993, the UK's Maytag division barely avoided disaster when it offered free airline tickets for every purchase of at least $150—and more than 200,000 customers applied for their free trips!

Pepsi-Cola had to contend with 800,000 winners in the Philippines when it gave out the wrong winning number in a competition. The multinational firm was hit with violent demonstrations. Pepsi finally settled the matter by paying $20 to every winning ticket holder.

At the same time, you should try to make sure that there will be a reasonable number of winners for your contest. Coca-Cola's 1992 Olympic Games promotion did not produce a single victor.

Promotional activities are gradually changing the way we shop. Requests for information and documentation, free trials, and club memberships have all revolutionized the promotional effort. Studies have unfortunately revealed declining brand loyalty since the early 1980s. John Philip Jones has said that it is now certain that consumers buy a group of four or five brands, rather than any specific one, and change from one to the other depending on the circumstances.[54]

A Needham Harper study showed that the percentage of consumers claiming that they try to stick with major brands dropped from 80% to 60% over an eight-year period. BBDO found that two-thirds of the consumers surveyed in 28 countries believed that no differences existed in brand quality among 13 different product categories.

For this reason it is never wise to overdo promotional efforts. Discounts and other promotional tools often work well in boosting product sales over the short term, but represent a real danger over the long term. While a promotional effort may achieve quick results, it is not likely to produce lasting ones.[55]

Prof. Don Schultz said, "One of the great hazards is that you will generate a group of consumers that are deal-conscious, and that you will destroy the price structure of your product...By emphasizing promotions, marketers are building a market of people who don't care if it is Dr. Pepper, 7-Up, or Coke. All they care about is that it's $1.09. You end up destroying the brand franchise that way."[56]

Lan Daykin, the editor of Brand Management Report, said: "When coupons were growing, they were used selectively by the man-ufacturer. Now it's almost automatic—if there's a promotion pushing into the warehouse, there's usually a coupon device to pull it out. And that has a negative effect, because in any given week, a consumer with a sharp eye can find coupons in almost any product group. I think what's being created is a very large group of consumers who are loyal to coupons, not brand."[57]

Many firms, such as Coca-Cola, Goodyear, Kellogg's, General Mills, Frito-Lay, Kraft, R. J. Reynolds and Procter & Gamble, realize that promotional campaigns will not solve all their problems.

Maxwell House is another company that suffered a tarnished image following excess promotion, and a $17.5 million decline in ad investments.

Minute Maid's marketing department had a difficult year when almost all of the company's marketing investments were applied to promotion. Over that same period, Tropicana, the company's main competitor, boosted its ad budget by $30 million per year.

Too many special offers of coupons in the 1980s helped reduce customer loyalty to certain liquor-industry brands. Even worse, the process ultimately marred the luxury image that the industry had sought to project.

"I think of advertising as the engine pulling a train. If you take away the engine, the train will roll along for a while but eventually [it] will slow," said Pierre Ferrari, Coca-Cola Foods' senior VP-consumer relations.[58]

The bottom line is that promotion can be effective for short-term strategies, while advertising involves a longer-term commitment. *Advertising Age* suggested that 65% of the money invested in marketing be applied to promotion, public relations, mass mailings and sponsorships.

Studies show that long-term sales begin to decline if the advertising/promotion ratio is less than 60-40. We know that advertising projects an image on long-term consumer attitudes and product image. A fair distribution of budgets between advertising and promotion provides an effective recipe.

In a successful firm such as IKEA, the general rule is for 65% of the marketing budget to be applied to advertising, 25% to promotion, and the rest to radio and outside advertising.

Goodyear Tire has decided to set aside promotions, and to apply its efforts toward brand building. "We converted a lot of the budget to promotion this year. That has to be corrected," said James DeVoe, VP-worldwide advertising for Goodyear.[59]

Sears has taken the same approach. "At this point, consumers are being assaulted by everyday low-price messages from so many different directions that they're not paying attention anymore," said Linda Hyde, VP-retail intelligence systems at Management Horizons.

In April 1994, General Mills took the initiative of cutting its cereal division's $600 million in promotional spending by 30%, and redirecting it toward developing new products and brand-building advertisements. Kellogg's followed, albeit more quietly.

Even Procter & Gamble and McDonald's are not safe from the negative effects of promotional abuse. In August 1992, Procter & Gamble announced its intention to eliminate all coupons for Pampers and Luvs disposable diapers. For McDonald's, the 1989 Scrabble game-card promotion failed to meet expectations.

"We're finding that consumers just don't react to 'You'll never find a deal like this again' advertising the way they once did," said Douglas Hickman, Fretter's VP-marketing and advertising. "Consumers are smarter and more sophisticated than ever before. They know that when our 'sale of the century' ends this week, they can find another similar sale somewhere else the next week."[60]

"A mentality focused on short-term sales goals and bonuses contributes to 'brand rape' in the marketplace," says Ogilvy and Mather's Worldwide Chairman-CEO Graham Phillips. For Maurice Saatchi, Saatchi & Saatchi Co. Chairman, "Advertising is a required investment in building strong brands."[61]

According to Gallup, the rising number of sweepstakes and contests tied to consumer products is more annoying than enticing to most consumers. AC Nielsen undertook a study of 862 packaged-goods promotions and discovered that more than 50% of them had no impact on sales, and that only 1 promotion in 10 generated a volume increase of 10% or better. In 1993, three studies found that coupon distribution declined or remained steady. This was the first year since 1970 that coupon distribution had not risen.[62]

Yet there will always be a place for intelligent promotions. Ivory promos challenged consumers to find bars of soap that were designed to sink; the postal service delivered 800,000 direct-mail designs to people who voted on whether a young or old Elvis should appear on a new commemorative postage stamp; and Absolut Vodka invited consumers to create their own ads using watercolor paints.

Promotional ads can always help you to build databases by gathering names and addresses through sweepstakes, rebates, free samples, and free gifts. Incidentally, the first-ever Olympic Fan Club started accepting members in January 1994, linking consumers and marketers in a database promotion tied to the 1996 Summer Games in Atlanta.

FLASH INFO

PROMOTIONAL PRODUCTS

Promotional items offer the great advantages of being affordable, of adding to the impact of other media, and of allowing themselves to be targeted at specific audiences.

The most popular promotional items in the 1990s were t-shirts, baseball caps, office accessories, and cups.

Studies show that 40% of those who receive promotional items can recall the advertiser's name after six months. Furthermore, 31% of all individuals used the item in question within a year of receiving it.[63]

SPONSORSHIP

Sponsorship is another phenomenon that has enjoyed excellent growth over the past few years. According to *Brandweek* magazine, worldwide sponsorship expenditures totaled $37.8 billion in 2004.[64] This amount should climb to $50 billion by 2006.

Companies boost their profiles and build goodwill by sponsoring cultural and athletic events.

The effects of sponsorship activities are wide-ranging and occasionally spectacular.

Athletic sponsorship represents about two thirds of total sponsorship investments, with the remainder almost equally divided between music festivals and trade shows, humanitarian causes and the arts.

Stadium scoreboards might not be as effective as 30-second TV spots in getting your message across, said the former president of CBS Sports, but given the right placement, it's going to get your brand out there.[65]

In 2004, it cost US $50 million for a sponsorship at the Athens Olympics. A study conducted by Decima Research during the Olympics confirmed the impact of this form of communication:

- 59% of all respondents said they were more likely to buy sponsors' products.

- 74% had an improved impression of the sponsor.

- 76% believed that the sponsor was the leader in its sector of activity.[66]

Athletic marketing stands out for the passion with which fans follow their teams. A Performance Research study showed that 80% of all fans are comfortable with players wearing logos on their gear.[67] Better yet, nearly 50% of golf enthusiasts said that they had tried to purchase sponsored products and services.

During the 2002 World Cup of Soccer, the 15 leading sponsors paid as much as US $24 million to have their names linked with the event. The FIFA World Cup was watched by some 1.5 billion TV viewers in all. A study by Frankel & Co. revealed that 59% of all viewers took note of sponsors' names during sports events, and that 54% had a better attitude toward sponsors.[68]

The ABCs of athletics and all other sponsorships are quite simple, and include three basic rules: 1) Target your audience; 2) Remain associated with an event over a long period; 3) Prepare to invest at least one dollar in advertising for every dollar you spend on sponsorship.[69]

When Nextel became the main sponsor of the NASCAR Championship in 2003, it signed a 10-year contract. Nextel replaced Winston, which had been associated with NASCAR since 1971. Winston had lent its name to the trophy that was given each year to the champion racer. The NASCAR series draws the largest US TV audience of any pro sport after NFL football.

Because of ever-increasing sponsorship costs—with an average $825,000 price tag in 2004—few companies become involved in major events. Rather, a new phenomenon has emerged known as *ambush marketing*.

Companies that do not hold sponsorship rights use ambush marketing to become indirectly linked to an event.

A company engaging in ambush marketing creates confusion in consumers' minds, enabling them to benefit indirectly from the positive fallout of sponsorship. The official sponsor is accordingly forced to share its visibility. Many companies have made use of this technique:

- At the 1984 Olympic Games, Kodak sponsored the American team. But Fuji was the official sponsor of the Games as a whole.

- At the 1988 Winter Olympics, Wendy's distributed posters illustrating winter sports scenes. At almost the same moment, McDonald's was investing considerable amounts as the event's official sponsor.

- In 1990, Coca-Cola became the official sponsor of the World Cup. Pepsi, however, threw a wrench in Coke's works by sponsoring the Brazilian team.

- For the 1992 Olympics, sports shoemaker Reebok became an official sponsor of the games. But advertising produced by Reebok's main competitor, Nike, used six players from the US national basketball team to feature its products. This strategy let Nike acquire some of the prestige associated with companies directly associated with the Olympic Games, without having to spend large sums.

- The most famous case of ambush marketing is without a doubt that of American Express. To offset Visa's "The Olympics don't take American Express" campaign, the American Express Co. launched its own offensive. The simple goal of this offensive was to thwart the efforts of Visa, the official sponsor of the Olympic Games being held in Barcelona. Amex achieved this goal by employing pictures of bullfights, an explicit reference to Spain, accompanied by the tagline "And remember, to visit Spain, you don't need a visa."[70]

FLASH INFO

STADIUM NAMING RIGHTS

Stadium Name	Sponsor	Home Teams	Avg. $/Year	Expires
Air Canada Centre	Air Canada	Toronto Maple Leafs, Raptors	$1.5 million	2019
Alltel Stadium	Alltel Corp.	Jacksonville Jaguars	$620,000	2007
American Airlines Arena	American Airlines	Miami Heat	$2.1 million	2019
American Airlines Center	American Airlines	Dallas Mavericks, Stars	$6.5 million	2031
America West Arena	America West	Phoenix Suns, Coyotes, Mercury	$866,667	2019
Ameriquest Field	Ameriquest Capital Corp.	Texas Rangers	$2.5 million	2034
Arco Arena	Atlantic Richfield	Sacramento Kings, Monarchs	$750,000	2007
Bank of America Stadium	Bank of America	Carolina Panthers	$7 million	2024
Bank One Ballpark	Bank One	Arizona Diamondbacks	$2.2 million	2028
Bell Centre	Bell Canada	Montreal Canadiens	N/A	N/A
Cinergy Field	Cinergy	Cincinnati Reds	$1 million	2002
Citizens Bank Park	Citizens Bank	Philadelphia Phillies	$2.3 million	2028
Comerica Park	Comerica	Detroit Tigers	$2.2 million	2030
Compaq Center	Compaq Computer	Houston Rockets, Comets	$900,000	2003
Conseco Fieldhouse	Conseco	Indiana Pacers, Fever	$2 million	2019
Continental Airlines Arena	Continental Airlines	New Jersey Nets, Devils	$1.4 million	2011
Coors Field	Coors Brewing	Colorado Rockies	N/A	INDEFINITE
Corel Centre	Corel	Ottawa Senators	$878,142	2016
Delta Center	Delta Airlines	Utah Jazz, Starzz	$1.3 million	2011
Edward Jones Dome	Edward Jones	St. Louis Rams	$2.65 million	2013
FedEx Field	Federal Express	Washington Redskins	$7.6 million	2025
FedEx Forum	Federal Express	Memphis Grizzlies	$4.5 million	2023
Wachovia Center	Wachovia Bank	Philadelphia 76ers, Flyers	$1.4 million	2023
TD Banknorth Garden	TD Banknorth (owner)	Boston Celtics, Bruins	N/A	2025
Ford Field	Ford Motor Co.	Detroit Lions	$1 million	2042
Gaylord Entertainment Center	Gaylord Entertainment	Nashville Predators	$4 million	2018
General Motors Place	General Motors	Vancouver Canucks	$844,366	2015
Gillette Stadium	Gillette	New England Patriots	N/A	2017
Great American Ball Park	Great American Insurance.	Cincinnati Reds	$2.5 million	2033
Gund Arena	Owners	Cleveland Cavs, Rockers	$700,000	2014
Heinz Field	H.J. Heinz	Pittsburgh Steelers	$2.9 million	2021
HP Pavilion	Hewlett-Packard	San Jose Sharks	$3.1 million	2016
HSBC Arena	HSBC Bank	Buffalo Sabres	$800,000	2026
Invesco Field at Mile High	Invesco Funds	Denver Broncos	$6 million	2021
Jacobs Field	Richard Jacobs	Cleveland Indians	$695,000	2014
KeyArena	Key Corp.	Seattle Supersonics, Storm	$1 million	2010

Lincoln Financial Field	Lincoln Financial Group	Philadelphia Eagles	$6.7 million	2022
M & T Bank Stadium	M & T Bank	Baltimore Ravens	$5 million	2018
MCI Center	MCI	Wash. Wizards, Caps, Mystics	$2.2 million	2017
Mellon Arena	Mellon Financial	Pittsburgh Penguins	$1.8 million	2009
Monster Park	Monster Cable	San Francisco 49ers	$1.5 million	2007
Miller Park	Miller Brewing	Milwaukee Brewers	$2.1 million	2020
Minute Maid Park	Coca Cola	Houston Astros	$6 million	2030
Nationwide Arena	Nationwide Insurance	Columbus BlueJackets	N/A	INDEFINITE
Network Associates Coliseum	Network Associates	Oakland A's	$1.2 million	2003
Office Depot Center	Office Depot	Florida Panthers	$1.4 million	2013
Pengrowth Saddledome	Pengrowth Mgmt.	Calgary Flames	$1 million	2016
Pepsi Center	PepsiCo	Denver Nuggets, Colorado Avalanche	$3.4 million	2019
Petco Park	PETCO	San Diego Padres	$2.7 million	2026
Phillips Arena	Royal Phillips Electronics	Atlanta Hawks, Thrashers	$9.3 million	2019
PNC Park	PNC Bank	Pittsburgh Pirates	$2 million	2020
Pro Player Stadium	Fruit of the Loom	Miami Dolphins, Florida Marlins	COMPANY BANKRUPT	N/A
Qualcomm Stadium	Qualcomm	San Diego Padres, Chargers	$900,000	2017
Raymond James Stadium	Raymond James Financial	Tampa Bay Buccaneers	$3.1 million	2026
RBC Center	RBC Centura Banks	Carolina Hurricanes	$4 million	2022
RCA Dome	RCA	Indianapolis Colts	$1 million	2004
Reliant Stadium	Reliant Energy	Houston Texans	$10 million	2032
Rexall Place	Katz Group	Edmonton Oilers	N/A	2013
Safeco Field	Safeco Corp.	Seattle Mariners	$2 million	2019
Savvis Center	Savvis Communications	St. Louis Blues	N/A	INDEFINITE
SBC Center	SBC Communications	San Antonio Spurs	$2.1 million	2022
SBC Park	SBC Communications	San Francisco Giants	$2.1 million	2024
Staples Center	Staples	Los Angeles Lakers, Kings, Clippers, Sparks	$5.8 million	2019
St. Pete Times Forum	St. Petersburg Times	Tampa Bay Lightning	$2.1 million	2014
Target Center	Target	Minnesota Timberwolves, Lynx	$1.3 million	2005
TD Waterhouse Centre	TD Waterhouse Group	Orlando Magic, Miracle	$1.6 million	2003
Toyota Center	Toyota	Houston Rockets	N/A	N/A
Tropicana Field	Tropicana	Tampa Bay Devil Rays	$1.5 million	2026
United Center	United Airlines	Chicago Blackhawks, Bulls	$1.8 million	2014
US Cellular Field	US Cellular	Chicago White Sox	$3.4 million	2025
Xcel Energy Center	Xcel Energy	Minnesota Wild	$3 million	2024

Source: ESPN

FLASH INFO

SPONSOR VISIBILITY

By linking up with an event, a sponsor seeks to maximize:

- Exclusive association with that event.
- Right to present itself as the official sponsor.
- Right to use the event's name, logo, and image.
- First rights of refusal as the advertiser of a televised rerun.
- Visibility on the event's website.
- Visibility on advertising and promotional materials.
- Visibility on derivative products.
- Opportunity for public relations activities.
- Opportunity to let consumers sample products.
- Tickets to events and so forth.

Many criteria can be used in assessing the value of sponsorships. They include number of visitors, visibility on an event's website and on its advertising material, the event's image, commercial potential, media coverage, references made to sponsors, and TV presence.

Sponsorship can also take a more subtle form. From the start of 1991's Desert Storm, manufacturers gave Coalition soldiers 60,000 free cases of Coke and Pepsi, 10,000 packs of Marlboro cigarettes, 5,000 Sony Walkmans, and 60,000 PolyGram cassettes. *Mother Jones* reported that each appearance of these products in televised reports was equivalent to the impact of a US$250,000 advertising investment.

On rare occasions, sponsorship can also create problems. In 1994, 18 NASCAR drivers—including Darrell Waltrip and Geoff Bodine—had agreed to use Hoosier tires at the Daytona 500. But during practice runs, two drivers of Hoosier-equipped cars were killed. These accidents suddenly raised questions about the tires' handling capabilities. By the day of the race, all 42 drivers were running on Goodyear Eagle tires, after Hoosier gave its contract drivers permission to switch for that race.[71] Upon investigation, NASCAR officials concluded that the tires weren't to blame. But the damage had been done.

PRODUCT PLACEMENT

Advertisers have for many years been ensuring visibility for their products in movies and on TV shows. This "product placement" technique lets companies build notoriety for their brands, reach captive audiences, avoid channel zapping, and shape a product's image.

Product placement has become a form of communication. A research study estimates that product-placement spending in the US reached a record $4.25 billion in 2005.[72] Major American studios generate more than an estimated $1 billion each year in placement income.

Product placement began in movies with *E.T.* In a key scene, a young boy tries to make contact with an alien by offering the creature some Reese's Pieces candy.

More recently, over 25% of the funding for the film *Minority Report* was generated through product placement efforts. Brands like Nokia, Lexus, and Gap were used one after the other by actor Tom Cruise. Some years earlier, the same actor had demonstrated the sales power of product placement by boosting sales of Oakley sunglasses by 80%, after wearing them in *Mission: Impossible II.*

In 2000, the film *Cast Away* devoted its first 30 minutes to promoting FedEx. Viewers were treated to views of the company's purple and orange logo, its trucks, packages, and a number of FedEx aircraft from the very start of the picture. The star himself was eventually revealed in the form of Tom Hanks playing a FedEx manager. The company's real president even appeared at the end of the feature!

In 2003, the producers of *The Matrix Reloaded* selected a concept car to be included in the film. This visibility enabled the car maker to reach out to a younger audience.

More than 20 brands were showcased in the James Bond film *Die Another Day*. Canadian viewers noted the presence of many Bombardier Ski-Doos. For the 40th anniversary of the James Bond series, Bombardier launched a James Bond snowmobile. This Canadian firm had previously used product placement on *Baywatch* to promote its Sea-Doos.

During the 2002 National Football League season, commentator John Madden used the Madden 2003 video game on a number of occasions during replays on Monday Night Football. Rather than show video replays of key scenes, Madden used the game that bore his name to illustrate his remarks. This tactic let Madden reach 10 million viewers each week.

If you wish to place your product through such means, take into account the positioning and the audience of a given film. Avoid putting your product in the hands of a bad guy. And be subtle. When film fans saw John Travolta drinking Diet Coke more than three times in *Domestic Disturbance*, they became indignant. If you make viewers feel you are up to something sneaky, you set their defense mechanisms in action. And that reduces the effectiveness of your investment.

SPENDING ON PRODUCT PLACEMENTS IN MEDIA, USA, 2004 (BILLIONS OF $)

TV:	$1,877.8
Film:	$1,254.6
Other:	$325.8
Total:	$3,458.1

Source: PQ Media in *Advertising Age*, April 4, 2005, p. 16.

FLASH INFO

TV ZAPPING

With the advent of the remote control, TV commercials have also undergone a reduction in their power to hold the viewer's attention. The impact of channel "zapping" on commercial viewing varies from study to study. According to AC Nielsen, between 3% and 5.2% of commercials are "zapped." Information Resources Inc. puts the figure at 10%, while Television Audience Assessment evaluates it at 39%.

Evening programs, half-hour programs, Saturday morning programs, and weekend sports shows are most likely to have their commercials "zapped." Younger audiences, however, flip channels more frequently than do older ones. Those commercials most avoided pertain to pain relievers, personal body hygiene, and deodorizers. The least zapped ads concern computers, chewing gum, and light beer. Ultimately, research has shown that most zapping occurs at the beginning and end of programs. So it is not surprising to learn that studies by McDonald's reveal higher recall for commercials during a program than those slotted during the station break.

In *The Want Makers,* Eric Clark highlights British research that showed that more than a quarter of the people who watched an edition of *News at Ten* failed to notice any of its commercials. Of that amount, 26% simply had not paid attention, 21% made a drink, 20% left the room, 11% were preoccupied with other things, 8% switched channels, 6% went to the toilet, and 5% talked to another person.

Chapter 6

What typefaces to use for your ad

Typefaces can serve to contradict or to enhance the meaning of your copy.

Typefaces have *personalities,* just like people. Some are masculine, others feminine. Some denote prestige, others may evoke a sense of weightiness, happiness, a good bargain, tradition, or a sense of modernism.

Graham Clifford, Chiat/Day/Mojo type director, expressed this idea in the following terms: "The typeface conveys 'hidden' messages—the 'tone of the voice' that is presented. Type has this unique ability to shout, whisper, persuade, ask, or demand. How the letters are put together to create words can substantially affect how we absorb the message. Will the viewer look at it, read it, memorize it, laugh at it or ignore it?"[1] This is why the characters you select for your text should match its personality.

Selecting your typeface is no easy task. Bolds imply strength. Characters that slant to the right are perceived as being dynamic. Those that lean to the left are considered to be filled with restraint. Slender letters create a sense of loftiness, while slim ones give the impression of distinction, refinement, and nobility. Cursive writing conveys a sense of energy; it has a sensational and perhaps an imperative quality.

The personality of a typographical character depends on its face, its slant, its weight, its proportion, the contrast between its downstroke and upstroke, and its serif.

The *typeface* or simply *face* is the printable part of the character, the part that provides the outline. We think of the face as a shape. Within a given typeface, certain characters contain designs of different size, in which case we say that the character has several faces (small, medium, and large).

The *slant* is the angle of the character relative to the baseline. The slant can be straight, or it can lean to the left or to the right.

The *weight* or *density* is the variation in the width of the lines that make up the character: extra light, light, book, medium, bold, extra bold, or heavy.

The *proportion* is the relative width of the characters: regular, condensed, or extended.

A letter's distinctive outline is formed by the *contrast between the downstroke and the upstroke* (the thick and thin strokes used in creating the character).

The *serif* indicates the way in which the strokes end on the baseline of a letter. Generally, there are considered to be four main families of characters as distinguished by the presence, absence, or shape of the serif (or finishing stroke).

Antique is a character without serifs. Based on Phoenician inscriptions, it appeared for the first time in England in 1816. The typeface was redesigned in 1927 by the English sculptor Eric Gill, and then by German designers such as Renner & Erbar. Antique has a contemporary look but it is tiring to read. It is cool, detached and best suited to titles.

Egyptian is a character with a rectangular serif and was originally found in Greek inscriptions. It was used in 1815 by Figgins and then in 1820 by Thorn. Attractive and seductive, this typeface has a certain weight or heaviness appropriate to the needs of advertising.

Didot is a modern typeface with a crisp, horizontal serif. It was perfected by F.A. Didot and imitated by Bodoni in the 18th century. The striking contrast between its thick and thin strokes gives this typeface a relatively strict and austere appearance. It is, above all, a character that is rational, logical, dry, and severe, and often used to announce important events.

Elzevir is an Old Style type, with strokes that end in a slanted, wedge-shaped serif. The typeface's structure is fashioned on calligraphic tracing executed with a broad pen. Found on Roman inscriptions, this typeface was used in the 15th century by Nicolas Jenson, and then by Aldus Manutinus and Claude Garamond. It is very beautiful and synonymous with culture, refinement, distinction, and nobility. These characters are perfectly suited for ad copy.

SELECTING A TYPEFACE

All typefaces should be selected to correspond with the product, its prospective buyers, the ad copy's length and format, the type of illustrations appearing in the ad, the main sales pitch, and the type of newspaper or periodical in which the ad is to appear. Moreover, the typeface should be both fashionable and easily *readable*. Such readability depends on seven factors:

1. Simplicity of the characters

Prospective customers will be more likely to read your text if it is printed in a typeface commonly found in magazines, newspapers, books, brochures, and ads. A few good examples are Century, Caslon, Times, Baskerville, Jenson, Futura, Franklin Gothic, Bembo, Garamond, and Goudy.

2. Character direction

Your characters should in most cases be horizontally aligned. Readers tend to dislike characters that appear in spirals, curves, or diagonals, and are hard to read. In a study conducted a few years ago, Daniel Starch compared two Lucky Strike ads.[2] In one case, the title was printed on a slant. In the other, it was horizontal. Readers had no trouble understanding either text, but they gave a higher readability score to the horizontal characters.

◆ *Readership rates are lower for diagonal, spiral, and vertical texts.*

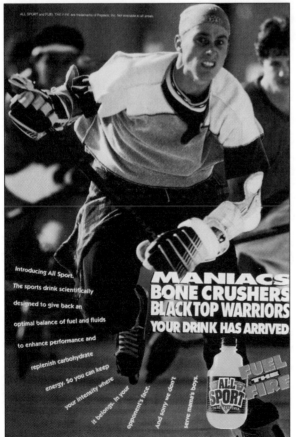

●——— **FLASH** INFO ———●

THE ROLES OF TYPEFACES...

IN BILLBOARDS

Drivers and passengers make up the biggest audience for outdoor media. The readability of your billboard will accordingly play a key role in its success.

A billboard should be visible for at least six to eight seconds if it is to work. This is a recognized standard for displays. At 80 km/h, a driver should be able to read a billboard from a distance of at least 100 meters. At 40 km/h, in a more urban area, a driver should be able to read a billboard ad that is doing its job properly from at least 30 meters.

IN PRINT AND ON THE WEB

The simple rule is to use classical characters.

●—————————————————————————●

3. Typeface size

Your copy should ideally be printed in 11-point type. Any larger, and the characters may seem a bit odd, any smaller and the text will be difficult to read. Readability is clearly impaired in type sizes of 8 points or less. Miles A. Tinker and Donald G. Paterson conducted a study in which the subject's eye movements were photographed as they read 6-point type. They discovered that for 6-point type there was a significant increase in fixation frequency, pause duration, and perception time. Regressions were also slightly increased.[3]

It's a good idea to start off with a drop cap if your copy is over 250 words. Drop caps are disproportionately large characters that almost miraculously draw the reader's attention, and stimulate their interest in reading. Drop caps also add class and style to your text, and thus, to your product as well.

4. Typeface color

Ad experts strongly recommend that you print your text in black on a white background, or at least in dark characters on a light background. Paterson and Tinker,[4] have reported that the most readable chromatic relationships, by decreasing order of readability, are:

1. Black on white
2. Green on white
3. White on white
4. Black on yellow
5. Red on yellow
6. Red on white

7. Green on red
8. Orange on black
9. Orange on white
10. Red on green
11. Black on purple

◆ *Logos, just like typefaces, have personalities, as illustrated by these examples from Kmart.*

Matthew Luckiesh conducted similar research and came up with slightly different results.[5] He discovered that the most visible combinations were, in descending order:

1. Black on yellow

2. Green on white

3. Red on white

4. Blue on white

5. White on blue

6. Black on white

7. Yellow on black

8. White on red

9. White on green

10. White on black

11. Red on yellow

12. Green on red

13. Red on green

It is a very poor idea to print white copy on a black or gray background. People read black on white texts 42% faster than they do those that are white on grey.[6] Moreover, 77.7% of all readers believe they read black on white texts faster than white on black ones.[7] The reading rates for white on black titles are similar to those for black on white.

Use a typeface with wider strokes for colored headlines, and make the heads a little larger than those in black. Why? Colored headlines need extra bulk to achieve the same contrast as black on white.

You'll boost your chances of being read by not using overly thick, thin, pale, or dark characters. You should also avoid printing text over pictures. Any layout that makes it difficult for the reader to perceive background or character shape gets lower-than-average reading rates.

◆ *Print a yellow headline on a black background for greater visibility.*

5. Character strength

You can use different graphic techniques to highlight a word or a group of words:

1. You can use *italics.*

2. You can write in CAPITALS.

3. You can use **bold characters.**

4. You can print in color.

5. You can use <u>underlining.</u>

6. You can frame or box your text.

7. You can circle your text.

8. You can use a *cursive style.*

9. You can mark or highlight your text.

I do not recommend that you place all of your text in italics. Typographic readability specialist Miles Albert Tinker said that a text consisting entirely of italic characters cuts down reading speed by 15 words per minute.[8] He added that 96% of those tested believed they read italic texts more slowly than those in standard characters.

Avoid printing in capitals. Texts that are printed in capitals are read about 18.9% more slowly than those in lowercase.[9]

6. Layout

Be careful about spacing between words. Words and letters that are either too close or too far apart needlessly impede the reading process. Tight lines also hinder the reading of very short or very long copy. Try not to use more than 40 characters per line.

Text columns of 20 characters or less interfere with the thought process. Those of 120 characters or more frustrate readers. Keep your text in columns of from 35 to 55 characters to avoid problems.

7. Character unity

Print ads should, as a general rule, never include more than two type-faces, and certainly no more than three. Too many different character types require numerous mental adjustments, and put off the reader.

Despite the scientific evidence, some ad experts continue to believe that any typeface can do the job. But reading experts know that this is not the case.

As Stephen Baker affirms in his book on *Advertising Layout and Art Direction,* "Many an advertisement gets little attention from the public only because of its hit-or-miss typography. The reader gets a quick impression from the page. The type looks inviting to read, or it does not."[10]

Chapter 7

The most effective layouts

A clear and simple layout will attract readers to your ad. Overdone layouts will drive them away. Helmut Krone, former artistic director for Doyle Dane Bernbach, said, "When you don't keep it simple and basic for the people, you're in trouble."[1]

If you make your ads look like little posters, you'll boost attention and reading rates.

The bigger your picture, the more attention your ad will draw, the more your copy will be read, and the more people will retain your message. Starch said that ads with the best results contain pictures that take up at least half the space. Ad copy, on the other hand, will rarely take up more than 30% of the area.

If an ad has multiple pictures, make sure one dominates.

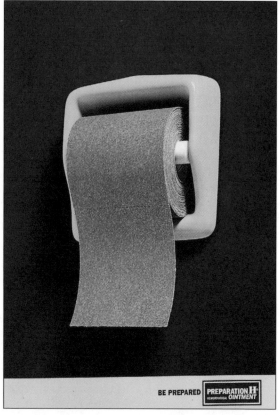

◆ *The simplest ads work best. Such ads are often tributes to effectiveness. Their layout is basic, and leaves plenty of space for the ad and the logo.*

Tossed fresh.
Tossed crisp.
Tossed all day long.

We start with fresh, crisp vegetables and greens. And we toss them together all day long. That's how we make sure every salad you order is as fresh as we can make it.

Because experts agree vegetables and greens are at their nutritional best when they're fresh. So at McDonald's, you'll find our Chef Salad, Chicken Salad Oriental and Garden Salad being tossed fresh, cool and crisp all day, every day.

Any other way just wouldn't be as good. Or as good for you.

For more information about our salads, and all our menu items, ask your McDonald's® Restaurant Manager, or call our Nutrition Information Center at (312) 575-FOOD.

IT'S A GOOD TIME FOR THE GREAT TASTE.

◆ *The breezier your layout, the more your ad will be read.*

Be consistent. Use similar formats, the same locations, the same typefaces, and the same kinds of layout.

Experience has shown that longer texts are read by more people if they are decorated with small pictures.

Some people think that margins, empty areas, and spacing between paragraphs are wasted space. Banish those thoughts! Breezy layouts allow you to highlight your headlines, your copy, and your pictures. They make it easier to read your text.

John Lyons has said, "One of the art director's most effective tools is the use of white space. White space acts as a relief, eliminates accessorized copy, and is both riveting and inviting to the reader. To the untutored eye, the urge to 'one up' blank space is contagious."[2]

Whenever possible, advertise in such special sections as sports, cars, fashion, food, and health. Special sections let advertisers blend the benefits of a trade magazine with those of a newspaper by reaching a local and targeted audience.

Specialized headings draw specific audiences, except on the front page. If you want to sell a cruise, you should advertise in the Travel section, where you will have a better chance of reaching your prospective customers. Special sections represent a good way of drawing readers and selling your products in a made-to-order environment. They sometimes put such sections away for later reference, a bit like magazines.

If you decide to advertise in a special section, take out a larger-than-average space. Most of your competitors will be grouped with you in a special section, so be sure to find some way to stand out.

◆ *Try to use white in your layouts. White not only attracts attention, but facilitates reading.*

You might consider giving your ad the appearance of a newspaper article, a magazine cover, or a comic strip. This is because most people have a tendency to be suspicious of advertising. Many people perceive most print advertising as being biased at the source, and so they simply skip over it. You can surmount this obstacle by imitating such cultural icons as comic strips and magazine covers. New York's Health Department successfully used English and Spanish comic strip-styled posters in the city's subways for its messages on AIDS.

Some advertisers try to dictate the nature of editorial content. In 1993, Mercedes-Benz said it would pull advertising from any specific issues that carried negative stories about the company. Such behavior may be deplorable, but it is also easy to understand. If you were a cigarette advertiser, would you like to be placed near an article on the dangers of smoking? I wouldn't.

If you are advertising a food product, try to provide a recipe. Marion Harper, founder of the Interpublic Group, said that ads with recipes are read by some 220% more readers than those without.[3]

If you use multiple facts in support of your product, use numbered points, rather than circles, bullets, or other icons in the margin. This approach will not only make it easier for readers to understand your message, but numbered points give the impression that you have something important to say. People are also used to the idea of creating numbered lists for dealing with complex matters.

●——— **MEDIA** ADVISORY ———●

THE ROLE OF LAYOUT...

IN BILLBOARDS

Size is not always the key factor in billboards, as it often is with newspaper and magazine ads. One study, in fact, showed that the two most important factors are location and design.[4]

Place your logo at the lower right of the billboard. Viacom has said that the "placement of a logo in the lower right-hand corner of a billboard has been shown to work very well."[5] The eye tends to scan a surface from left to right and from top to bottom. If you place your logo in the lower right, it will be the last element to be seen and recognized.

IN MAGAZINES

Vertical layouts (with the picture at the top and ad copy below) are often extremely effective in magazine ads. In a study conducted a few years ago, American advertising expert Mills Shepherd said that 35 of the best read magazine ads used vertical layouts.[6]

IN DAILY NEWSPAPERS

Use special sections whenever possible, and get off the beaten track occasionally. Purchase central island displays in the stock listings, or ads on the front page of a section.

IN WEEKLIES

Advertisers in weeklies often tend to include a great deal of information. They believe that the more they say, the more convincing they will be. The opposite is true. The simpler and sweeter your ad, the better it will work.

ON THE WEB

Stay away from *pop-ups* and avoid traditional formats. The website *Ask Jeeves* eliminated pop-ups first and traditional banners next. Also make sure to use contextual ads. For example, if an article about a computer virus is posted to a site, your ad for anti-virus software would appear. The three companies that provide this kind of service are Overture Services, Google, and Primedia.

◆ *White spaces, a clear and simple layout, and the sense of movement will attract people's attention to your advertising.*

SEVEN LAYOUT STYLES THAT WORK

Your ad layout should be designed to boost the attention your message receives and to make your ad easier to read. Here are seven ways of organizing your ad's headlines, text, images, and logo, based on your particular needs.

1. Picture window

This is the most popular layout style. The visual takes up to two thirds of the ad space. It is accompanied by a one-line title and a text broken down into two or three columns.

With this sort of layout, you are best off with *vertically* organized pages, containing a photo on top, a title below the image, and copy after the titles. A *vertical* layout with the picture on top, the title directly beneath it, and text farther down, always works miracles.

The *horizontal* page layout (with photograph on one side of the page and copy on the other) should be avoided. People are accustomed to seeing text beneath illustrations. If a text is written to the left or to the right of an illustration we simply won't read it. When Dove soap changed its layout from vertical to horizontal, readership plunged from 64% to about 50%.[7]

2. Type specimen

This layout style captures attention by emphasizing the headline. It is often used in ads by airlines, banks, computer firms, and insurance companies.

3. Copy heavy

Use this kind of layout if copy is the dominant factor in your concept. The image will take up less space, and the headline will only take one or two lines.

4. Circus

Despite appearances, a circus layout is well organized and intended to generate excitement. A series of minor elements combine to create a consistent whole.

5. Frame

Like a framed table, the text is entirely surrounded by different graphic elements in this kind of layout, which is often used to advertise fashion products and jewelry.

6. Silhouette

The copy in a silhouette layout literally surrounds the product or object by following its contours and outline. Silhouettes are used in alcohol and cosmetics ads.

7. Color layout

Color layouts take the form of a double-page ad and are dominated by images. The color ad creates a visual contrast that is likely to draw the reader's attention. Color layouts are used for car ads.

◆ *Layouts that simulate movement always attract attention.*

SIZE AND FORMAT

Returns on an ad largely depend on size. The bigger your ad, the more attention it will draw.[8]

In a study published in the *Journal of Advertising Research*, Verling Troldahl and Robert Jones considered four factors (ad size, type of product being advertised, ratio of copy to illustration, and number of points considered in the advertising copy) and their impact on ad readership. They learned that 40% of all readers will read an ad based on its size.[9] Product type, on the other hand, only matters for 19% of all readers. Thirty-nine percent of readers are attracted by an ad's artistic qualities.

There is a relationship between your ad's size and the attention it commands. Double-page spreads capture more reader attention than do single-page ads, which in turn get more attention that do half pages. However, the attention your ad draws is not directly proportional to the space it occupies.[10]

Surveys on newspaper and magazine ads have led to the discovery of the "square root" rule, whereby reader attention only increases by the square root of the increase in an ad's size.[11] That means you would have to quadruple an ad's size to double the amount of attention it draws.

Although double-page ads cost twice as much, they are recommended. In mass circulation magazines, double-pages generate 25% more attention and readership than do single-page spreads.[12] In trade magazines, double-page ads generate 37% better readership than single pages.[13] Gallup & Robinson have said that double-page ads give your product importance and prestige.

The return on an ad does not depend on a publication's size. Researcher Lawrence Ulin compared readership and retention rates for a single-page ad appearing in *Reader's Digest* (small format) with those for an ad in large-format *Life* magazine. Ulin discovered that there was no difference between the large and small formats. In other words, readers assess an ad not based on absolute size, but relative to the format of the publication in which it appears.

An ad's shape may affect its returns. When Starch compared a quarter-page ad printed in a single column with a square ad of the same size, he observed that recognition and readership for the columnar ad were 29% higher than in the square version.[14]

The larger your ads, the more consumers will believe that your company is credible and solid. In his book, *The 27 Most Common Mistakes in Advertising*, Alec Benn noted that readers associate an ad's size with that of the advertiser's company.[15] In other words, readers assume that small businesses will use small ads, and big ones will purchase larger ones.

Big ads provide better returns in industrial than in commercial advertising.[16]

If you are producing a double-page magazine spread, make sure not to lose your title, copy, or illustration in the central margin.

If your ad extends over more than one page, make sure to produce a connection between each page through such means as repeating the brand name on each page, by using ellipses, by spreading the headline over two opposite pages, and by using the same background for all pages.

THE BEST POSITIONS FOR BEING NOTICED

I don't think a top-rate location will save a bad ad. However, if you are preparing to deploy a powerful campaign and can afford a little bit extra, make note of the following facts:

1. Ads appearing on the front, inside front, and inside back covers are read by 30% more people than ads located on inside pages.[17]

2. Ads on the back cover obtain 64% more readership than copy located within a magazine.[18]

3. Readership of ads appearing in the first 10% of a magazine is 10% better than average.

4. Placing an ad in a magazine's first seven pages should produce an especially high response rate.[19]

5. The recall of ads placed in the front of a magazine is higher than in the back. Studies recommend avoiding the last quarter in particular and the second half in general, of a magazine.[20]

6. A recent study by Starch showed that ads placed in the first third of a magazine are noticed by 12% more readers than those in its last third.[21]

7. Readership is equal for right- and left-hand pages. However, in direct marketing, Bob Stone has said that right-hand pages generate 15% more response coupons than do their left-hand counterparts.[22]

8. The centre of a magazine gives good results, particularly if most ads appear in the front or back.

9. Bleed ads generally obtain higher readership.

10. Readership for ads at the top of a page is generally higher than for those at the bottom.

11. Readership is usually higher than average for ads containing recipes or coupons.[23] A study conducted on women's readership revealed that ads involving contests do not perform as well as standard ads that do not promote such events.[24]

12. One page consisting of a paper of a different density than the other pages in a magazine gives good results.

13. A page that is slightly smaller than those used in the rest of the magazine works well.

14. A single foldout page in a magazine tends to work well.

◆ *Foldout cover pages work well in magazines if the additional space helps get the message across. This Gatorade ad is an excellent example of this technique. Above: The image with the foldout closed. Below: After it is opened.*

15. Even if they cost twice as much, double-page ads should be considered. They generate higher levels of reader involvement and they attract more attention. According to Gallup & Robinson, they make the product appear important and prestigious. Jo Marney recalls that impact studies have revealed that double pages, on average, beat single pages in eliciting favorable reactions toward the product.

16. Pop-ups (ads that assume a three-dimensional form when you open a magazine's page) and holograms are very costly, but obtain significant results. Transamerica Corporation invested $3 million in 1986 (or 35% of its total advertising budget) on a pop-up that appeared in the centre of *Time* magazine. It took 560 people a total of 420,000 hours to put together the ad, which appeared in 6 million copies of this well-known magazine. A survey showed that 96% of *Time's* readers remember having seen the ad, 91% read more than half of it and 69% of *Time's* readers had a very positive opinion of the company.[25]

17. A gatefold that works uses traditional methods of attracting reader attention, such as bright colors, an interesting illustration, and a clever technique for getting readers to open the gatefold. My most valuable source of information, Starch Readership Service, gives the following advice on achieving an efficient gatefold: show off the product and highlight the brand name. The inside front cover is the most common position for a gatefold. Most gatefolds are the standard "single flap" kind—essentially, a three- or four-panel advertisement with an outside one-panel "teaser", and another panel facing it, accompanied by another two or three panels that function as a single unit once the teaser page has been lifted.

18. Brochures and small guides inserted in magazines give good results—at the expense, however, of adjacent ads. An eight-page John Hancock special obtained a recall rate of 40%, the 20-page American Booksellers Association insert, 50% and the 24-page Kmart insert promoting the Olympic Winter Games, 83%.

K-Mart sponsored a 24-page Olympic Winter Games booklet in an issue of *Time* magazine as phase one of an overall campaign designed "to highlight the giant retailer's accelerated push towards brand quality, and away from its earlier focus on price." A study by Beta Research showed that five out of every six *Time* readers recalled seeing the special section in the issue.

A 4-page B&W special unit for a new IBM corporate campaign published in *Time* achieved a 43% recall rate. Even better, 93% of the respondents who remembered the four-page unit reported that they had read a portion of it.

An Impression study conducted on the special 12-page advertising section for Thomas J. Lipton Inc., showed that 38% of subjects remembered having seen or read the special section. Of those surveyed, 87% enjoyed the special advertising section, and 59% expressed strong interest in trying "new" Lipton products after reading the ad.

Calvin Klein used a 116-page "outsert" of black-and-white photos in *Vanity Fair* at a reported cost of $1 million to make sure it was well noticed.

Some agencies have, however, become upset about inserts and other methods used to break through magazine advertising clutter, because these techniques appear to have an undesirable effect on the readership of adjacent ads. "The inserts have the ability to change the entire feel of the magazine," said Frank MacNamara. "You'll always flip immediately to that insert, which cuts down the possibility of other advertising being seen."

◆ *Using color in an otherwise black and white ad can boost its impact and draw attention to the brand and product. Those objects that are printed in color can really stand out!*

19. Advertising placed upside down or sideways, like Glenmore Distilleries' or Sisley's advertising, can be efficient if you want to convey an image of versatility. It adds an element of intrigue.

20. Holograms and talking ads are very expensive but well worth it. In 1987, Carillon Importers' Absolut Vodka used a musical ad that played "Jingle Bells." That ad cost $1 million in production and media, and ran in just two publications. However, Richard Costello, president of Absolut's agency, TBWA New York, said, "That advertising got us $8 million in free publicity."

In 1990, Absolut used a talking ad, and Finlandia vodka sported a 3-D hologram.

COLOR OR BLACK-AND-WHITE ADS?

The use of color is strongly recommended for advertising, even if it costs more than black-and-white:

1. *Color ads attract attention.* A study by Daniel Starch of a sample of 23,000 ads pertaining to a variety of products showed that four-color ads achieved far more visibility, whatever their size, than those in black-and-white or in just two colors.[26] A similar study conducted on more than 25,000 ads appearing in different American publications achieved identical results.[27] Full-page color ads, in short, achieve 45% more attention than full-page black-and-white ones.[28]

2. *Color ads boost readership.* All else being equal, the addition of one color boosts readership by 22%, while the addition of two or three colors boosts it by 68%.[29] A study conducted on 109,460 ads in trade magazines confirmed Starch's discoveries: black-and-white pages were read by an average of 33% of all readers, while 44% read full-page color ads.[30]

◆ *Color pictures generally work better than those in black and white. But this does not mean color images are better in every case. It all depends on your goal. If you want to tickle the imagination, black and white will serve very well. The mysterious ambiance created by black and white images is naturally vibrant. Black and white pictures can also inspire serious thought or give your product a sense of age and tradition.*

247

3. *Retention is enhanced by color ads.* Color ads generally enjoy twice the retention of those in black-and-white.

4. *Color ads boost your product's prestige.*[31] The use of color in print tends to boost the status and prestige of the advertiser, brand, or service in question. Consumers perceive the use of color as a demonstration of strength, power, and sturdiness.[32]

5. *Color ads sell.* In the case of ads promoting sales or discounts, the addition of one color to a black-and-white ad should generate an additional 41% in revenues.[33] Better yet, one color ad in an otherwise black-and-white ad campaign should make sales soar.[34]

6. *Color ads give life to your pictures.*[35] Products appear more appetizing. Your subject appears more lively, attractive, and real. Color is particularly important when advertising food products.

7. *Color ads enhance certain aspects of your message.* In a daily black-and-white newspaper or in a black-and-white ad, the use of color enhances the impact of your ad by drawing attention to the essential ingredient: the brand or the product.

8. *Color ads identify your brand.* They make it easier for customers to recognize your product: 7-Up is green, Coke is red, Pepsi is blue, Hertz is yellow, Avis is red, and National is green.

The use of color can also help emphasize an important change in your company. In 1994, Xerox unveiled a new red and pixilated "X" symbol, and a black-and-red corporate logo. This change was designed as a modification of the old blue "Xerox" logo, to draw more attention to Xerox's entry into areas outside of copying. This effort showcased the company's involvement in electronic products such as scanners and fax machines.[36]

THE IMPORTANCE OF COLOR

7-Up	*Green*
Coke	*Red*
Pepsi	*Red and blue*
Hertz	*Yellow*
Avis	*Red*
National	*Green*
Campbell	*Red and white*
Kodak	*Yellow*
Fuji	*Green*
Visa	*Blue and gold*
Pennzoil	*Yellow*
Castrol	*Green and red*
STP	*Red and blue*
Quaker State	*Green*

CONCLUSION

When asked for his predictions on print advertising in the 21st century, Philip W. Sawyer, VP at Roper Starch Worldwide, declared: "Visually complex advertising won't produce results, so advertisers will learn that simple means are effective."[37]

Chapter 8

The hidden meanings of different colors

If you decide to advertise in color, you should realize that color is more than a gimmick for catching attention. It also helps establish atmosphere and alter emotions.

You'll boost your chances of success by understanding that through the process of synesthesia—or a secondary sensation that accompanies an actual perception—color creates a sense of quality, lightness, softness, hardness, strength, prestige, price, temperature, purity, taste, fragrance, femininity, or masculinity.

Some years ago, Louis Cheskin, director of a company that conducted studies on color, asked housewives to try the detergents contained in three different boxes, and to decide which would be best to wash delicate fabrics.[1] The first box was yellow, the second blue, and the third had yellow dots on a blue background. Although the boxes held the same contents, the different packaging elicited varying reactions among the housewives. They felt the detergent in the yellow box was too strong and destroyed the fabric. They said the detergent in the blue box was ineffective and failed to wash properly. But they said the detergent in the blue and yellow box gave excellent results.

During another study, a group of women were offered two samples of the same beauty cream. One was in a pink jar, the other in a blue one. The women were asked to identify the more effective product. More than 80% said that the cream in the pink jar was softer, more delicate and more effective than the one in the blue container.[2] However, the composition of both products was identical.

Ad experts have long known that a particular color can make all the difference between success and failure. The right color can in fact boost a product's sales:

- The success of Lucky Strike and Marlboro cigarettes is at least partly due to a change in the colors of their packs.

- In the car industry, Cooper showed that color is one of three key criteria used in selecting a car (the two others being price and quality).[3]

- Some years ago, the orange-colored soft drink Orange Crush was sold in small dark-brown bottles. After Jim Nash Associates redesigned the container to make it larger, clear and more modern in appearance, enabling consumers to see the product's orange color—rather than concealing it from them, as with a medication—company vice-president A. E. Repenning reported that sales tripled within a month.

- Berni Corporation claims that when it changed Canada Dry's sugar-free ginger ale label can from red to green and white, sales shot up by more than 25%.[4]

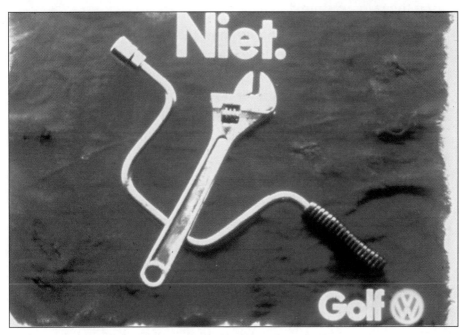

◆ *Color works very much like images in creating an impact on the subconscious mind. Consumers forge psychological relationships between the color of an ad, that of the product's packaging, and its content. Red is the most dynamic color and evokes a sense of force, buoyancy, and energy.*

- Nynex colored its pay phones yellow to attract more callers.

- Lever Brothers sold Lux soap in bars of different colors—pale pink, light green, turquoise, and yellow—rather than just the usual yellow, to make it the market's first luxury toilet soap.

- In the 1990s, Italy's Benetton put up ads featuring young people in colorful undergarments. These hues allowed the manufacturer to generate a sense of happiness and joy in its ads, for more than a decade. More recently, Apple scored a big success with its blue and tangerine iMac computers. Next, Gillette relaunched its Venus razors for women with a brilliant concept: the razor was pink!

- In the casino sector, studies show that such dark colors as black, red, purple, and blue draw players' attention for longer periods of time. We know that bright red machines work well in catching players' eyes. But after a few moments, they move on to machines sporting more subtle tones. For that reason, brighter machines are placed at the ends of the rows, and the blue and green ones in the centers.

- In 2004, M&M's introduced bolder colors for its candies. "We've always had color as a unique point of difference, but we wanted to reinforce that message in a fresh, contemporary way." The new M&M's feature a brighter mix of colors, including a brightened yellow and blue, as well as a larger M, and an updated package.[5]

Unfortunately, many advertisements and packaging color schemes do not evoke any association of ideas, and bear no relation whatsoever to the product. There are a few classic examples of packaging errors: promoting a decaffeinated coffee in a bright, exciting red that does not, and is not meant to excite; offering a sleeping pill in a stimulating yellow; and presenting sugar in a "bitter" green package.

People don't just buy a product; they also buy its colors.

THE HIDDEN MEANINGS OF COLORS

Each color has a range of emotional meaning.

1. Red

For many years, red-and-white packaging could sell almost any product. This was not just a matter of chance. Red is "The" advertising color. It symbolizes love, warmth, sensuality, and passion. It is also identified with revolution, bloodshed, the diabolical, and eternal hellfire. It is the most violent and most dynamic color, with the greatest potential for action. It expresses the joy of conquest and of revolution.

◆ *You can use red for any kind of warning or off limits notice.*

Red boosts blood pressure, muscular tension, and respiratory rate. It is the color of driving and urgent eroticism. While a deep red is perceived as being severe, traditional, and rich, a burgundy red is seen as being luxurious and elegant. Cherry red is sensual. A medium red represents activity, strength, movement, and passionate desire. A light red signifies strength, buoyancy, energy, joy, and triumph. You can use red:

- For firefighting products.

- For all products that convey a sense of virility—such as sports cars, cigarettes, and shaving cream—because this color gives off a particularly masculine aura.

- For all impulsively purchased consumer goods, like chocolate and chewing gum.

- For a promise of quality and value for all food products, and is sufficiently neutral to be used with any item.

- For all notices and warning signs.

Fast food restaurant owners are putting red's properties to good use when they paint their dining rooms in this color. This system encourages customers to hurry up, thus increasing the total number of customers served.

Workers tend to spend less time in red toilets than in blue ones for the same reasons.

2. Orange

Orange evokes a sense of warmth, fire, sun, light, and autumn, with the accompanying psychological effects of eagerness, stimulation, and youth. In large quantities, orange speeds up the heart rate without affecting blood pressure. Frivolous beyond measure, orange is not taken seriously and has no status. Orange is an excellent color for ravioli, prepared dishes, and for meat and tomato-based preserves.

●————**MEDIA** ADVISORY ———●

THE ROLE OF COLOR...

ON TV

In contrast with other media, TV commercials can seduce consumers through a careful mix of sound, image, color, and movement.

IN BILLBOARDS

Use distinctive colors.

IN MAGAZINES

Most magazines permit high-quality color reproduction. This is an important factor in ads for food, alcohol, clothing, and cards.

IN DAILIES AND WEEKLIES

Modern equipment has vastly enhanced color reproduction in newspapers. This is excellent news for advertisers.

●————————————————————————●

3. Yellow

Yellow is happy, vibrant, and friendly. It represents good humor and joy in living. It is fresh and bright and, like orange, conveys a sense of warmth and illumination. Yellow is particularly good in attracting customer attention, especially when mixed with black. In marketing, yellow stands for "low priced." This color is used by Subway, McDonald's, Cheerios, and Yellow Shoes. Yellow is also well suited to products associated with corn, lemon, and sun cream.

TRANS: HAPPINESS IS A STOLI, BECAUSE ONLY

STOLI IS REAL RUSSIAN VODKA

◆ *Yellow is happy, vibrant, and friendly.*

4. Green

Green solicits calm and restfulness. It serves to reduce blood pressure and to dilate the capillaries. It is a symbol of good health, freshness, and nature. This color is often used for canned vegetables and for tobacco products, especially those that are mentholated.

These days, green is more popular than ever. The color is associated with ecological values and with the environment. Green is also the color of hope. The suicide rate at the once black Blackfriar's Bridge in London has been cut by one third since it was painted green.

People perceive food products that are packaged in green to be less fatty, to contain fewer calories, and to be richer in proteins. This color is widely used for the packaging of frozen foods.

5. Blue

Blue makes people think of the sky, water, the sea, space, the air, and travel. It is associated with ideas of wonder, freedom, dreams, and youth. It is a calm, relaxing, and transparent color that inspires a sense of peacefulness, relaxation, and wisdom. It symbolizes security and conservatism. It is also a color of wealth, trust, and security.

Evoking a sense of freshness in its paler shades, blue seems cool in its deeper tones. Blue is well suited to frozen foods (to give the impression of ice) and to all beverages, such as beer, soft drinks, bottled water, etc., particularly when accompanied by yellow. The coldest color is blue-green.

Oddly, we tend to avoid blue foods and beverages as a carryover from previous eating habits. We prefer the colors of nuts, roots, and ripe fruits, such as white, red, brown, and yellow.[6]

◆ *Blue is a reassuring, relaxing, and peaceful color.*

6. Purple

Purple is a cool red in both the physical and psychological sense of the word. There is something morbid, nonfunctional, and sad about this color. Purple is rarely used in advertising, except perhaps to give a product a sense of royalty.

7. Brown

Brown is associated with the earth, woodlands, warmth, and comfort. It represents healthy living and daily work. It expresses a desire for ownership and the search for material well-being. Brown is a masculine color that conveys a sense of class and professionalism. It can be used to sell anything to men.

◆ *Black confers a sense of distinction, nobility, and class.*

8. Black

Black is associated with ideas of death, bereavement, and solitude. It assumes the qualities of night and its impenetrable character. Black is a color with no hope or future. At the same time, black conveys a sense of nobility, distinction, and elegance. It has a sophisticated character that is well suited to high-quality products such as perfumes or wines.

Black is often used in advertising because it is very useful in establishing contrasts. Furthermore, black sets off any surrounding colors.

9. White

As bright as it may be, white tends to convey a sense of silence and coolness. In large quantities, white can be dazzling. Alone, it creates a sense of emptiness that is almost bursting with possibilities.

◆ *Black is ideal for creating contrasts, and helps set off any adjacent colors.*

◆ *White suggests cleanliness. In the company of blue, it also suggests freshness.*

White symbolizes purity, perfection, trendiness, innocence, chastity, youth, calm, and peace. It personifies cleanliness, particularly when accompanied by blue. White is the ideal companion for all colors, as it makes them appear deeper and fuller.

10. Gray

Gray expresses a sense of doubt. Its paleness evokes a sense of fright, age, and death. Gray is by far the dirtiest color. At the same time, a metallic gray conveys a sense of strength, exclusivity, and success.

11. Pink

Pink is timid and romantic. It suggests gentleness, femininity, affection, and intimacy.

12. Pastels

Favre and November, two experts on color, have said that the characteristic features of pastel hues are the softening and dilution of the qualities of the colors from which they originate. They represent intimacy and affection.

LOVE IS RED AND SEX IS PINK

Color is related to the emotions. Henry C.L. Johnson, an expert on motivational studies, performed intensive research on this issue and presented his conclusions in an article in *Marketing/Communications*.[7] The following list is largely drawn from that publication:

A

action—brown
affliction—purple
anger—red, orange
authority—black
autumn—brown
award—blue

B

beauty (divine)—yellow
beauty (human)—green
belligerence—red, orange

C

chaos—violet
cold—blue
confidence—yellow
constancy—blue
contentment—green

D

dawn—pink
death—black, violet
dedication—violet
demon—blue
dignity—purple
distinction—yellow
dominance—red, orange

E

earthiness—brown
enchantment—violet
enlightenment—yellow
envy—green
esteem—yellow
eternal life—green
excellence—yellow
excitement—red

F
faith—blue
fellowship—brown
fertility—brown
fever—red, orange
fidelity—blue
fire—yellow
flesh—pink
friendship—green
frugality—purple
fruitfulness—green
fulfillment—red
fury—red, orange
G
gold—yellow
gourmet—brown
grief—black
H
health—green
holiness—white
honor—blue
hope—green
human emotions—red
humility—blue, black
I
immateriality—blue
immortality—blue
impressive—violet
innocence—silver, white
intangible—blue
intelligence—yellow
intimate—pink
introverted—blue

J
joy—pink, silver, green
K
knowledge—yellow
L
leisure—green
love (human)—red
love (divine)—violet
love (physical)—red, orange
loyalty—black
lurking catastrophe—violet
M
masculinity—brown
maturity—brown
melancholy—purple
menace—violet
mourning—blue, black
mystery—blue, violet
N
nothing—blue
O
oppression—violet
P
passion—red, orange
passivity—blue
piety—violet
playfulness—yellow
power—blue, black
purity—white, yellow
R
radiance—yellow
recessiveness—blue
royal—black

S

sacrifice—red, orange

sadness—blue, black

serviceability—black

sex—pink

shadow—blue

slaughter—red, orange

solitude—violet

sorrow—black

spirituality—blue, violet

sport—brown

strength (fiery)—red, orange

strength (physical)—brown

superstition—violet

T

tenderness—blue

terror—blue, violet

triumph—red, orange

truce—white

truth—blue

U

understanding—yellow

V

valor—red, orange

value—yellow

vegetable—green

vegetable growth—red, orange

victory—red, orange

virility—brown

W

warmth (atmosphere)—brown

warmth (inner)—red, orange

wisdom—silver

COLOR COMBINATIONS

You should be aware of what your main colors symbolize when producing billboards or print ads. You should also understand what color pairs represent. Readers will not react to the individual colors of a pair, but rather to the set of sensations produced by the pair.

Here are some basics on this topic:

- A combination of *red and yellow* signifies a desire to conquer and a desire for novelty. The psychological impact of applying these characteristics is achieved when you use red and yellow for such sources of energy as fuel pumps or matchbooks.

- A combination of *red and green* signifies a desire for self-affirmation, authority, and security. It is recommended if you want to create an impression of strength and solidity for maintenance products, for example.

- A combination of *red and blue* signifies a desire for conquest, and a need for intimate and erotic contact. The red and blue combination is well suited to the packaging of beauty products, or for paper used in writing love letters.

- A combination of *red and black* signifies pent-up excitement that is ready to take the form of aggressive impulses. "The devil wears red and black in the theater or in the movies," wrote Max Lüscher. "Before he says a single word, he is recognized by the psychological impact of his outfit."

- A combination of *yellow and blue* is very dynamic. It suggests power, effectiveness, speed, and energy.

- A combination of *blue and pink* suggests softness, childhood, and breeziness. It stimulates the consumer's maternal instincts and protective feelings. It is well suited to beauty products and baby products.

- A combination of *red and white* gives an impression of cleanliness and of a healthy character.

- A combination of *blue and white* creates a sensation of freshness and healthiness. It also evokes a fresh and cheerful temperament.

- A combination of *green and blue* suggests restfulness, freshness and nature.

- A combination of *white and black* gives your ads a sense of rigor, solemnity, chic, and good taste.

- A combination of *yellow, red, and blue* is joyful and animated.

- A combination of *yellow, red, orange, green, and brown* evokes thrift, ripe tropical fruits, sun, and escape.

- *Multicolored* combinations suggest the dynamism, joy, and energy of young children.

Colors suggest different degrees of *temperature*. The so-called stimulating and dynamic colors—yellow, orange, and red—are warm. They affect the sympathetic nervous system and glandular activity. They cause blood pressure, and the respiratory and pulse rates, to rise.

Blue, green, and purple, on the other hand, are considered to be calm, restful, cool colors. They act on the parasympathetic system. They decrease attention and the pulmonary and cardiac rates.

You have an average of one tenth of a second to get a reader interested in your ad. To retain the interest of readers, an ad must capture their attention at a single glance. Some colors work better than others in drawing such attention.

◆ *A combination of red and green is powerful and creates a sense of strong contrast.*

◆ *Red and blue together create a powerful contrast.*

◆ *The combination of yellow and black has an explosive quality.*

Under normal circumstances, warm colors catch the eye more successfully and are visible from greater distances than are cool ones. Bright orange and red-orange win hands down in this category. Used in moderate doses they attract more attention than any other colors. In excess, however, they trigger anxiety.

This is why orange is so commonly found on price mark-down labels, and occasionally on different kinds of packaging, as well as on billboards overlooking major thoroughfares.

Red is most visible in the dark, followed by green, yellow, and white. Blue and purple are the most difficult colors to distinguish in poor lighting.

Complementary colors (red and green, blue and yellow, purple and orange) produce the strongest contrasts when juxtaposed. Red appears even brighter on a green background. The same rule applies with white and black. Butchers tend to use these contrasting properties when they place bits of parsley on their meats to make them appear fresher.

Color alters the perceived *weight* of objects. In 1926, Carl Warden and Ellen Flynn concluded that black seemed to be the "heaviest" color, followed by red, gray, and purple (of equal weight), and then by blue, green, yellow, and white.[8] French expert Maurice Déribéré subsequently revealed that darker colors (which contain greater percentages of black) are "heavy", and brighter colors (which contain large percentages of white) are "light."

An experiment conducted in an American factory showed that heavy black crates that were handled each day appeared lighter to the men performing this task when they were painted bright green.

During another study, crates that had been painted bright yellow were perceived to be lighter than crates of the same weight that were painted dark brown. The person loading the bright yellow crates actually felt less tired after a day's work than he did with the dark brown ones.

Darker hues also make objects look smaller. A white figure on a black background appears bigger than a black figure of the same size on a white background. If we take three crates of equal size, the red one will appear smallest, the white largest, and the blue will seem to fall between the two in size. The three vertical stripes in the French flag must have the following proportions to be perceived as equal in size when seen from a distance: blue—33%, white—30%, and red—37%.

John Hedgecoe once reported that "the impact of these combinations has a psychological basis." Focal distance is greater for red and yellow than it is for blue and green. When we look at different colors, the eye must constantly refocus to compensate for the different wavelengths.

Colors appear to *move*. White, which is an active color, seems to spill over beyond its boundaries, while passive black seems to withdraw within itself. Red seems to leap out toward the viewer, while blue seems to shirk away.

Colors are also perceived to have different *tastes*. Yellow-green and greenish-yellow are "acidic." Yellow-orange and red are "sweet." Pink is "sugary." Blue, brown, olive green, and purple are "bitter." Yellow is "spicy." Grayish-green and grayish blue are "salty."

Consumers also associate colors with *fragrances*. Orange is "peppery." Green is a bit "spicy." Purple and lilac are "fragrant." Light, pure, and delicate colors evoke the fragrance of a sweet perfume. On the other hand, dark, disturbing, and warm colors evoke unpleasant odors.

Colors are also associated with *sounds*. Purple is bass, yellow is treble, and red is noisy.

In terms of touch, red is perceived as hot, square, and protruding. Yellow is pointy and triangular. Blue is cool, slick, slippery, and round.[9]

The desire to express the qualities of different colors is merely an attempt to confirm the sensations that these colors arouse in our minds. The feelings that colors produce are so subtle and delicate that words are inadequate to express them properly.

To make life easier for the advertising community and to ensure that Barbie's pink and IBM's blue are always the same shades and hues, a young graphic designer named Lawrence Herbert created the Pantone chart.

His company now generates annual revenues of some $2 billion. This chart enables graphic artists and printers to speak the same language on matters of color, anywhere in the world.

WHAT COLORS ARE MOST LIKED—AND HATED?

Some colors tend to please and others to displease. Eysenk summarized research conducted by 40 statisticians among a total sample of 21,000 subjects in different countries.[10] He concluded that from most to least popular, colors could be ranked as follows:

- Blue
- Red
- Green
- Purple
- Orange
- Yellow

Primary colors are generally better liked than intermediate hues.

If we consider gender-based preferences, it would seem that women prefer blue over red, and men like blue more than green.

Among different shades of color, pink comes to mind first. Beige, azure blue, light blue, light green, pale yellow, and navy blue follow. Greenish-yellow is the shade that makes people most uncomfortable, followed by olive green and gray. Blue-yellow, blue-green, blue-red, and yellow-red are described as being the most pleasant combinations.

It should be noted that color preferences change with age.[11] Young people prefer pure and dazzling colors, like red and yellow. Older folks prefer softer hues and darker, less intense colors.

Studies have shown that the poor and less cultivated masses like intense colors such as red and orange. Those with greater social standing and higher levels of culture tend to like cool, soft hues and shades.[12]

Before using a color in a foreign market, make sure that it triggers no negative connotations. Colors do not have the same attributes everywhere. In Japan, white is the color of mourning, while black plays this role in western society. In Egypt and Syria, green is the national color, and it would be considered in bad taste to use it on packaging.

THE SYMBOLISM OF LINES AND SHAPES

Lines and shapes contribute to the meaning of your illustration or product, in the same manner as colors. In what would become a famous experiment, Louis Cheskin demonstrated that a tube decorated with circles was perceived as a better quality container than one decorated with triangles.

Two hundred women used two different skin creams in this study.[13] These women were then asked which cream worked better. Nearly 80% said that the product contained in the tube with circles was far better than the other. However, both tubes held the same product.

Some shapes give the impression of density, of viscosity, and of weight. Others express a sense of fluidity and lightness. In a study, Raymond Loewy, the world's best known industrial designer, offered 500 people equal quantities of beer, some contained in long slim bottles made of transparent glass, and others in short squat and opaque bottles. Neither style bore labels.

After the tasting, Loewy asked his guests to tell him which bottles contained the lighter beer. Although all of the bottles held the same contents, 98% of the respondents said the slimmer bottle had the lighter beer.[14]

People generally perceive lines and directions as follows:[15]

- Fine lines express simplicity, daintiness, and lightness.

- Thick lines suggest strength and energy.

- Heavy lines give an impression of resoluteness and violence.

- Long lines create a sense of liveliness.

- Short lines give a sense of resolve.

- Broken lines produce a sense of hectic motion.

- Straight lines suggest calm, restfulness, peace, stability, security, and peace of mind.

- Straight vertical lines give a sense of the infinite, height, buoyancy, warmth, activity, and obstruction. An ascending vertical line is always synonymous with spirituality and progress, and conveys a positive sense. A descending vertical line, which signifies earthly possessions and regression, is negative.

- A curved line evokes a sense of gentleness, grace, elegance, flexibility, good cheer, fantasy, movement, youth, and instability.

- Oblique lines convey a sense of movement and of falling. Lines tilted to the right are associated with positive feelings. They are dynamic and seem to advance. Those that tilt to the left, on the other hand, are associated with negative feelings and seem to regress.

- Quadrilateral lines evoke a studious atmosphere.

In the case of shapes:

- Circles are soft, sensual, and feminine.

- Squares are hard, dry, cold, and masculine.

- The triangle is the most virile and aggressive shape. When seated on a base, a triangle suggests calm and stability. Set on its tip, however, it conveys an impression of lightness and imbalance.

◆ *Diagonals suggest motion. Those leaning to the right are associated with positive feelings.*

"Should a man's hat be packed in a round box, for example? (A hexagonal shape is more acceptable)," pondered Stephen Baker in *Visual Persuasion,* "Should a woman's toilet soap be oval or square? (Oval is more desirable.) Should detergents be packaged in square boxes? (Yes. Detergents have been found to sell more quickly if they connote masculinity—power and action—even though buyers are mainly women)."[16]

Should breakfast cereals come in square containers? Yes. Square containers convey a sense of power, abundance, and generosity, which is well suited to what people expect from their morning meal.

◆ *Lines and shapes add to the meaning established by your logo. You create a sense of strength and power by increasing the number of angles and points.*

REVIEW

Once you decide to use colors, shapes, and lines in your ads, your choices of which to employ should be based on such objective criteria as visibility and readability, as well as on such subjective criteria as the ideas that these graphic elements evoke.

Chapter 9

When to use and when to avoid comparative advertising

Comparative advertising first appeared in the United States in 1930 when Sears took out print ads to compare its tires with eight other national brands. In 1931, Firestone did just as Sears had done,[1] but its comparative ads were rejected by a variety of newspapers, including the *Chicago Tribune* and the *New York Daily News*. One year later, Plymouth published an ad that asked consumers to "Look at All Three."[2] By June, Plymouth's sales had soared 218% from the previous year. Comparative advertising was born.

Even though it has not found favor with certain companies or large agencies, comparative advertising is currently a common practice in the United States, Canada, Great Britain, Sweden, and Australia.

In 1964, Wilkie and Farris said that 15% of all advertising is comparative.[3] A decade later, the figure had climbed to 20%. In 1982, 23% of all ads made reference in one way or another to the competition, a clear acknowledgement of the importance of comparison.

Many ad experts believe in the effectiveness of comparative advertising. Experience would seem to prove them right. Pepsi, Burger King, Savin, Carefree, and Suave shampoo have significantly increased their market shares through comparative advertising.

Political campaigns have played a role in this trend. In the United States, George Bush's victory over Mike Dukakis in the 1988 presidential election was generally attributed to the negative advertising produced against Dukakis by Bush adviser Roger Ailes. Negative advertising played a key role in Canada's 2004 federal election, and enabled Paul Martin's team to smear Conservative Party head Stephen Harper.

Comparative advertising has the simple goal in business and politics of identifying and devaluing the competition.

According to Stanley Tannenbaum, chairman of Kenyon and Eckhardt: "It is a mistake to condemn comparative advertising as ineffective, confusing and a disaster to our business just because some advertisers do not know how or when to use it. You can't look a few swaybacked nags in the mouth and then conclude that horse racing is headed for disaster."[4]

Few consumers, however, like comparative advertising. More than 41% don't think it's "right," because the facts presented do not permit a fair comparison. Furthermore, 37% believe that the facts are usually exaggerated. And 36% think that advertisers should emphasize their own strong points rather than attempt to demean the competition.[5] For William LaMothe, chairman and CEO of Kellogg's, "comparative advertising is a lazy way to sell your product."[6]

Much has been written on this topic,[7] and most of the discussion boils down to two key questions:

1. When should you use comparative advertising?

2. When should you avoid it?

BETTER THAN AVERAGE PERFORMANCE

Comparative advertising can work:

1. If your product holds a small market share, if you're new to the market, or if you're not well known[8]

The leader is naturally in a strong position. To boost your results, you will have to get people to change their minds about the leader. This was Tylenol's strategy when it advertised that aspirin could irritate the stomach lining. Tylenol is now the number one pain reliever in the United States with 30% of the market, ahead of Anacin, Bayer, Bufferin, and Excedrin. This achievement represented a remarkable exploit in a market that had been dominated by aspirin.

2. If you can prove that your product is better

Give consumers the reasons why they should buy your product along with the reasons they should avoid those of the competition.

A study by Research Systems Corp. claimed that competitive TV spots carrying brand-differentiating messages improve the odds of achieving superior persuasion scores. "Including a competitive product as a point of reference for consumers will help them understand the advantage one product has over another," said Mark Gleason, RSC executive VP.[9]

Savin has used comparative advertising in recent years to demonstrate its superiority over Xerox. In one of these ads, the company told consumers that Sa~~

~~dier than those of the comp~~

shot up from $60 million to $200 million, and Savin installed more copying machines than any of its competitors.

In the US, Burger King was successful in reigniting its sales by demonstrating exactly how it cooks its hamburgers on TV. In England, however, the firm's ads proclaimed that Burger King hamburgers contain 41% more beef than do those of McDonald's.

Improved packaging can also boost the sales effort. John Lyons said, "Scope's new plastic bottle helped gain more than a stride in the share race with Listerine. I remember the commercial we created to introduce it. In slow motion, we dropped both Scope's new plastic bottle and Listerine's glass bottle onto a hard-tile bathroom floor and froze at the hit point, as a pair of bare tootsies stood surrounded by flying glass from the Listerine bottle."[10]

3. If there is no special preference or loyalty for any particular brand

Undecided consumers are always receptive to new information.[11]

4. If your budget is less than your competitor's

Comparative advertising lets you place yourself on the same level as the leader, as Burger King did with McDonald's.

5. If your company is the victim of comparative advertising[12]

Undecided consumers are always receptive to new information. Responding to the competition will let you reply, set things straight, and ultimately give you a chance to come out on top.

However, this may not be a simple procedure. As Larry Light points out, "If the number-one brand counterattacks, the consumer may be led to believe that the original advertising had a point. History has indicated this always increases the credibility of the original attack."[13]

Shortly after Coca-Cola replied to Pepsi-Cola's repeated attacks, Pepsi's market share surged from 8% to 18% in Dallas.[14]

There are, however, some exceptions. Hertz's response to Avis's comparative advertising allowed Hertz to win back 5% of the 10% in market share it had lost within six months. Such results tend to show that market impact also depends on the actual response.

6. If your product is truly original

New products find easier acceptance than existing ones. Expressions like "lead-free gas," "sugar-free Coke", and food "without additives" are all examples of how new products can be compared to more traditional ones.

7. For industrial ads

When your readership is likely to take a logical approach to your ad, direct comparisons with other brands often yield excellent results.

8. When you have tried everything else without success

Comparative advertising is your ultimate weapon. After a number of unsuccessful ad campaigns, Vivitar decided to test two brands in a side-by-side demonstration.[15] The ad proclaimed Vivitar's superiority, and sales took off. Vivitar soon acquired second place in its market with a 10% share.

..., but it's the only time to kick a leader. [16]

The worldwide recall of all Perrier bottles due to the discovery of some bottles containing an abnormally high level of benzene cost $260 million dollars ($48.6 million in communications, $201 million to redeem and destroy the bottles, with operational costs estimated at $18 million).

WORSE THAN AVERAGE PERFORMANCE

Comparative advertising is not recommended:

1. If you dominate the market

There is usually no reason for the leader to draw consumer attention to its rivals.[17] If the market leader uses comparative advertising, it tends to boost the credibility of other brands. When a leader goes after its competitors, consumers get the message that their products are better.

2. If there is no difference between your product and those of the competition

There is no point in using comparative advertising if you cannot show why people should buy your products rather than those of the competition. In an article published in *Sales and Marketing Management*, John Trytten wrote that comparative advertising only works when it is based on solid facts.[18]

3   If you have a tight budget

Most comparative advertising campaigns are expensive and continue over a long period. Pepsi's attempts to take on Coca-Cola, for example, have persisted for years.

4. If consumers buy your product for emotional rather than logical reasons

Revlon doesn't advertise that its lipsticks succeed in seducing 69% more men than do Maybelline's.

SHOULD YOU CLEARLY IDENTIFY YOUR COMPETITOR?

A study by Philip Levine showed that TV commercials that named competitive brands were perceived as being more complicated and less credible than ads that did not.[19] However, the Batten, Barton, Durstine & Osborn agency indicates that products with small market shares are more likely to identify the competition.[20]

Hank Seiden said, "People totally believe commercials that mention competitors' names. They assume that if you show or talk about a competitor's product, what you say in the commercial must be true or you could never run it on the air. They know that your competition could not only force you to take the commercial off the air, but would sue you for all you're worth."[21]

Gillette, Ford, 3M, and Avis have shown that naming the competition can pay off. Avis obviously never specifically named the leader, Hertz, when it launched its "We're #2" campaign. But any consumer who was familiar with the car rental market knew the name of the competitor in question. Similarly, people realized that Kodak was the target when 3M referred to the company "in the yellow box."[22]

Cola. Once he gets a Pepsi, his usual style returns. Another version was created for use in countries—including Germany, Italy, Greece, and Spain—that prohibit competitors from being named or shown. In that one, Mr. Hammer is handed a white cup containing a cola drink, but no Coca-Cola can or label is seen."[23]

WARNING

Don't produce a comparative ad that puts you in a face-to-face confrontation with the market leader. An ad that directly takes on consumer habits will always boomerang against its promoters.

To compete with a well-established leader, you must find a gap in its armor and then reveal this weakness to consumers. You can say that your product is less expensive, that you use better ingredients, or that your product is not plagued with the inconveniences of the one produced by the competition. But you have to say more than it's merely better.

Chapter 10

The 5 effects of repetition

A s we near the end of this book, I have a final piece of advice: *keep repeating your ads as long as they sell.* An ad published one day and not the next is a failed ad.

Conducting an ad campaign means beating on the same drum for weeks or months. Napoleon once said, "Repetition is the best argument!" The same rule applies in advertising.

Many ads have, in fact, failed because they lacked adequate weight. This problem occurs if advertisers fail to purchase adequate broadcast time, or print space, and repeat ads.

Repetition is such a powerful strategy that a study has shown that 9 out of 10 buyers of your product will continue to look at your ads even after buying your product.[1] This process increases the likelihood of your customers being happy with their purchases.

research shows that our memories tend to forget. As far back as 1885, Hermann Ebbinghaus revealed the importance of repetition. Many subsequent studies have shown that increased repetition normally results in increased product notoriety and sales.[3]

●———— MEDIA ADVISORY ————●

THE ROLE OF REPETITION:

ON TV

Maintaining a set of television commercials over the long term is widely recommended. Keep your pitch alive as long as possible, and repeat it often. By preserving minimal advertising weight, you ensure the effectiveness of your message.

IN RADIO

Radio is an advertising media that requires a high frequency of repetition. You should repeat your commercials as often as possible to build up your product's notoriety, and to stimulate consumer reaction.

A three-week consecutive campaign is recommended to boost the audience recall rate of a particular message, and thus develop the brand's renown.

ON BILLBOARDS

You need to purchase the most advertising weight possible if you decide to use billboards. Billboard awareness rates are an important asset. Viacom reports that there is no major decline in notoriety until six weeks following the conclusion of an outdoor ad campaign.

IN MAGAZINES

The biweekly or monthly appearance of many magazines will not permit the generation of high frequencies over the short- or mid-term. These frequencies will often prevent you from creating a sense of immediacy or of exploiting an unusual event.

IN DAILY NEWSPAPERS

In the 1960s, 80% of all people read a newspaper each day, compared with only 60% today. This is one more reason why you should repeat your ads.

IN WEEKLIES

Research has shown that the more often readers are exposed to ads, the more likely they will develop a positive feeling toward the product in question. Have you overexposed your message? Relax. According to a recent study, just 7% of the public felt that it has seen ads appearing in weeklies too often.

WHAT REPETITION CAN DO FOR YOU

Numerous researchers have studied the effects of repetition.[4] Here are five "miracles" that repetition can perform for your advertising campaign.

1. Repetition boosts the likelihood of exposure to your ads

The more often readers are exposed to an ad, the more likely they are to see it. To reach approximately 95% of a publication's readership, Daniel Starch estimated that an ad should be repeated:

- 13 times if it was noticed by 20% of the readership during its first appearance;
- 8 times if it was noticed by 30% of the readership during its first appearance;
- 6 times if it was noticed by 40% of the readership during its first appearance;

- 4 times if it was noticed by 50% of the readership during its first appearance;

- 3 times if it was noticed by 60% of the readership during its first appearance.[5]

Ad repetition thus serves to enhance your product's visibility. Research has also shown that the purchase of a familiar product generally produces satisfaction (81%), while the purchase of an unknown item is perceived as risky (82%).[6] Many sales have been lost because consumers are not adequately aware of your product.

2. Repetition improves product image

The more often people are exposed to an ad, the more their positive feelings toward the product are likely to increase.[7] According to Simmons Market Research Bureau, this is one of the reasons why ad experts repeat their ads as often as possible. It has been shown that consumers learn, over time, to recognize and to like such brands.[8]

The MITS Altair 8800 was the first personal computer. But today this product no longer exists. The company's founders, unfortunately, did not believe in advertising. Apple, on the other hand, which was launched two years later, is still part of our lives. It revolutionized the advertising world and turned the Super Bowl into an advertising event.

If you boost the frequency of your ads, people will come to believe that you are a leader in your industry, that you have more experience, that you offer the best service, and, most importantly, that you are financially secure.[9]

Recall rates among trade magazine readers rose 26% when advertisers placed two or more ads in the same issue.[10]

But beware of the risk of market saturation! While one ad alone is not likely to achieve observable results, excessive frequency over a certain time frame is likely to cause readers to reject your product.

Cahners Publishing has said that an ad becomes exhausted between the 10th and 21st weeks following the launch of a campaign.[11]

To overcome the monotony of ad repetition, you might consider using different variations of your headline, copy, layout, slogan, typeface—or any other portion of the ad. Each ad can then simultaneously appeal to the public's sense of familiarity and novelty. You will recreate a share of the ad's original impact and enhance its effect on those who saw it previously.

In recent years, various advertising campaigns have made successful use of some types of continuity. Some good examples are the campaigns waged by Wrigley, American Express, Absolut, Calvin Klein, and Jack Daniel's.

3. How the sequencing and frequency of your ad's appearances influence the learning process

This phenomenon was very well illustrated by an experiment conducted in 1958 by Hubert A. Zielske. In this study, Zielske exposed a sample of households to a set of 13 ads appearing at different frequencies.[12] In an initial subgroup, the frequency was set at one exposure (one ad) per week for 13 weeks. In a second subgroup, the frequency was set at one exposure every four weeks for 52 weeks. To prevent the results from being skewed, Zielske made sure that respondents were only interviewed once throughout the study.

After compiling the results, Zielske concluded that an ad that appears on several occasions within a short time frame obtains a higher recall rate than an ad shown at broader intervals. However, such an ad was less likely to be recalled over the long term.

What should we make of Zielske's experiment? You should emphasize repetition over time in your advertising and promotional efforts to launch a product. However, if you wish to support an established product or build a long-term image for it, you should space out your ads.

RECALL BASED ON EXPOSURE

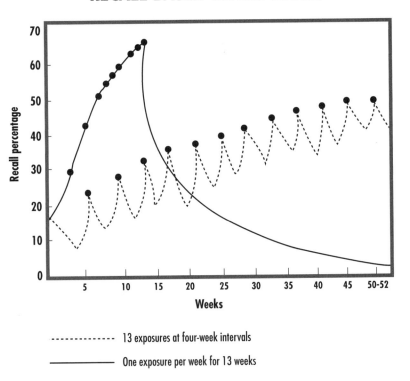

- - - - - - - - - - - - 13 exposures at four-week intervals

———————— One exposure per week for 13 weeks

The following chart compares recall rates for an ad that appeared once a week for 13 weeks to that for an ad that appeared once every four weeks. It is clear that the more concentrated exposure yielded higher recall rates than exposure over a four-week period. Over the long-term, however, exposure that is spaced over longer intervals will produce higher recall rates.

4. Interrupting your campaign will result in a loss of recall

The moment you stop advertising, recollection of your campaign will drop off sharply and will continue to diminish over time.

The reader recall rate after Zielske's 13th mailing was 63%. This figure dropped to 32% within four weeks of the final mailing, then 22% after six weeks, 15% after eight weeks, 10% after 17 weeks, and, finally, to only 4% at the end of the year.[13]

According to Byron Galway, vice-president of the 243 Group, "When advertising is cut—during a recession or for whatever reason—the notoriety of a product diminishes and the market sales for the product go down. When advertising stops, people forget."[14]

Take Hershey's, for example. The company was leader of a sector in which advertising was almost unknown. During the 1973 cocoa crisis, which included among its effects increased prices charged by cocoa producers, Hershey's cut its ad budgets while the competition reacted by investing massively in advertising. Hershey's soon dropped out of first place, and despite a remarkable 1981 comeback, has still not been able to recover its original position.

Maxwell House is another good example of a company that made the mistake of cutting its ad budgets. The firm slashed its ad media investments in 1987 from $60 million to $13.5 million.[15] Maxwell House's closest competitor, Folgers, was quick to snatch away a large share of its market. Maxwell House was sufficiently disturbed by this loss that it returned to its former ways the following year by putting $73 million into advertising and cutting its promotional activities.

When Kodak stopped advertising its batteries in October 1990, sales of Duracell and Energizer immediately took off.[16]

The manufacturers of Tampax tampons recently realized that the brand's slump in sales was due to a cut in ad budgets.[17]

In 1994, TCBY Enterprises took to the airwaves for the first time in three years, hoping to reverse a plummet in revenues from $29.5 million in 1989 to $6.6 million in 1993.[18]

5. Repetition boosts sales

Repetition brings customers into the store and boosts sales. In 1963, DuPont established a link between growth in sales and the number of ads produced during a campaign.[19] The Missouri Valley Petroleum Corporation subsequently noted that a doubling of its ad budget resulted in a huge increase in sales over a three-year period.[20]

It is no surprise that major corporations have invested colossal sums in advertising. Worldwide advertising expenditures increased seven-fold from 1950 to 1996. According to Universal McCann, international advertising investments were $656 billion in 2003, half of which was spent in North America. In the United States, 2.5% of the GDP is spent on advertising each year.

Apple bought all of the ad space in certain US magazines to announce the launch of its Macintosh in 1984. In October 1991, Calvin Klein spent $1 million on a 116-page insert in *Vanity Fair*.

TOP 10 ADVERTISERS–1955

USA	1955 (in millions)
General Motors	$170
Procter & Gamble	$85
General Foods	$75
Ford Motors	$72
Chrysler Corp.	$68
Colgate-Palmolive	$62
General Electric	$60
Lever Bros.	$55
National Dairy Products	$35
Distillers Corp.-Seagrams	$30

Source: "100 leading advertisers," *Advertising Age,* June 27 2005, p. S-17

TOP 10 ADVERTISERS–2004

USA	2004 (in millions)
General Motors Corp.	$3,997
Procter & Gamble	$3,919
Time Warner	$3,283
Pfizer	$2,957
SBC Comunications	$2,686
DaimlerChrysler	$2,462
Ford Motors	$2,458
Walt Disney	$2,241
Verizon Communications	$2,197
Johnson & Johnson	$2,175

Source: 100 leading advertisers, *Advertising Age,* June 27 2005, p. S-2.

FLASH INFO

COST OF A 30-SECOND COMMERCIAL
DURING THE SUPER BOWL

Year	Channel	Cost (US$)
1996	NBC	1,085,000
1997	FOX	1,200,000
1998	NBC	1,291,100
1999	FOX	1,600,000
2000	ABC	2,100,000
2001	CBS	2,200,000

Source: Nielsen Monitor-Plus

22 GOOD LEADS

Your campaign won't work just because you are spending large amounts of money. Success ultimately depends on the quality of your ads and the strategy you use. We know that with a given sum of money:

1. You will be better off advertising in one market at a time rather than going nationwide from the start.

2. You will be better off spending money in one city than in several.

3. You will be better off spending too much money in one media (TV, print, billboard, etc.) than not enough in several.

4. You will do better to spend too much money in one media than not enough in several.[21]

5. A series of commercials is better than just one.

6. Repetition helps consumers remember your brand, but too many ads over too short a period may be poorly received. Repetition aids consumer learning, but too much too soon may be counter-productive. Heavy media weight may wear out new messages at an accelerated rate.

7. Ads for products with longer shelf lives (such as cars, cameras, and stereos) lose their effectiveness more gradually than ads for frequently purchased items. The negative effects of high-frequency campaigns can be sidestepped by building different ads around a single theme.

8. The more time between each repetition, the longer you can use an ad.

9. If you have a slim budget, a single ad will work better than many in reinforcing consumer retention.

10. If you know when people will be most likely to buy your product, be sure to advertise just before sales pick up.

11. A persuasive ad with a modest budget will prove more effective than a so-so ad with a big budget.[22]

12. Humorous ads lose their effectiveness more quickly than classical ads.

13. A persuasive TV spot that runs at a lower gross rating point far outperforms a less persuasive spot run at a high gross rating point when it comes to purchasing intent, according to the Research Systems Corporation.[23]

14. Studies show that a 15-second TV spot works 60% to 80% as well as a 30-second commercial, which in turn is 70% to 90% as effective as a 60-second ad.

15. When you purchase television and radio time, make sure to *double-spot*. Doublespotting means buying two commercials on the same show. This strategy increases the likelihood that the audience will be exposed to your message.

16. If you can afford it, employ *roadblocking* techniques. This means placing the same commercial on multiple TV channels.

17. If your budget is limited, use the same ads over and over.

18. Don't stop advertising during a recession.[24] Studies by the American Business Press[25] (1974-1975), McGraw-Hill[26] (1974-1975 and 1981-1982), and the Harvard Business Review[27] (1974-1975), have considered the relationships between advertising, sales, and recessions. These studies showed that businesses that failed to cut their ad budgets during recessions did better in subsequent years than those that did.[28]

19. Cut your ad budget in wartime. When the Gulf War broke out, a number of nationwide advertisers, like Procter & Gamble, Sears, Pepsi-Cola, McDonald's, Pizza Hut, Toyota, Miller, Kodak, Ford, AT&T, and American Express, reduced their ad placements. "I don't think [advertising is] proper. There's a backlash potential, and you have to ask, what would you gain from it?" said Louis Schultz, executive VP-director of media services, Lintas: USA.[29]

    Coca-Cola circulated a directive stating that none of its ads should appear in a news bulletin or report pertaining to the war. Chevron cancelled $4 million of media purchases, and TWA eliminated all print ads and TV commercials.[30]

    On the 50th anniversary of the Japanese attack on Pearl Harbor, Japanese manufacturers halted their ads in American media for more than a month. When the second Iraq War broke out in 2003, a number of advertisers, including Volkswagen and Royal

Caribbean Cruises, pulled their commercials off TV. Adolph Coors did likewise, while Procter & Gamble decided to avoid all advertising during news bulletins and programs devoted to the Iraq War.[31]

20. It is better to appear too sensitive than not sensitive enough. During the first anniversary of the 9-11 tragedy, Fox News announced that it would not broadcast any commercials. Advertisers such as Dell, General Motors, Gillette, and Pepsi decided not to advertise their products that day, since they believed the distressing images were not conducive to sales. Nextel, on the other hand, decided to sponsor the presentation of CBS's documentary on 9-11. USAir indefinitely canceled all advertising in the wake of the September 8, 1994 crash of a Boeing 737-300 jet outside of Pittsburgh, which killed all 132 people aboard. Other carriers also suspended or modified their ad accounts.[32]

21. Advertise in publications that have a high interest-response rating. A study conducted by *Reader's Digest* indicates that the higher the consumer's interest is toward the publication in which your advertisement appears—not to be confused with circulation—the higher your advertisement will score on an appreciation scale.

   The Wall Street Journal reported that studies conducted by Simmons Market Research Bureau and Cahners Publishing Company revealed how reader involvement can significantly influence ad recall ability. A reader casually perusing a publication was found to recall a given ad only 34% of the time, while readers deeply immersed in their material recalled a given ad 52% of the time.[33] The study also found that the greater a reader's interest in a publication, the more likely he or she will be not only want to read an ad, but to rate the product over its competitors. Reader involvement also increases believability, purchase intent, and a reader's perception of an ad's effectiveness.

Similar phenomena have in fact been observed with TV commercials. Attention to commercials and their recall percentage increases with program preference. Generally, highly rated programs are more valuable to advertisers than are shows with low ratings. Studies show that viewer attention to poorly rated shows is approximately 22% lower than the attention rating for more highly rated programming.

22. Avoid placing your ads in the same sections as those of your competitors. In a 1989 study conducted among University of Cincinnati undergraduates, Robert Kent, a marketing professor at Drexel University, found that exposure to two competing commercials decreased brand-name recall by more than 25% and advertising-claim recall by roughly 40%.[34]

Research by McDonald's suggests that the effectiveness of commercials is severely reduced when they are scheduled near a competitive spot. Specifically: 1) If a competitor's commercial runs within 30 minutes of your spot, the effectiveness of your commercial message is reduced by 18%; 2) If the competitor's commercial is scheduled within 10 minutes, the loss in impact is 46%; and 3) If the two commercials run back-to-back, the loss in effectiveness is 58%.[35]

DO ADS WORK BETTER IN SOME SEASONS THAN IN OTHERS?

First appearances would suggest that North American media consumption is stable year round. Nothing could be further from the truth.

The time that people spend watching *TV* varies seasonally, being about equal in the spring and fall, dropping about 20% in summer (June, July and August), and peaking in winter (January, February and March).

◆ *Get the best results by repeating your ads on a seasonal basis. Time your ad campaigns to slightly precede or follow peak sales periods.*

Television is not the only media with seasonal peaks and valleys. It seems that people spend about 5% more time reading *magazines* and *newspapers* in the summer than other seasons. The slowest months for these media are July, early August, and January. Advertisers tend to favor the fall and spring.

Billboards also work better in some seasons than others. Recall rates for billboard campaigns are 5% to 6% higher in summer and fall.

Contrary to popular belief, people do not spend more time listening to the *radio* in the summer. However, summertime ad campaigns often include radio spots. Radio helps offset the smaller TV audience during the warm season.

Because it is warmer and people spend more time outside, TV ratings drop during the summer, while billboard performance climbs for the same reasons. That is why media plans often include billboard use during the summer, since studies indicate their effectiveness slightly increases during that period.

ONE OR MORE TYPES OF MEDIA?

Concentrate your purchases in a few different media. As we said earlier, it is generally preferable to spend too much on one media than not enough on several.

Concentration is a key principle of advertising repetition. It is better to maintain a high presence in a small number of locations than a diluted presence in many.

If you have $10,000 to invest in advertising, don't make the mistake of spreading yourself too thin. Select a major media like the radio and a secondary media like brochures. In addition to limiting yourself to a single major media, concentrate your ads within a few broadcasts.

If your budget is less than $50,000, concentrate your efforts in two or three media at most. Identify three particularly profitable periods of the year and purchase your advertising accordingly.

Michael Corbett, author of *33 Ruthless Rules of Local Marketing*, insisted that the most important rule is to dominate a media.[36]

Your ads won't work five times better just because you use five radio stations. And they won't work better just because you use TV, billboards, and radio, rather than just television. Most importantly, you should *concentrate* your efforts.

Before moving on to a second media, you must do very good work with the first. You should aim for a higher saturation rate than the level normally required to inform a target group alone.

HOW OFTEN SHOULD YOU REPEAT YOUR MESSAGE?

It is widely believed that your audience needs to be exposed to your message at least three times for it to work.

Herbert Krugman has said that the first exposure is very special.[37] Like the first exposure to any kind of stimulation, the prevailing reaction is, "What is this?" During the second exposure, the consumer says, "I've seen that before." The second exposure encourages the consumer to think about the offer. The consumer either likes it or not in the third exposure. That's when sales are made.

A direct marketing ad must be repeated at least six times to have a reasonable degree of effectiveness. The number of response coupons will continue rising until the ad has been published ten times.[38] Over a ten-week cycle, the first three weeks of publication represent 20% of all sales, while the last four weeks represent about 50% of all sales.

It is always profitable to concentrate your purchases in the biggest markets. Don't spread yourself too thin, but do learn to identify your primary market.

To increase your advertising's effectiveness a notch, you will do better by over-investing in your primary market and under-investing in secondary ones. In the United States, that would mean over-investing in the ten most important markets. In Canada, that would mean over-investing in Toronto, Vancouver, and Montreal, and under-investing in other Canadian cities. By the same token, it also means over-investing in Ontario and under-investing in the other provinces.

According to AC Nielsen, Ontario receives 44% of Canada's advertising investments. Advertisers as a rule make sure to over-invest in Ontario and under-invest in the rest of Canada.

DISTRIBUTING YOUR REPEAT ADS

Some small businesses want to advertise all year round. It would be wonderful if you could advertise 52 weeks of the year. Unfortunately, this is rarely possible.

To boost the effectiveness of your ad purchases, learn to limit yourself to two or three key periods of the year. Concentration is a key consideration in media placement. Whatever your advertising budget, research teaches us that it is always better to concentrate your repeat ads over time. Rather than advertising every two weeks for six months, place your ad every week for three or four weeks, and repeat this process on two or three occasions.

In advertising, it is important to "limit yourself and always be highly selective. You are better off maintaining a high presence in a few selected periods than being less present throughout the year," according to American ad expert Hobson.

Be realistic: most small businesses (particularly micro-enterprises) lack the budgets to buy ad space throughout the year. It is difficult to catch anyone's eye in Toronto for less than $500,000.

There is also another reason not to constantly bombard customers with your ads. Research shows that, after a certain point, some ads lose their ability to attract an audience. Beyond a certain threshold, they lose their effectiveness.

If you fail to obtain noticeable effects with a single ad, too many ads over a given period may cause a backlash among your readers.

The distribution curve of your ad budget reflects spending strategies throughout your campaign. It is rarely possible for small businesses to advertise 52 weeks of the year. They should learn to select two or three key periods. There are six different ways of planning your repeat ads over time:[39]

1. Constant repetition

This means regularly repeating your ad to produce a uniform degree of exposure. This tactic is recommended if you advertise well-known products with constant sales over time.

2. Seasonal repetition

This strategy involves tailoring your repeat ads to appear just prior to, or during key sales periods. Seasonal repetition is best suited to such products as: lawn mowers, swimming pools, moving firms, and snow blowers.

The sales of almost all products are seasonal. Some are associated with holidays, and others have to do with the different seasons or the climate.

In North America, Christmas generates some 40% of all cell phone sales. January represents 20% of sales by fitness clubs, while fall generates another 15% of enrolments.

Take advantage of these phenomena by placing your ads just before sales volumes climb. This will not only serve to refresh the memories of existing customers, it will give you visibility at the time people are starting to think about your product.

Jo Marney says: "In all these cases, advertising usually begins ahead of the consumer-buying season when people might first begin thinking of such products. Don't fail to utilize the psychological beginnings of seasons. Women's interest in spring usually begins about 67 days ahead of the season. Interest in summer and fall starts 14 days ahead of each of these seasons. And preoccupations with winter start about 36 days before the beginning of winter."[40]

In 1994, the computer industry spent more than $100 million in advertising during the 105 days before Christmas to persuade consumers to buy their products.[41]

3. Periodic repetition

Periodic repetition involves brief bursts of ads at regular intervals. It is recommended for advertising during maintenance campaigns, for products that are in mature or declining phases, and if your ads are humorous in nature.

4. Irregular repetition

This strategy involves repeating your ads at irregular intervals. Use it to monitor irregular customer traffic or to modify cycles of behavior. Fitness centers usually use irregular repetition to ensure that their ad investments coincide with the three biggest enrolment periods: New Year's, the start of summer, and the back-to-school period.

5. During product launch

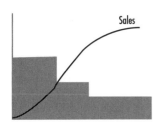

This strategy involves producing lots of advertising during the launch of a new product to get people to try it out and like it. It is probably the best formula for small businesses. Use it for launch campaigns and to get people to take advantage of a new promotional campaign.

When Helene Curtis launched Vibrance shampoo, the company spent $55 million. Procter & Gamble Co. put $60 million in advertising behind Aleve in its first year.[42]

Colgate spent about $40 million in the first six months of '95 to introduce Colgate Baking Soda & Peroxide with Tartar Control toothpaste.[43]

Sterling Health USA set aside $116 million for the launch of Bayer Select non-aspirin pain reliever.

IBM Corp. invested $20 million in three months for the new Aptiva multimedia computer.[44] Industry executives estimate that the average marketing cost per designer fragrance launch has risen from $4 million to nearly $16 million over the last four years.[45]

In 1994, ad expenditures on America's top 10 political campaigns totaled about $1 billion.[46]

6. Intensive repetition

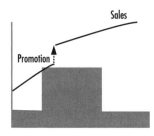

This strategy involves producing intensive ads to elicit a strong and fast response, as with the distribution of samples and discount coupons. I recommend this strategy to get people to try your product, to buy it a second time, or to make multiple purchases.

In 1885, Thomas Smith wrote:

- "The first time a man looks at an advertisement, he does not see it.
- The second time he does not notice it.
- The third he is conscious of its existence.
- The fourth time he faintly remembers having seen it before.

- The fifth time he reads it.

- The sixth time he turns up his nose at it.

- The seventh time he reads it through and says, "Oh bother!"

- The eighth time he says, "Here's that confounded thing again!"

- The ninth time he wonders if it amounts to anything.

- The tenth time he thinks he will ask his neighbor if he has tried it.

- The eleventh time he wonders how the advertiser makes it pay.

- The twelfth time he thinks perhaps it may be worth something.

- The thirteenth time he thinks it must be a good thing.

- The fourteenth time he remembers that he has wanted such a thing for a long time.

- The fifteenth time he is tantalized because he cannot afford to buy it.

- The sixteenth time he thinks he will buy it some day.

- The seventeenth time he makes a memorandum of it.

- The eighteenth time he swears at his poverty.

- The nineteenth time he counts his money carefully.

- The twentieth time he sees it, he buys the article, or instructs his wife to do so."[47]

This holds true today.

Advertising: art or science?

When asked if advertising is an art or a science, Jules Arren, one of the first experts in this field, replied:

"Advertising will never evolve into a precise science like mathematics. Advertising operates in a variety of ways, has a great flexibility and is extremely complex, in fact it is like the human spirit. The human factor has too large a role in the calculations of advertising, thus making it difficult to boil down into exact theories and formulas.

"That does not mean that in advertising, as in psychology, there are no laws or general rules that should be understood and applied. If we classify the sciences, by separating the mathematical sciences, which alone are exact because they consider abstractions, we notice that if the object studied is concrete, real, alive, complex, the exact laws become uncertain and rare, and their reasoning becomes empirical. Between mathematics and meteorology, the science of advertising occupies a space neighboring psychology.

Without question, advertising has to follow a certain methodology and utilize simple calculations that would relate it to an imperfect science, true enough, but not an art.

We should force ourselves by accurate observation and experimentation to formulate new laws, to calculate with increasing exactitude the fixed values of an advertising success; to formulate the axioms with greater precision , and not to fall into the trap of awaiting genius, nor to leave your success to good fortune."[1]

I concur with this viewpoint. I do not believe advertising is an exact science, but I also do not believe that personal opinions or intuition go a long way in producing successful ad campaigns.

Ad creators around the world proclaim that advertising is an art and that anyone who disagrees with them is wrong. Who are they to make such a claim? What proof do they have?

Coca-Cola's former head of marketing, Sergio Zyman, once said that ad agencies have taken refuge in the joyful mystery of creation. For Zyman, advertising is a science in which everything breaks down into precise figures. Its activities include experimentation, control, analysis, tweaking, and the reproducibility of results. That is why ad impact should be assessed in terms of sales generated.

Bill Bernbach once said: "Today, everybody is talking creativity, and frankly, that's got me worried. I fear all the sins we may commit in the name of creativity. I fear that we may be entering an age of phonies."[2]

Helmut Krone claimed that advertising is confused. "This word 'creativity' has gotten totally out of hand, and I feel sorry for the clients. They're not getting a fair shake. The name of the game seems to be: make nonsense commercials. If they mean something, they're not creative enough."[3]

I personally believe that the best way to conduct a successful campaign is to apply a certain number of well-tested principles.

"Unfortunately, when commercials are as common as a car horn in New York—and maybe as effective—it's ironic that [top executives] say we know less now about the effectiveness of advertising than we did 40 years ago," says Mr. Chris Whittle, Chairman of Whittle Communications.[4]

You will never get anyone to buy your product without promising something in return. Do you think consumers will buy your product just because they like you? I really doubt it. But many ad people refuse to believe this principle.

One rule is certain and will never change: *advertising's job is to sell, and the surest way to achieve this goal is by learning the rules of the trade.*

Notes

Introduction

1. Goodrum, Charles and Helen Dalrymple. *Advertising in America,* New York, Abrams Harry, 1990; Baker, Stephen, *Visual Persuasion,* New York, McGraw-Hill, 1961.

2. Newspaper Association of America. *What Makes a Good Newspaper Ad?,* 1993.

3. Morris, Desmond. *Bodywatching: A Field Guide to the Human Species,* New York, Crown Publishers, 1985, p. 13.

Chapter 1

1. Reeves, Rosser. *Reality in Advertising,* New York, Alfred A. Knopp, 1961, p. 47.

2. "Exclusive: Teens' Take On Brands," *Advertising Age,* February 21, 2005, p. S-4.

3. Meskill, John. "The Media Mix", *4A Media Letter,* January 1979, p. 1-2.

Chapter 2

1. Ries, Al and Jack Trout. *Positioning: The Battle for your Mind,* New York, Warner Books, 1986, p. 6.

2. Rapp, Stan and Tom Collins. *The Great Marketing Turnaround,* New York, Plume Book, 1992, pp. 16-17.

3. Williams, Christopher. "Home Depot Enters New Growth Phase," *National Post,* October 11, 2004, p. FP.6.

4. Packard, Vance. *The Hidden Persuaders,* New York, David McKay Company, 1957, p. 46.

5. Ries, Al and Jack Trout. *Bottom-Up Marketing,* New York, McGraw-Hill, 1989, p. 127.

6. Sshlosberg, Harold. "A Comparison of Five Shaving Creams by the Method of Constant Stimuli", *Journal of Applied Psychology,* vol. 25, n° 4, August 1951, pp. 401-407.

7. Allison, Ralph and Kenneth Uhl. "Influence of Beer Brand Identification on Taste Perception", *Journal of Marketing Research,* vol. 1, n° 3, August 1964, pp. 36-39.

8. Pronko, Nicholas and W. Bowles. "Identification of Cola Beverages. 1. First Study", *Journal of Applied Psychology,* vol. 32, n° 3, June 1948, pp. 304-312; "Identification of Cola Beverages. II. A Further Study", *Journal of Applied Psychology,* vol. 32, n° 5, October 1948, pp. 559-564; "Identification of Cola Beverages. III. A Final Study", *Journal of Applied Psychology,* vol. 33, n° 6, December 1949, pp. 605-608; Pronko, Nicholas and D.T. Herman. "Identification of Cola Beverages. IV. Postcript", *Journal of Applied Psychology,* vol. 34, n° 1, February 1950, pp. 68-69.

9. Ries, Al and Jack Trout. *Positioning: The Battle for your Mind,* New York, Warner Books, 1986, p. 30.

10. Carpenter, Gregory S. and Kent Nakamoto. "Consumer Preference Formation and Pioneering Advantage", *Journal of Marketing Research,* vol. 26, n° 3, August 1989, pp. 285-298; Robinson, William T. "Sources of Market Pioneer Advantages: The Case of Industrial Goods Industries", *Journal of Marketing Research,* vol. 25, n° 1, February 1988, pp. 87-94; Robinson, William T. and Claes Fornell. "Sources of Market Pioneering Advantages in Consumer Goods Industries", *Journal of Marketing Research,* vol. 22, n° 3, August 1985, pp. 305-318; Urban, Glen, Theresa Carter, Steve Gaskin and Zofia Mucha. "Market Share Rewards Pioneering Brands: An Empirical Analysis and Strategie Implications", *Management Science,* vol. 32, June 1986, pp. 645-659.

11. Boston Consulting Group. "The Rule of Three and Four", *Perspectives,* n° 197, 1976; The Boston Consulting Group in John Rossiter and Larry Percy. *Advertising & Promotion Management,* New York, McGraw-Hill, 1987, p. 53.

12. Buzzell, Robert. "Are There 'Natural' Market Structures?", *Journal of Marketing,* vol. 45, n° 1, Winter 1981, pp. 42-51.

13. Lubliner, Murray J. "Old Standbys' Hold Their Own", *Advertising Age,* September 19, 1983, p. 32.

14. Howell, Debbie. "Another Day, Another Dollar," *Chain Store Age,* New York, Spring 2005, p. 8.

15. Ibid.

16. McConnell, Douglas. "The Price-Quality Relationship in an Experimental Setting", *Journal of Marketing Research,* vol. 5, n° 3, August 1968, pp. 300-303.

17. Andrews, Robert and Enzo R. Valenzi. "The Relationship Between Price and Blind-Rated Quality for Margarines and Butters", *Journal of Marketing Research,* vol. 7, n° 3, August 1970, pp. 393-395.

18. Levitt, Harold J. "A Note on Some Experimental Findings About the Meaning of Price", *The Journal of Business,* vol. 27, n° 3, July, 1954, pp. 205-210.

19. Scitovszky, Tibor. "Some Consequences of the Habit of Judging Quality by Price", *The Review of Economic Studies,* vol. 12, Summer 1945, pp. 100-105.

20. Stafford, James E. and Ben Enis. "The Price-Quality Relationship: an Extension", *Journal of Marketing Research,* vol. 6, n° 4, November 1969, p. 456-458.

21. Tull, Donald, R. A. Boring and M. H. Gonsior. "A Note on the Relationship of Price and Imputed Quality", *The Journal of Business,* vol. 37, n° 2, April 1964, pp. 186-191.

22. Koten, John. "Teen-Age Girls, Alas, Are Big Consumers-But Poor Customers", *The Wall Street Journal,* November 9, 1984, pp. 1, 24.

23. Busch, Anita. "Sexier the Better, Student Body Says", *Advertising Age,* February 5, 1990, p. S-1.

24. American Association of Magazine Publishers. "A Documentary on the Power of Magazines", *Newsletter of Research,* n° 55, December 1987, p. 5.

25. Clark, Eric. *The Want Makers,* New York, Penguin Books, 1990, pp. 181-182.

26. Newspaper Association of America (1993). Teens and Newspapers: 10 surprises.

27. ICR. *Girl Power, Teen Girls Spend More Than Boys,* 2005.

28. "How to Advertise to the 50-Plus Market", Bozell, n° 10.

29. Ward, Adrienne. "Senior-Slanted Media Reap Auto Bounty", *Advertising Age*, July 24, 1989, pp. S-21-22.

30. American Association of Magazine Publisher. "A Documentary on the Power of Magazines", *Newsletter of Research*, n° 55, December 1987, p. 10.

31. Speros, James. "Why The Harley Brand's So Hot", *Advertising Age*, March 15, 2004, p. 26.

32. U.S. Census Bureau.

33. Kim, Junu Bryan. "Doing the Right Thing - Two Approaches", *Advertising Age*, July 1, 1991, p. 18.

34. "Tetley Brings Round Tea Bags to U.S.", *Advertising Age*, April 15, 1991, p. 12; Winters, Patricia, "Tetley Round Tea Bags Challenge No 1 Lipton", *Advertising Age*, January 1, 1993, p. 2.

35. Twedt, Dik Warren. "How Important to Marketing Strategy Is the Heavy User?", *Journal of Marketing*, vol. 28, n° l, January 1964, pp. 71-72.

36. "Absolut Built on the Edge", *Advertising Age*, April 9, 1990, p. 55.

37. Freeman, Laurie, "Animal Uproar", *Advertising Age*, February 26, 1990, p. S-2.

38. "Kodak Fun Saver", *Advertising Age*, July 6, 1992, p. S-22.

39. Rosenthal, Rachel. "Good Old Things in New Packages", *Advertising Age*, August 1, 1994, p. 12.

40. Coombes, Andrea. CBS MarketWatch.com, October 9, 2002.

41. Warner, Lloyd, Marchia Meeker and Kenneth Eells. Social Class in America, Gloucester (Mass.), P. Smith, 1957, 274 p.

42. "Perrier: the Astonishing Success of An Appeal to Affluent Adults", *Business Week*, January 22 1979, pp. 64-65; Finkelman, Bernice. "Perrier fours Into U.S. Market, Spurs Water Bottier Battle", *Marketing News*, September 7, 1979, pp. 1-9.

43. Donaton, Scott. "Self Sorts Women by Attitudes", *Advertising Age*, October 16, 1989, p. 32

44. Pillsbury's News. "Pillsbury's Research Identifies Five Clusters of American Eaters", San Diego, Febuary 13, 1988.

45. Van den Bergh, Bruce G. "Feedback: More Chickens and Pickles", *Journal of Advertising Research*, vol. 21, n° 6, December 1982, January 1983, p. 44; see also Van den Bergh, Bruce G., Janay Collins, Myrna Schultz and Keith Adler. "Sound Advice on Brand Names", *Journalism Quarterly*, vol. 61, n° 4, Winter 1984, pp. 835-840.

46. "A Rose by any other Name..." *Advertising Age*, October 31, 1994, p. 39.

47. Sexton, Richard. *American Style*, San Francisco, Chronicle Books, 1987, p. 17.

48. "Style is Substance for Ad Success: Light", *Advertising Age*, August 27, 1979, p. 3.

49. Fisher, Christy. "Nestle's Chocolate Aero Targets Women", *Advertising Age*, April 5, 1993, p. 4.

50. Meyers, Janet. "Black and Decker Ups Share in Hardware", *Advertising Age*, July 24, 1989, p. 28.

51. Deveney, Kathleen. "Why Outlook Is Murky for Clear Products", *The Globe and Mail*, March 16, 1994, p. A9.

Chapter 3

1. Krugman, Herbert E. "What Makes Advertising Effective?", *Harvard Business Review*, vol. 53, n° 2, March-April 1975, p. 96.

2. Dupont, Luc. *Images That Sell*, Sainte-Foy, White Rock Publishing, 2000, pp. 7-9.

3. Beatson, Ronald. "Reaching United Europe Won't Be a Simple Task", *Advertising Age*, April 9, 1990, p. 31.

4. Plisken, Robert. "Some of the Most Carefully Chosen Words Are Pictures", In *Advertising. An Omnibus of Advertising*, prepared by *Printers' Ink*, pp. 113-146.

5. Caples, John. *Tested Advertising Methods*, Englewood Cliffs, N.J., Prentice Hall, 1987, p. 212.

6. Martineau, Pierre. *Motivation in Advertising*, New York, McGraw-Hill, 1957, pp. 125-126.

7. Hepner, Harry. *Advertising, Creative Communications with Consumers*, New York, McGraw-Hill, 1964, p. 462.

8. Hepner, Harry. *Advertising, Creative Communications with Consumers*, New York, McGraw-Hill, 1964, p. 462.

9. McCollum/Spielman. "And a Child Shall Lead Them: A Review of Commercials Featuring Children", *Topline*, December 1986.

10. Whittler, Tommy E. "The Effects of Actors' Race in Commercial Advertising: Review and Extension", *Journal of Advertising*, vol. 20, n° 1, 1991, pp. 54-60.

11. Thomaselli, Rich. "MLB Reversal Fuels Ad Boundary Debate", *Advertising Age*, May 10, 2004, pp. 3, 65.

12. Roman, Kenneth and Jane Maas. *How to Advertise,* New York, St. Martin's Press, 1976, p. 34; Maas, Jane. *Better Brochures, Catalogs and Mailing,* New York, St. Martin's Press, 1981, p. 21.

13. Hopkins, Claude. *Mes succès en publicité,* Paris, La Publicité, 1927, pp. 110-111 and pp. 140-141.

14. Swasy, Alicia. *Soap Opera: The Inside Story of Procter & Gamble,* New York, Times Books, 1993, p. 107.

15. McDonald's. "McDonald's 1981", *Basic Media Seminar Manual, McDonald's Corporation,* 1980, p. 2.

16. Teinowitz, Ira and Steven W. Colford. "Old Joe a Winner Even with Ad Ban", *Advertising Age,* August 16, 1993, pp. 1, 37; Levin, Gary. "Poll: Camel Ads Effective With Kids", *Advertising Age,* April 27, 1992, p. 12; Wells, Melanie, "Mezzina/Brown Rides Joe Camel into Notoriety", *Advertising Age,* April 11, 1994, p. 46.

17. Atkinson, Claire. "Brawny Man Now A Metrosexual", *Advertising Age,* February 16, 2004, p. 8.

18. Ogilvy, David. "We Sell. Or Else", *The Advertiser,* Summer 1992, p. 22.

19. Lafayette, Jon. "Scandal ruts focus on ad visuals", *Advertising Age,* November 26, 1990, p. 62.

20. Bauer, Raymond Augustine and Stephen A. Greyser. *Advertising in America, the Consumer View,* Boston, Division of Research, Harvard Business School, 1968, pp. 173-177.

21. Mayer, Martin. *Madison Avenue USA,* New York, Pocket Books, 1958, p. 66.

22. Schwab, Victor O. *How to Write a Good Advertisement,* New York, H. Wolff, 1942, p. 9.

23. Caples, John. *Tested Advertising Methods,* Englewood Cliffs (N.J.), Prentice Hall, 1987, p. 205.

24. Baker, Michael and Gilbert A. Churchill Jr. "The Impact of Physically Attractive Models on Advertising Evaluations", *Journal of Marketing Research,* vol. 14, n° 4, November 1977, pp. 538-555.

25. Smith, G. H. and R. Engel. "Influence of a Female Model on Perception Characteristics of an Automobile", *Proceedings of the 76th Annual Convention of the American Psychological Association,* vol. 3, 1968, pp. 681-682.

26. Steadman, Major. "How Sexy Illustrations Affect Brand Recall", *Journal of Advertising Research,* vol. 9, n° l, March 1969, pp. 15-19.

27. Alexander, Wayne and Ben Judd Jr. "Do Nudes in Ads Enhance Brand Recall?", *Journal of Advertising Research,* vol. 18, n° 1, February 1978, pp. 47-50.

28. Myers, Gerry. *Targeting the New Professional Woman,* Chicago, Probus, 1994, p. 157.

29. Cohen, Dorothy. *Advertising,* Glenview (Illinois), Scott Foresman, 1988, p. 514.

30. Pfau, M. and R. Parrott. *Persuasive Communication Campaigns,* Boston, Allyn & Bacon, p. 126.

31. "Nuprin's Ad Smash Hit", *Advertising Age,* October 14, 1991, p. 3.

32. Hovland, C. and W. Weiss. "The Influence of Source Credibility on Communication Effectiveness", *Public Opinion Quarterly,* 15, 1951, pp. 635-650; Schulman, G. and C. Worrall. "Salience Patterns, Source Credibility, and the Sleeper Effect", *Public Opinion Quarterly,* 34, 1970, pp. 371-382; Warren, I. "The Effect of Credibility in Sources of Testimony on Audience Attitudes Toward Speaker and Message", *Speech Monographs,* vol. 6, 1969, pp. 456-458.

33. Friedman, Hershey H. and Linda Friedman. "Endorser Effectiveness by Product Type", *Journal of Advertising Research,* vol. 19, n° 5, October 1979, p. 70.

34. Fisher, Christy. "Garfield's Suite Role Gets Cut", *Advertising Age,* June 18, 1990, p. 14.

35. "Can Celebrities Really Sell Products?", *Marketing & Media Decisions,* September 1984, pp. 64-66.

36. Atkin, Charles and Martin Block. "Effectiveness of Celebrity Endorsers", *Journal of Advertising Research,* vol. 23, n° 1, February-March 1983, pp. 57-61.

37. "The '80s", *Advertising Age,* January 1, 1990, p. 23.

38. Fisher, Chrysty. "Butterfinger", *Advertising Age,* July 5, 1993, p. S-9.

39. Sloan, Pat. "Calvin Klein Underwear", *Advertising Age,* July 5, 1993, pp. 5-12.

40. Kahle, Lynn R. and Pamela M. Homer. "Physical Attractiveness of the Celebrity Endorser: A Social Adaptation Perspective", *The Journal of Consumer Research,* vol. 11, n° 4, March 1985, pp. 954-961; Swasy John L. and James M. Munch. "Examining the Target Receiver Elaborations: Rhetorical Question Effects on Source Processing and Persuasion", *The Journal of Consumer Research,* vol. 11, n° 4, March 1985, pp. 877-886.

41. Alsop, Ronald, "Jaded TV Viewers Tune Out Glut of Celebrity Commercials", *The Wall Street Journal,* February 7, 1985, p. 33.

42. Winters, Patricia. "Diet Colas Deap Comparative Tactic", *Advertising Age,* January 21, 1991, p. 24.

43. "Can Celebrities Really Sell Products?", *Marketing & Media Decisions,* September 1984, pp. 64-66.

44. Geiger, Bob. "The Good Guys Finish First", *Advertising Age*, March 5, 1990, p. S-1.

45. Mandese, Joe. "Steward, Cosby Top Q Ratings: Where's Mike?", *Advertising Age*, August 31, 1992, pp. 3, 40.

46. Advertising Age Roundup, "Endorsement Slump", *Advertising Age*, April 8, 1991, p. 3; Levin, Gary. "Baseball's Endorsement Shutout", *Advertising Age*, February 15, 1993, p. 16.

47. Ibid.

48. Vaske, Hermann. "There Is No Excuse for Bad Work", Archive, vol. 6, December 1993, p. 15.

49. *The Wall Street Journal* advertisement.

Chapter 4

1. Fox, Stephen. *The Mirror Makers,* New York, Vintage, 1984, p. 113.

2. Janis, Irving L. and Seymour Feshbach. "Effects of Fear Arousing Communications", Journal of Abnormal and Social Psychology, vol. 48, n° 1, January 1953, pp. 78-92.

3. Marney, Jo. "The Headline's the Thing", *Marketing*, November 17, 1986, p. 8.

4. Reeves, Rosser. *Reality in Advertising*, New York, Alfred A. Knopf, 1961, p. 47.

5. Howard, John and Jagdish N. Sheth. *The Theory of Buyer Behavior,* New York, John Willey & Sons, 1969, pp. 147-148.

6. Brock, Timothy, Stuart M. Albert and Lee Alan Becker. "Familiarity, Utility and Supportiveness as Determinants of Information Receptivity", *Journal of Personality and Social Psychology,* vol. 14, n° 4, 1970, pp. 292-301.

7. Ogilvy, David. *Confessions of an Advertising Man*, New York, Athenaeum, 1966, p. 111.

8. Swasy, Alecia. *Soap Opera: The Inside Story of Procter & Gamble*, New York, Random House, 1993, p. 89.

9. Berlyne, Daniel E. "Conflict and Information Theory Variables as Determinants of Human Perceptuel Curiosity", *Journal of Experimental Psychology*, vol. 53, n° 6, June 1957, pp. 399-404; "Novelty and Curiosity as Determinants of Exploratory Behaviour", *The British Journal of Psychology,* vol. 41, parts 1 and 2, September 1950, pp. 68-80.

10. Levinson, Jay Conrad. *Guerrilla Marketing Excellence,* New York, Houghton Mifflin Company, 1993, p. 37.

11. Honomichl, Jack J. "The Ongoing Saga of Mother Baking Soda", *Advertising Age,* September 20, 1982, pp. M-2, M-3 and M-22.

12. Plummer, Joseph. "Outliving the Myths", *Journal of Advertising Research,* February-March 1990, p. 27.

13. Clancy, Kevin and Robert Shulman. *Marketing Myths That Are Killing Business,* McGraw-Hill, New York, 1993, p. 81.

14. Hopkins, Claude. *My Life in Advertising/Scientific Advertising,* Lincolnwood, Illinois, 1986, p. 191.

15. Rapp, Stan and Thomas L. Collins. *MaxiMarketing,* Paris, McGraw-Hill, 1988, p. 46.

16. Berelson, Bernard and Gary Steiner. *Human Behavior: An Inventory of Scientific Findings,* Harcourt, Brace & World, 1964, p. 540.

17. Strunk, William and E. B. White. *The Element of Style,* New York, Collier MacMillan, 1959, pp. 15-16.

18. Percy, Larry and John Rossiter. "10 Ways to More Ads Via Visual Imagery Psycholinguistics", *Marketing News,* February 19, 1982, p. 10.

19. Martineau, Pierre. *Motivation in Advertising,* New York, McGraw-Hill, 1957, p. l.

20. Marney, Jo. "In the End It's All a Matter of Words", *Marketing,* January 4, 1982, p. 9.

21. Levinson, Jay Conrad. *Guerrilla Advertising,* Boston, Houghton Mifflin Company, 1994, p. 176.

22. Johnson, Bradley and Jennifer Lawrence. "From Beer to Diapers, 'Ultra' Is the Ultimate Tag", *Advertising Age,* July 15, 1991, pp. 3, 13.

23. Freeman, Laurie and Patricia Winters. "Extra! Extra! Read All About It", *Advertising Age,* May 22, 1989, p. 12.

24. Rudolph, Harold. *Attention and Interest Factors in Advertising Survey, Analysis, Interpretation,* New York, Funk & Wagnalls Company with Printers' Ink Publishing Co., 1947, pp. 46-47.

25. Miller, George A. "The Magical Number Seven, Plus or Minus Two: Some Limits on Our Capacity to Process Information", *Psychological Review,* vol. 63, n° 2, 1956, pp. 81-87.

26. Caples, John. *Tested Advertising Methods,* Prentice Hall, Englewood Cliffs, 1987, p. 38.

27. Marney, Jo. "Delivering the Promise", *Marketing,* June 7, 1982, p. 12.; *Laboratory of Advertising Performance,* New York, McGraw-Hill Research, 1950, Data Sheet # 3200.

28. McGraw-Hill. *Laboratory of Advertising Performance,* New York, McGraw-Hill Research, 1950, Data Sheet 3200.

29. Marney, Jo. "The Headline's the Thing", *Marketing,* November 17, 1986, p. 8.

Chapter 5

1. Rossiter, John R. "The Increase in Magazine Ad Readership", *Journal of Advertising Research,* vol. 28, n° 5, October-November 1988, pp. 35-39.

2. *The Wall Street Journal* advertisement.

3. *The Wall Street Journal* advertisement.

4. Starch, Daniel. *Measuring Advertising Readership and Results,* New York, McGraw-Hill, 1966, p. 103.

5. Roman, Kenneth and Joel Raphaelson. *Writing that Works,* New York, Harper & Row, 1981, p. 2.

6. Politz, Alfred. "Dilemma of Creative Advertising", *Journal of Marketing,* vol. 25, n° 2, October 1960, p. 1.

7. Starch, Daniel. "Why Readership of Ads Has Increased 24 %", *Advertising & Selling,* August 1946, p. 47.

8. Flesch, Rudolph. *How to Test Readability,* New York, Harper & Brothers, 1951, 56 p.

9. McGuire, William. "The Nature of Attitude and Attitude Change", in Gardner Linsley and Elliot Aronson. *The Handbook of Social Psychology, Reading,* Massachusetts, Addison-Wesley Publishing Co., vol. 3, 2nd edition, 1968, chapter 21, pp. 136-314.

10. Burnett, Leo. *Communications of an Advertising Man,* Chicago, Leo Burnett Co., 1961, p. 246.

11. Packard, Vance. *The Hidden Persuaders,* New York, David McKay Company, Inc., 1957, p. 152.

12. Graham, Judith. "Electronics Retailers Tone Down", *Advertising Age,* December 4, 1989, p. 6.

13. Woolf, James D. "Salesense in Advertising... Outstanding Advertising Need Not Stretch the Truth", *Advertising Age,* March 18, 1957, p. 81.

14. Hovland, Carl and Wallace Mandell. "An Experimental Comparison of Conclusion-Drawing by the Communicator and by the Audience", *Journal of Abnormal and Social Psychology*, vol. 47, n° 3, July 1952, pp. 581-588.

15. Caples, John. *Tested Advertising Methods*, Englewood Cliffs, Prentice Hall, 1987, pp. 138-139.

16. Hodgson, Richard S. *The Dartnell Direct Mail and Mail Order Handbook*, Chicago, The Dartnell Corporation, 1964, p. 390.

17. Newman, Joseph W. and Richard Staelin. "Prepurchase Information Seeking for New Cars and Major House-hold Appliances", *Journal of Marketing Research*, vol. 9, n° 3, August 1972, pp. 249-257.

18. O'Toole, John. *The Trouble with Advertising: A View from the Inside*, New York, Times Books, 1985, pp. 3-4.

19. Bearden, William O. and Terence A. Shimp. "Warranty and Other Extrinsic Cue Effects on Consumers' Risk Perceptions", *Journal of Consumer Research*, vol. 9, n° l, June 1982, p. 38-46; Sexton, Richard. *American Style*, San Francisco, Chronicle Books, 1987, p. 17.

20. Shuchman, Abe and Peter Riesz. "Correlates of Persuasibility: the Crest Case", *Journal of Marketing Research*, vol. 12, n° 2, February 1975, pp. 7-11.

21. Lord, Laura. "The Club", *Advertising Age*, July 5, 1993, pp. 5-19.

22. Serafin, Raymond. "Cars Squeeze Mileage From Awards", *Advertising Age*, June 4, 1990, p. 36.

23. Hopkins, Claude. *My Life in Advertising/Scientific Advertising*, Lincolnwood (Illinois), Crain Books, 1986, p. 119.

24. Hume, Scott. "Clinton Serves MCD's a PR Feast", *Advertising Age*, December 14, 1992, p. 6.

25. Bly, Robert. *The Copywriter's Handbook: A Step-by-step Guide to Writing Copy that Sells*, New York, Dodd, Mead & Company, 1985, pp. 22-23.

26. Cone, Edward F. "Terrific! I Hate it", *Forbes*, June 27, 1988, pp. 130-132.

27. Weinberger, Marc G. and Harlan E. Spotts. "Humor in U.S. Versus U.K.-TV Advertising", *Journal of Advertising*, vol. 18, n° 2, 1989, pp. 39-44.

28. Madden, Thomas J. and Marc G. Weinberger. "Humor in Advertising: A Practitioner View", *Journal of Advertising Research*, vol. 24, n° 4, 1984, p. 23-29.

29. McCollum Spielman. "Focus on Funny", *Top Line*, vol. 3, n° 3, July 1982.

30. Madden, Thomas J. and Marc G. Weinberger. "The Effects of Humor on Attention in Magazine Advertising", *Journal of Advertising,* vol. 11, n° 3, 1982, pp. 8-14.

31. Stewart, David M. and David H. Furse. *Effective Television Advertising,* Lexington (MA), D.C. Heath and Company, Chicago, 1986.

32. Weinberger, Marc G. and Leland Campbell. "The Use and Impact of Humor in Radio Advertising", *Journal of Advertising Research,* vol. 31, December/January 1991, pp. 44-52.

33. Madden, Thomas J. "Humor in Advertising: Applications of a Hierarchy of Effects Paradigm", *Journal of Advertising Research,* 1982.

34. Madden, Thomas J. and Marc G. Weinberger. "Humor in Advertising: A Practitioner View", *Journal of Advertising Research,* vol. 24, n° 4, 1984, p. 23-29.

35. Madden, Thomas J. and Marc G. Weinberger. "Humor in Advertising: A Practitioner View", *Journal of Advertising Research,* vol. 24, n° 4, 1984, p. 23-29; Ogilvy Center, 1985 and Biel and Bridgwater, 1990 in "Does Commercial Liking Matter?", *Topline.*

36. Gelb, Betsy and George M. Zinkhan. "The Effect of Repetition on Humor in a Radio Advertising Study", *Journal of Advertising Research?,*vol. 14, n° 4, 1985, pp. 13-20, 68.

37. Madden, Thomas J. and Marc G. Weinberger. "Humor in Advertising: A Practitioner View", *Journal of Advertising Research,* vol. 24, n° 4, 1984, p. 23-29.

38. Landler, Mark and coll. "What Happened to Advertising", *Business Week,* September 23, 1991, p. 71.

39. Schultz, Don E. and William A. Robinson. *Sales Promotion Essentials,* Lincolnwood (Illinois), NTC Business Books, 1989, p. 6.

40. "Free Standing Inserts Remain Stable as Couponing Consolidates", NCH Promotional Services Ltd., SR0103, March 2003.

41. Hume, Scott. "Couponing Reaches Record Clip", *Advertising Age,* February 3, 1992, p. 1; "Coupon Capitals", *Advertising Age,* August 1990, p. 14.

42. Hume, Scott. "Redeeming Feature", *Advertising Age,* February 4, 1991, p. 35.

43. Rapp, Stan and Tom Collins. *The Great Marketing Turnaround,* New York, Plume Book, 1992, p. 29.

44. Holmes, John H. and John D. Lett. "Product Sampling and Word of Mouth", *Journal of Advertising Research,* vol. 17, n° 5, October 1977, pp. 34-40.

45. Sloan, Pat and Scott Donaton. "Sampling Smells Sweet for Scent Biz", *Advertising Age,* August 3, 1992, p. 17.

46. Barnes, Julian. "Fast-Food Giveaway Toys Face Rising Recalls", *The New York Times,* August 16, 2001, p. A1.

47. Hopkins, Claude. *My Life in Advertising/Scientific Advertising,* Lincolnwood (Illinois), 1986, p. 105.

48. Cahners Advertising Research Report. "How Important to Readers is the Mention of Price in an Advertisement?", *Cahners Advertising Research Report,* New York, 1979, n° 115.

49. Marney, Jo. "Proof that it Pays to Advertise During Times of Economic Slowdown", *Marketing,* December 14, 1981, pp. 24 and 26.

50. Anonyme. "Supermarket Psych-Out", *Tufts University Health & Nutrition Letter,* New York, vol. 16, n° 11, January 1999, pp. 1, 3.

51. Winters, Patricia. "Rapt Up in Packages: Special Designs Can Offer Marketing Value", *Advertising Age,* December 3, 1990. pp. 4, 40.

52. Winters, Patricia. "MagiCan Maladies", *Advertising Age,* May 21, 1990, p. 3, 62; "Coke and Gadgetry's Pitfalls", *Advertising Age,* June 4, 1990, p. 20.

53. Thomaselli, Rich. "Who Really Reaps Mileage Rewards?", *Advertising Age,* June 20, 2005, p. 12.

54. Jones, John Philip. *What's in a Name?,* Massachusetts, Lexington Books, 1986, pp. 2-3, p. 106.

55. Guadagni, Peter and John D. C. Little. "A Logic Model of Brand Choice Calibrated on Scanner Data", *Marketing Science,* vol. 2, Summer 1983, pp. 203-238; Gupta, Sunil. "Impact of Sales Promotion on When, What, and How Much to Buy", *Journal of Marketing Research,* vol. 25, n° 4, November 1988, pp. 342-355; Neslin, Scott A., Caroline Henderson and John Quelch. "Consumer Promotions and the Acceleration of Product Purchases", *Marketing Science,* vol. 4, Summer 1985, pp. 147-165.

56. Haugh, Louis J. "Questioning the Spread of Coupons", *Advertising Age,* August 22, 1983, p. M-31.

57. English, Mary McCabe. "Like it or Not, Coupons Are Here to Stay", *Advertising Age,* August 22, 1983, pp. M-26, M-27, M-28.

58. Freeman, Laurie and Jennifer Lawrence. "Brand Building Gets New Life", *Advertising Age,* September 4, 1989, p. 3.

59. Serafin, Raymond. "Goodyear Back to Brand Building", *Advertising Age,* December 4, 1989, p. 14.

60. Graham, Judith. "Electronics Retailers Tone Down", *Advertising Age,* December 4, 1989, p. 6.

61. "O&M's Phillips Decries 'Brand Rape'", *Advertising Age,* May 14, 1990, p. 52.

62. Rapp, Stan and Tom Collins. *The Great Marketing Turnaround,* New York, Plume Book, 1992, p. 19.

63. Levinson, Jay Conrad. *Guerrilla Marketing Excellence,* New York, Houghton Mifflin Company, 1993, p. 74.

64. Clancy, Kevin and Dan Belmont. "Top of Mind", *Brandweek,* vol. 45, n° 29, August 9, 2004, p. 25.

65. Thomaselli, Rich. "Nielsen Measures Sports Sponsorship", *Advertising Age,* May 3, 2004, p. 14.

66. Marney, Jo. "CARF Plans for the Future", *Marketing,* March 27, 1989, p. 10.

67. Schlossberg, Howard. "Fans Favors Corporate Sponsors in Tennis", *Marketing News,* July 22, 1991.

68. Hume, Scott. "Sports Sponsorship Value Measured", *Advertising Age,* August 6, 1990, p. 22.

69. Hansen, Flemming and Lene Scotwin. "An Experimental Enquiry into Sponsoring: What Effects Can Be Measured?", *Marketing and Research Today,* August 1995, pp. 173-181; Kerstetter, Deborah and Richard Gitelson, "Attendee Perceptions of Sponsorship Contributions to a Regional Art Festival", *Festival Management & Event Tourism,* n° 2, 1995, pp. 203-209.

70. Levin, Gary. "AmEx's Olympics Ambush May Goad IOC into Action", *Advertising Age,* Febuary 10, 1992, p. 2.

71. Richard, Leah. "Hoosier Tire's 'Rookie Mistake'", *Advertising Age,* March 7, 1994, p. 46.

72. PQ Media in *Advertising Age,* April 4, 2005, p. 16.

Chapter 6

1. Clifford, Graham, "Type Casting", *Creativity,* May, 1990, p. 8.

2. Starch, Daniel. *Measuring Advertising Readership and Results,* New York, McGraw-Hill, 1966, pp. 75-76.

3. Paterson, Donald G. and Miles A. Tinker. "Influence of Size of Type on Eye Movement", *Journal of Applied Psychology,* vol. 26, n° 2, April 1942, pp. 227-230.

4. Paterson, Donald G. and Miles A. Tinker. "Eye Movement in Reading Type Sizes in Optimal Une Widths", *Journal of Educational Psychology*, vol. 34, n° 9, December 1943, pp. 547-551.

5. Luckiesh, Matthew. *Light and Color in Advertising and Merchandising*, New York, D. Van Nostrand, 1923, pp. 246-251.

6. Tinker, Miles Albert. *Legibility of Print*, University Press, Ames, Iowa (Iowa state), 1963, p. 146; Tinker, Miles Albert and Donald G. Paterson. *How to Make Type Readable: A Manual for Typographers, Printers and Advertisers*, New York, Harper & Brothers Publishers, 1940, p. 120.

7. Starch, Daniel. *Principles of Advertising*, New York, Garland Publishing Inc., 1985, pp. 668-669; Paterson, Donald G. and Miles A. Tinker. "Studies of Typographical Factors Influencing Speed of Reading: VI Black Type Versus White Type", *Journal of Applied Psychology*, vol. 15, n° 3, June 1931, pp. 241-247.

8. Tinker, Miles A. *Legibility of Print*, Ames, Iowa, Iowa State University Press, 1963, p. 55.

9. Breland, Keller and Mariam Kruse Breland. "Legibility of Newspaper Headlines Printed in Capitals and Lower Case", *Journal of Applied Psychology*, vol. 28, n° 2, April 1944, pp. 117-120.

10. Baker, Stephen. *Advertising Layout and Art Direction*, New York, McGraw-Hill, 1959, pp. 91-98.

Chapter 7

1. Vaske, Hermann. "On One Hand You have the Saatchis, and on the Other, Mother Teresa", *Archive*, vol. 2, 1989, p. 9.

2. Lyons, John. *Guts*, New York, Amacom, 1989, p. 38.

3. Harper, Marion. *Getting Results from Advertising*, New York, Funk & Wagnalls Co., 1948, p. 41.

4. Telcom For Independent Outdoor Advertising. "A Study of Outdoor Advertising Sign Placement", 1979.

5. Mediacom.

6. Baker, Stephen. *Visual Persuasion: The Effect of Pictures on the Subconscious*, New York, McGraw-Hill, 1961, chapter 3.

7. Hepner, Harry Walker. *Advertising: Creative Communications with Consumers*, New York, McGraw-Hill, 1964, p. 469.

8. Hendon, Donald W. "How Mechanical Factors Affect Ad Perception", *Journal of Advertising Research*, vol. 13, August 1973, pp. 39-45.

9. Troldahl, Verling C. and Robert L. Jones. "Predictors of Newspapers Advertisement Readership", *Journal of Advertising Research,* vol. 5, n° 1, March 1965, pp. 23-27.

10. Godin, Seth and Chip Conley. *Business Rules of Thumb,* New York, Warner Books, 1987.

11. Hendson, Donald Wayne. "How Mechanical Factors Affect Ad Perception", *Journal of Advertising & Search,* vol. 13, n° 4, August 1973, p. 40.

12. Godin, Seth and Chip Conley. *Business Rules of Thumb,* New York, Warner Books, 1987.

13. Reed Elsevier Business Information Research. *Is Advertising Readership Influenced by Ad Size,* n° 110.

14. Starch, Daniel. *Measuring Advertising Readership and Results,* New York, McGraw-Hill, 1966, pp. 73-75.

15. Benn, Alec. *The 27 Most Common Mistakes in Advertising,* New York, Amacom, 1978, p. 35.

16. Rossiter, John and Larry Percy. *Advertising & Promotion Management,* New York, McGraw-Hill, 1987, p. 622.

17. Printers' Ink. "Is Preferred Position Worth It?", *Printers' Ink,* August 25, 1961, pp. 43-44.

18. Ibid.

19. Stone, Bob. *Successful Direct Marketing Methods,* Chicago, Crain Books, 1979, p. 112.

20. Liesse, Julie. "Finding the Perfect Print Ad", *Advertising Age,* August 13, 1990, p. 25.

21. "Average Readership of All One-Page 4-Color Ads by Page Position In Magazines", *Starch Tested Copy,* vol. 1, n° 2, June 1989.

22. Stone, Bob. *Successful Direct Marketing Methods,* Chicago, Crain Books, 1979, p. 112.

23. Starch. "Do Reader Offer Ads Par Off", *Starch Tested Copy,* vol. 1, n° 13, pp. 1-4.

24. Starch. "Readership of Sweepstakes Advertisement", *Starch Tested Copy,* vol. l, n° 15, pp. 1-4.

25. Gentalen, Tiit. "Transamerica Pop-Up Unit Awareness", *Time Marketing Information,* September 1986, ME n° 9074; "The Transamerica Pop-Up Unit Advertising Effectiveness Study", *Time Marketing Information,* October 1986.

26. Starch, Daniel. *Measuring Advertising Readership and Results,* New York, McGraw-Hill, 1966, p. 60.

27. Printers' Ink. "What Stirs the Newspaper Reader", *Printers' Ink,* June 21, 1963, pp. 48-49.

28. Starch INRA Hooper, 1992 in Fast Consulting, *Why Use Color?,* 1993.

29. Starch, Daniel. *Measuring Advertising Readership and Results,* New York, McGraw-Hill, 1966, p. 61.

30. Reed Elsevier. "How Is Advertising Readership Influenced by Ad Size and Color", *Business Information Advertising Performance Studies,* 1992.

31. Starch, Daniel. *Measuring Advertising Readership and Results,* New York, McGraw-Hill, 1966, p. 31; Runyon, Kenneth. *Advertising and the Practice of Marketing,* Columbus, Charles E. Merrill Publishing Co., 1979, p. 239.

32. Wheatley. "Measuring the Effect of ROP Color on Newspaper Advertising", 1966.

33. Austin, Larry and Richard Sparkman. "The Effect on Sales of Color in Newspaper Advertisements", *Journal of Advertising,* vol. 9, n° 4, 1980, pp. 39-42; voir aussi Gardner, Burleigh B. and Yehudi A. Cohen. "ROP Color and its Effect on Newspaper Advertising", *Journal of Marketing Research,* vol. 1, n° 2, May 1964, pp. 68-70.

34. ARF/ABP. *Does the Use of Four-Color Advertisement in a Specialized Business Magazine Advertising Campaign Increase Sales?,* 1984-1985.

35. Wheatley. "Measuring the Effect of ROP Color on Newspaper Advertising", 1966.

36. "Xerox Corp.", *Advertising Age,* August 8, 1994, p. 37.

37. Levin, Gary, "More Nudity, but Less Sex", *Advertising Age,* November 8, 1993, p. 37.

Chapter 8

1. Cheskin, Louis. *Business without Gambling: How Successfull Marketers use Scientific Methods,* Chicago, Quadrangle Books, 1963; *Color Guide for Marketing Media,* New York, Macmillan, 1954; *How to Predict What People will Buy,* New York, Liveright Pub. Corp., 1957; *Why Peoples Buy: Motivation Research and its Successful Application,* New York, Liveright Publishing Corporation, 1959.

2. Cheskin, Louis. *Secrets of Marketing Success,* New York, Trident Press, 1967, p. 111.

3. Cooper, Mimi. "The Color of Money May Actually Be Fuchsia", Direct Marketing, vol. 34, May 1994, pp. 66-67.

4. Alsop, Ronald. "Color Grows More Important in Catching Consumers' Eyes", *The Wall Street Journal*, November 29, 1984, p. 37.

5. Thompson, Stephanie. "M&M's Wraps Up Promo With Color," *Advertising Age*, March 8, 2004, p. 4.

6. Morris, Desmond. *Manwatching: A Field Guide to Human Behavior*, New York, Harry N. Abrams Publishers Inc., 1977, pp. 302-303.

7. Johnson, Henry C.L. "Love is Red, Power is Blue, Sex is Pink: What Color Are You?" *Marketing/Communications*, May 1968, p. 103.

8. Warden, Carl and Ellen L. Flynn. "The Effect of Color on Apparent Size and Weight", *The American Journal of Psychology*, vol. 37, n° 3, 1926, pp. 398-401.

9. Favre, Jean-Paul and Andre November. *Color and und et Communication*, *Zurich*, ABC Editions, 1979, p. 30.

10. Eysenk, R .J. "A Critical Experiment Study of Color Preferences", *American Journal of Psychology*, vol. 54, n° 3, July 1941, pp. 385-394.

11. Johnson, Douglas. *Advertising Today*, Chicago, Sciences Research Associates Inc., 1978, p. 103.

12. Ward, Philip. *Advertising Fundamentals*, Scranton, Intext Publisher, 1970, p. 649.

13. Cheskin, Louis. *Secrets of Marketing Success*, New York, Trident Press, 1967, p. 110.

14. Loewy, Raymond. *Never Leave Well Enough Alone*, New York, Simon and Schuster, 1951, pp. 199-200.

15. Baker, Stephen. *Visual Persuasion: The Effect of Pictures on the Subconscious*, New York, McGraw-Hill, 1961, chapter 3.

16. Baker, Stephen. *Visual Persuasion: The Effect of Pictures on the Subconscious*, McGraw-Hill, New York, 1961, chapter 3.

Chapter 9

1. "Comparisons Become Invidious in Rivalry for Tire Market", *Business Week*, April 22, 1931, p. 10 in Sellars, Ronald Kay. *A Study of the Effectiveness of Comparative Advertising for Selected Household Appliances*, The Louisiana State University and Agricultural and Mechanical Col., Marketing, PhD thesis, 1977, pp. 2-3.

2. Harris, King. "How Slirling Getchell Chased Walter Chrysler - and Hired a Mail Boy", *Advertising Age,* July 31, 1967, pp. 59-62.

3. Wilkie, William L. and Paul W. Farris. "Comparison Advertising: Problems and Potential", *Journal of Marketing,* vol. 39, n° 4, October 1975, p. 8.

4. McCollum/Spielman. "Success Factors in Comparative Advertising", *Topline,* December 1978, vol. 1, n° 2, p. 2.

5. Starch. *The Gaver Story: When Position Does Make a Difference,* vol. l, n° 9, October 1989, pp. 1-4.

6. "Cereal", *Advertising Age,* April 1, 1991, p. 33.

7. Barry, Thomas E. and Roger L. Tremblay. "Comparative Advertising: Perspective and Issues", *Journal of Advertising,* vol. 4, n° 4, 1975, pp. 15-20; Boddewyn, Jean J. and Katherin Marton. *Comparison Advertising: A Worldwide Study,* New York, Hastings House, 1978, chapter 7; Prasad, V. Kanti. "Communication Effectiveness of Comparative Advertising: A Laboratory Analysis", *Journal of Marketing Research,* vol. 12, n° 2, May 1976, pp. 128-137; Tannenbaum, Stanley and Andrew G. Kershaw. "For and Again Comparative Advertising", *Advertising Age,* July 5, 1976, pp. 25-26 and 29.

8. Droge, Cornellia and Rene Darmon. "Associative Positioning. Strategies Through Comparative Advertising: Attribute Versus Overall Similarity Approaches", *Journal of Marketing Research,* vol. 24, November 1987, p. 223-232; "Creating a Mass Market for Wine", *Business Week,* March 15, 1982, pp. 102-118; Jain, Subhash C. and Edwin C. Hackleman. "How Effective is Comparison Advertising for Stimulating Brand Recall?", *Journal of Advertising,* vol. 7, n° 3, 1978, pp. 20-25.

9. Rickard, Leah. "New Ammo for Comparative Ads", *Advertising Age,* February 14, 1994, p. 26.

10. Lyons, John. *Guts,* New York, Amacom, 1989, p. 136.

11. Tyler, William. "Comparison Advertising: A Powerful Selling Tool When It Is Not Abused", *Advertising Age,* April 21, 1975, pp. 58 and 60.

12. Gorn, Gerald J. and Charles B. Weinberg. "The Impact of Comparative Advertising on Perception and Attitude: Some Positive Findings", *The Journal of Consumer Research,* vol. Il, n° 2, September 1984, pp. 719-727.

13. Rosenthal, Edmond M. "Comparative Advertising: Weapon or Fad?", *Marketing Times,* vol. 23, September-October 1976, p. 13.

14. Giges, Nancy. "PepsiCo Ad Insists: No Question - Coke Drinkers Prefer Pepsi", *Advertising Age,* July 19, 1976, pp. 2 and 66.

15. Swayne, Linda Sue Eggeman. *Comparative Advertising as Corporate Strategy: An Investigation of Key United States Industries,* North Texas State University, Marketing, PhD thesis, 1978, p. 49.

16. Winters, Patricia. "Perrier Rivals Refuse to Make Waves", *Advertising Age,* March 12, 1990, p. 74.

17. Golden, Linda L. "Consumer Reactions to Explicit Comparisons in Advertisements", *Journal of Marketing Research,* vol. 16, n° 4, November 1979, pp. 517-532; Levine, Philip. "Commercials that Name Competing Brands", *Journal of Advertising Research,* vol. 16 , n° 6, December 1976, pp. 7-14; Shimp, Terence A. and David C. Dyer. "The Effects of Comparative Advertising Mediated by Market Position of Sponsoring Brand", *Journal of Advertising,* vol. 7, n° 3, Summer 1978, pp. 13-19; "Creating a Mass Market for Wine", *Business Week,* March 15, 1982, pp. 102-118.

18. Trytten, John. "It's Easy as Pie: Nothing Can Compare with a Bad Comparative Ad", *Sales and Marketing Management,* July 12, 1976, p. 61.

19. Levine, Philip. "Commercials that Name Competing Brands", *Journal of Advertising Research,* vol. 16, n° 6, 1976, pp. 7-14.

20. "Underdog Wins in Naming Names: BBDO", *Advertising Age,* March 10, 1975, p. 56.

21. Roberts, Jack. "Comparative Advertising... I'm O.K... You're Not O.K..." American Association of Advertising Agencies, Charlotte, (North Carolina), November 13, 1973 in Swayne, Linda Sue Eggeman. *Comparative Advertising as Corporate Strategy: An Investigation of Key United Stated Industries,* North Texas State University, Marketing, PhD thesis, 1978, p. 50.

22. Swayne, Linda Sue Eggeman. *Comparative Advertising as Corporate Strategy: An Investigation of Key United Stated Industries,* North Texas State University, Marketing, PhD thesis, 1978, p. 24.

23. Bowes, Elena and David Kilburn. "Coke Hits Pepsi's Hammer", *Advertising Age,* July 15, 1991, p. 33.

Chapter 10

1. Newspaper Association of America (1993). *Ten Top Reasons to Advertise.*

2. ARF/ABP. *How Long Does it Take to See the Results of a Specialized Business Magazine Advertising Campaign,* n° 100, 1984-1985.

3. Lieberman Associates & Marketmath Inc. "A Study of the Effectiveness of Advertising Frequency in Magazines", 1979-1980.

4. Appel, Valentine. "On Advertising Wear Out", *Journal of Advertising & Search*, vol. 11, n° l, February 1971, pp. 11-13; Britt, Steuart Henderson, Stephen C. Adams and Allan S. Miller. "How Many Advertising Exposures Per Day?", *Journal of Advertising Research*, vol. 12, n° 6, December 1972, pp. 3-9; Calder, Bobby J. and Brian Sternthal. "Television Commercial Wearout: An Information Processing View", *Journal of Marketing Research*, vol. 17, n° 2, May 1980, pp. 173-186; Carrick, Paul M. Jr. "Why Continued Advertising Is Necessary: A New Explanation", *Journal of Marketing*, vol. 23, n° 4, April 1959, pp. 386-398; Craig, C. Samuel, Brian Sternthal and Clark Leavitt. "Advertising Wearout: An Experimental Analysis", *Journal of Marketing Research*, vol. 13, n° 4, November 1976, pp. 365-372; Ehrenberg, Andrew S.C. "Repetitive Advertising and the Consumer", *Journal of Advertising Research*, vol. 14, n° 2, April 1974, pp. 25-33; Greenberg, Allan and Charles Suttoni. "Television Commercial Wearout", *Journal of Advertising & Search*, vol. 13, n° 5, October 1973, pp. 47-53; Krugman, Herbert E. "Why Three Exposures May Be Enough", *Journal of Advertising Research*, vol. 12, n° 6, December 1972, pp. 11-14; Naples, Michael J. *Effective Frequency... The Relationship Between Frequency and Advertising Effectiveness*, New York, Association of National Advertisers Inc., 1979, 140 p.; Ostheimer, Richard H. "Frequency Effects Over Time", *Journal of Advertising Research*, vol. 10, n° l, February 1970, pp. 19-22; Ray, Michael L., Alan G. Sawyer and Edward C. Strong. "Frequency Effects Revised", *Journal of Advertising Research*, vol. 11, n° l, February 1971, pp. 14-20; Ray, Michael L. and Alan G. Sawyer. "Repetition Models: A Laboratory Technique", *Journal of Marketing Research*, vol. 8, n° 1, February 1971, pp. 20-29; Zielske, Hubert A. "The Remembering and Forgetting of Advertising", *Journal of Marketing*, vol. 23, n° 3, January 1959, pp. 239-243.

5. Starch, Daniel. *Measuring Advertising Readership and Results*, New York, McGraw-Hill, 1966, p. 97.

6. Newspaper Association of America (1993). *Ten Top Reasons to Advertise.*

7. Zajong, Robert B. "Attitudinal Effects of Mere Exposure", *Journal of Personality and Social Psychology Monograph Supplement*, vol. 9, n° 2, part 2, June 1968, pp. 1-27; Harrison, Albert A. "Exposure and Popularity", *Journal of Personality*, vol. 37, n° 3, September 1969, pp. 359-377.

8. Grush, J. E. and K. L McKeogh. "The Finest Representation that Money Can Buy: Exposure Effects in the 1972 Congressional Primaries", Chicago, May 1975, in Baron, Robert A. and Donn Byrne. *Social Psychology: Understanding Human Psychology*, Boston, Allyn and Bacon Inc., 1977, p. 221; Simmons Market Research Bureau in Cahners Advertising Research Report, *Does Advertising Exposure Have a Positive Influence On Brand Perceptions and the Likelihood of Future Product Usage*, 1993-1994.

9. Gordon Publications. *How Do Size, Color and Frequency of Advertisements Influence Buyers' Impressions of a Supplier,* n° 131.

10. Cahners Advertising Research Report. Does *"Remember Seeing" Increase Two Or More Ads Are Placed By The Same Company In The Single Ussus Of A Specialized Business Magazine,* n° 2001.16.

11. "A Disturbing New Study on 15 Seconds Commercials", *Canada Newsletter,* April 1989, pp. 1-2.

12. Zielske, H. A. "The Remembering and Forgetting of Advertising", *Journal of Marketing,* vol. 23, n° 3, January 1959, pp. 239-243.

13. Zielske, H. A. "The Remembering and Forgetting of Advertising", *Journal of Marketing,* vol. 23, n° 3, January 1959, p. 240.

14. Galway, Byron T. "To Cut or not to Cut?", *Marketing & Media Decisions,* April 1981, p. 34.

15. Dagnoli, Judann. "Maxwell House Gets Reheated", *Advertising Age,* November 27, 1989, p. 1.

16. Liesse, Julie. "How the Bunny Charged Eveready", *Advertising Age,* April 8, 1991, pp. 20, 56. p. 229.

17. Freeman, Laurie. "Tampax: Poorly Managed Franchise Must Stop Slide", *Advertising Age,* October 3, 1994, p. S-10.

18. "TCBY is Back on the Air", *Advertising Age,* April 25, 1994, p. 57.

19. Becknell, James C. Jr. and Robert W. McIsaac. "Test Marketing Cookware Coated with Teflon", *Journal of Advertising Research,* vol. 3, n° 3, September 1963, pp. 2-8.

20. Sevin, Charles H. "What We Know About Measuring Ad Effectiveness", *Printers' Ink,* July 9, 1965, pp. 47-53.

21. Hobson,W. "Three Basic Principles in Campaign Planning" *The Selection of Advertising Media,* Londres, Mercury House, Business Books Limited, 1968, p. 174-182, in Littlefield, James E. *Readings in Advertising: Curent View Points on Selected Topics,* St-Paul, West Publishing Co., 1975, pp. 242-248.

22. "Commercial Wearout and Pool Guidelines: an Approach to Estimating the Number of Commercial Executions Required in an Advertising Campaign", March 1983, pp. 3-4.

23. Teinowitz, Ira. "Ad Message, not Frequency, Sells", *Advertising Age,* December 1989, p. 31.

24. Levin, Gary. "Recession Lesson: Don't Cut Ads", *Advertising Age,* November 26, 1990, p. 12.

25. *The Wall Street Journal*'s advertisement; *How Advertising in Recession Periods Affects Sales*, New York, American Business Press Inc., 1979.

26. *The Wall Street Journal* advertisement, McGraw-Hill Research, Report No. 5262.1, Laboratory of Advertising Performance.

27. *The Wall Street Journal* advertisement,

28. Dhalla, Nariman K. "Advertising as an Antirecession Tool", *Harvard Business Review*, January/February 1980.

29. "Marketers Slash Ads as War Erupts", *Advertising Age*, January 21, 1991, pp. 1, 54.

30. Tansey, Richard, Michael R. Hyman and Gene Brown. "Ethical Judgements About Wartime Ads Depicting Combat", *Journal of Advertising*, vol. 21, n° 3, September 1992, pp. 54-74.

31. Berk, Christina Cheddar. "Procter & Gamble Continues To Pull Ads From News Programs", *The Wall Street Journal*, April 1, 2003, p. B8.

32. "USAir, Other Airlines Ground Ads After Crash", *Advertising Age*, September 12, 1994, p. 2.

33. Cahners Advertising Research Report. "How Long Do Advertisements Draw Inquiries?", *Cahners Advertising Research Report*, New York, 1979, n° 240.3.

34. Mandese, Joe. "Rival Spots Cluttering TV", *Advertising Age*, March 4 1991, p.6.

35. McDonald's. "1981 Basic Media Seminar Manual, McDonald's Corporation", 1980, p. 15.

36. Corbett, Michael. *33 Ruthless Rules of Local Marketing*, Houston, Breakthru Publishing, 1988, p. 123.

37. Krugman, Herbert. "Why Three Exposures May Be Enough", *Journal of Advertising Research*, April 1991.

38. Cahners Advertising Research Report. "How Long Do Advertisements Draw Inquiries?", *Cahners Advertising Research Report*, New York, 1979, n° 240.3.

39. Brisoux, Jacques E., Rene Y. Darmon and Michel Laroche. *Advertising Management*, Toronto, John Wiley & Sons, 1984, p. 420.

40. Marney, Jo. "Check Seasoning in your Mix", *Marketing*, April 19, 1982, p. 20.

41. Johnson, Bradley. "PC Marketers Put $100M on the Line", *Advertising Age*, November 12, 1994, p. 3.

42. DeNitto, Emily. "P&G's Aleve Quickly Joins Top Pain Killers", *Advertising Age*, December 5, 1994, p. 3.

43. Sloan, Pat. "Colgate Packs $40M Behind New Toothpaste", *Advertising Age*, December 12, 1994, p. 36.

44. "IBM's Aptiva Ignites with $20M in Ads", *Advertising Age*, September 26, 1994, p. 47.

45. Sloan, Pat. "Leaders Follow Scent to Growth in Fragrances", *Advertising Age*, September 28, 1994, p. 30.

46. Colford, Steven W. "Plot-Filled Election Tally Hits", *Advertising Age*, September 26, 1994, p. 46.

47. Smith, Thomas. *Hints to Intending Advertisers*, London, 1885, in Leo Bogart. *Strategy in Advertising: Matching Media and Messages to Markets and Motivation*, Chicago, Crain Books, 1984, p. 207.

Conclusion

1. Arren, Jules. *Comment il faut faire de la publicité*, Paris, Pierre Lafitte & Co. Éditeurs, 1912, pp. 35-36.

2. Ogilvy, David. "We sell. Or Else.", *The Advertiser*, Summer 1992, p. 21.

3. Vaske, Hermann. "On One Hand You Have the Saatchis, and on the Other, Mother Teresa", *Archive*, vol. 2, 1989, p. 9.

4. Spethmann, Betsy. "Census Data-Base Adds up to Success", *Advertising Age*, April 15, 1991, p. 6.

Bibliography

Aaker, Davis and John Myers. *Advertising Management,* Englewood Cliffs, Prentice-Hall, 1987, 564 p.

Baker, Stephen. *Advertising Layout and Art Direction,* New York, McGraw-Hill, 1959, 324 p.

Baker, Stephen. *Visual Persuasion,* New York, McGraw-Hill, 1961, n.p.

Bayan, Richard. *Words that Sell,* Chicago, Contemporary Books, 1984, 127 p.

Benn, Alec. *The 27 Most Common Mistakes in Advertising,* New York, Amacom, 1978, 156 p.

Bly, Robert W. *The Copywriter's Handbook,* New York, Owl Books, 1990, 368 p.

Bogart, Leo. *Strategy in Advertising,* Chicago, Crain Books, 1984, 406 p.

Burnett, Leo. *Communications of an Advertising Man,* Chicago, Leo Burnett Co., 1961, 350 p.

Caples, John. *Making Ads Pay,* Dover Publications, 1957.

Caples, John and Fred E. Hahn. *Tested Advertising Methods,* Englewood Cliffs, N.J. Prentice Hall, 1998, 304 p.

Cheskin, Louis. *Why People Buy : Motivation Research and Its Successful Application,* New York, W. W. Norton & Company, 1959, 348 p.

Cohen, Dorothy. *Advertising,* Glenview, Scott Foreman, 1988, 626 p.

Corbett, Michael. *33 Ruthless Rules of Local Marketing,* Houston, Breakthru Publishing, 1995, 199 p.

Cossette, Claude and Nicolas Massey. *Comment faire sa publicité soi-même,* Montréal, Les Éditions Transcontinental, 2002, 345 p.

Dichter, Ernest. *The Strategy of Desire,* Garden City, Transaction Publishers, 2002, 314 p.

Dobrow, Larry. *When Advertising Tried Harder,* New York, Friendly Press, 1984, 205 p.

Dupont, Luc. *Images that Sell,* Sainte-Foy, White Rock Publishing, 2000, 272 p.

Favre, Jean-Paul and André November. *Color and und et communication,* Zurich, ABC Verlag, 1979, 167 p.

Flesch, Rudolf. *How to Test Readability,* New York, Harper & Brothers, 1951, 56 p.

Glatzer, Robert. *The New Advertising,* New York, The Citadel Press, 1970, 191 p.

Hopkins, Claude. *My Life in Advertising and Scientific Advertising,* Lincolnwood, Crain Books, 1986, 318 p.

Kobliski, Kathy. *Advertising Without an Agency,* Central Point (Oregon), The Oasis Press, 2001, 192 p.

Martineau, Pierre. *Motivation in Advertising : Motives That Make People Buy,* New York, McGraw-Hill, 1971, 210 p.

Ogilvy, David. *Ogilvy on Advertising,* New York, Vintage, 1985, 224 p.

Percy, Larry and John R. Rossiter. *Advertising Strategy,* New York, Praeger Publishers, 1980, 301 p.

Rapp, Stan and Thomas Collins. *MaxiMarketing,* New York, McGraw-Hill, 1988, 377 p.

Reeves, Rosser. *Reality in Advertising,* New York, Alfred A. Knopp, 1961, 153 p.

Ries, Al and Jack Trout. *Positioning : The Battle for Your Mind,* New York, McGraw-Hill, 1987, 649 p.

Roman, Kenneth and Jane Maas. *How to Advertise,* New York, Thomas Dunne Books, 2003, 256 p.

Rossiter, John and Larry Percy. *Advertising & Promotion Management,* New York, McGraw-Hill, 1987, 649 p.

Schultz, Don and William Robinson. *Sales Promotion Essentials,* Lincolnwood, NTC Business Books, 1989, 234 p.

Starch, Daniel. *Measuring Advertising Readership and Results,* New York, McGraw-Hill, 1966, 270 p.

Stone, Bob and Ron Jacobs. *Successful Direct Marketing Methods,* Chicago, McGraw-Hill, 2001, 608 p.

Strunk, William and Eb White. *The Elements of Style,* New York, Collier MacMillan, 1959, 71 p.

Tinker, Miles and Donald Paterson. *How to Make Type Readable,* New York, Harper & Brothers Publishers, 1940, 209 p.